The Seven 'I's of Modi's India

Through The Eyes Of An NRI

Anant Chetan

The Seven 'I's of Modi's India

Made with ❤ on the Notion Press Platform
www.notionpress.com

CONTENTS

PREFACE

What defines a nation's progress? Is it measured by the number of highways and skyscrapers, or by the evolving identities and aspirations of its people? Over the past decade, India has experienced a remarkable transformation, navigating the crossroads of tradition and modernity, growth and inclusivity, and ambition and introspection. These changes demand a closer look, not just to understand where India stands today but also to contemplate where it is headed.

As an Indian who has lived abroad for much of his adult life, I've had the privilege of observing my homeland through the dual lens of an insider and an outsider. This unique perspective has allowed me to appreciate the strides India has made while also questioning the challenges it continues to face. Living in Europe and the UK, I've seen how societies address issues of governance, identity, and progress—sometimes offering parallels to India's journey, and at other times providing stark contrasts. This book is born from the confluence of those observations, reflections, and questions.

The idea for *The Seven 'I's of Modi's India* came from an attempt to distil a decade of change into key themes that encapsulate the essence of the country's evolution. The "Seven 'I's" emerged as a framework to explore this transformation, encompassing Infrastructure, Industrialization, Innovation, Immunity, Ideology, Identity and Institutions. Each chapter delves into one of these themes, examining how it has shaped and been shaped by India's policies, society, and global standing. Although the book presents a particular sequence for the 'I's, they do not necessarily need to be read in that order. You can explore each 'I' independently, starting with the one that resonates the most with you.

Between 2014 and 2024, India has undergone shifts that are as ambitious as they are contentious. The construction of highways and smart cities reflects an era of rapid infrastructural growth, while the push for digital governance has brought both efficiency and debate. Social initiatives have sought to redefine inclusion, even as protests and unrest reveal the complexities of a diverse democracy. The rise of India's global influence is undeniable, yet it invites the question: How do we balance soft power with internal cohesion?

This book isn't about statistics—it's about countries, societies and people: their aspirations, struggles, and resilience in the face of change. It's about the identities we unconsciously adopt and the biases we carry, often without realizing their influence. It asks the tough questions: Did the promises of "*Achhe Din*" materialize? Were the skeptics justified in their doubts? And, most importantly, what lies ahead for a nation as vast and diverse as India?

The book does not aim to provide definitive answers but rather to provoke thought, spark conversation, and encourage readers to view India's journey through their own unique perspectives. It is not intended as a partisan commentary but as an exploration of a nation navigating its aspirations, conflicts, and realities. To achieve this, I draw comparisons between events in India and similar occurrences in countries like Germany, the Netherlands, and the UK, where I have primarily lived over the past decade. Rather than prescribing what is right or wrong, this book is meant for people like myself who are still deliberating, seeking more context and clarity to draw their own conclusions. Are we truly heading in the right direction?

These are the reflections I hope to explore with you. And of course, if you would like to share your opinions, thoughts, remarks, reviews or get in touch, please do reach out via my personal blog www.infiniteseaofopportunities.com.

I invite you to join me in this journey—to reflect on how far we've come, how far we have to go, and the paths we might take along the way. Together, let's explore the seven 'I's that define India today and imagine what they might reveal about its future.

Anant Chetan

Portsmouth, UK

PROLOGUE

It was a typical afternoon when I returned from the university, tired but relieved that the day's classes were over. As I checked my phone, a text from my cousin popped up: "Bro, 500 and 1000 rupee bills will be invalid from midnight today." My initial reaction was confusion, followed by indifference. "So what?" I thought. After all, how could a change in currency impact my daily life or for that matter anyone else's life? What's the big deal?

My reaction was probably from the lost faith or lost hope in the Modi Government. In 2014, after decades of monotonous post-independence politics characterized by sluggish growth and unfulfilled promises, a wave of optimism swept across the nation. A party other than the Indian National Congress came to power with a decisive full majority, breaking the long-standing political inertia. Many hailed this as India's "Black Swan" moment—a rare and transformative event that could potentially reshape the nation's future. With a dynamic new leader at the helm, there was a palpable sense of hope. People envisioned sweeping reforms that would ignite economic growth, create jobs, and establish India as a global powerhouse, ushering in a long-awaited era of progress and prosperity.

However, in reality, the Modi government's first two years were painfully uneventful, a stark contrast to the wave of optimism that had swept the nation in 2014. Initiatives like Swachh Bharat, while well-intentioned, barely scratched the surface of the monumental challenges facing the country. Mann Ki Baat, a radio program meant to connect the prime minister with citizens, often felt detached from ground realities, offering platitudes in place of solutions. Meanwhile, the nation was gripped by chilling headlines of mob lynchings—each case more harrowing than the last, with the Akhlaq case standing out as a symbol of a fractured society.

To add to this, the prime minister's repeated exhortations to pay taxes and open accounts under the JAM Trinity (Jan Dhan, Aadhar, Mobile) initiative seemed disconnected from the day-to-day struggles of the average citizen. The air was heavy with despair and uncertainty. A question loomed over every conversation: where were the '*acche din*'—the promised days of prosperity and progress? Or was this bleak and unsettling reality the true face of '*acche din*'?

But, then came demonetization. At first, I dismissed it. "So what if the government invalidates certain currency bills?" I thought. Little did I know, this seemingly simple announcement would herald one of the most dramatic economic decisions in India's modern history, shaking not just wallets, but the very fabric of the nation. But as I followed the news over the next month, the magnitude of the decision became clear. It was a seismic event that jolted the nation awake—not just physically, as people queued for hours outside banks, but emotionally and spiritually. For the first time in decades, it felt as though the very soul of the country had been stirred.

What followed next was nothing short of exhilarating, an unrelenting cascade of transformative events that pushed the adrenaline rush higher and higher. It felt as though a humble cart had been transformed into a Ferrari, speeding faster every second. Before the demonetization tremors had even settled, the Goods and Services Tax (GST), a significant tax reform aimed at unifying India's fragmented tax system by replacing multiple indirect taxes with a single, streamlined structure was introduced; shaking the system once more. This was quickly followed by the landmark ban on Triple Talaq—a historic step towards gender justice and equality in India. For decades, the practice of Triple Talaq had marginalized countless Muslim women, often leaving them destitute and without legal recourse. Its abolition signaled a commitment to safeguarding the rights of women, setting a precedent for progressive reform within personal laws—and then the unthinkable—the abrogation of Article 370. Nobody—

absolutely nobody—anticipated such a bold and unexpected move.

The Citizenship Amendment Act (CAA) was next, igniting nationwide debates and protests. Then came the airstrikes in 2019, which stirred patriotic fervor like never before, uniting the nation in a surge of collective pride. Following this, Mission Shakti showcased India's prowess in space warfare with the successful ASAT (Anti-Satellite) test. This milestone not only cemented India's position as a global power in advanced defense technologies but also fundamentally altered the nuclear dynamic in the region. It was a strategic response to Pakistan's nuclear blackmail, sending a clear message about India's capabilities and resolve. The momentum didn't stop there: the contentious Farm Bills, the ambitious National Register of Citizens (NRC), the long-awaited building of the Ram Mandir, and for the first time, inviting private players into the space sector. It felt as though the government was on a relentless mission to transform every aspect of the nation within an incredibly short span of time.

Politics had never been this captivating. The pace was relentless, almost too fast to comprehend. For me, it was both exhilarating and overwhelming—like witnessing a high-stakes blockbuster unfold in real time. Each announcement brought another dramatic twist, keeping the nation on edge. I found myself thoroughly entertained, yet the sheer velocity of change demanded constant effort to stay informed and make sense of it all. Every time the prime minister addressed the nation, the same thought raced through my mind: "What's next? What could possibly be coming next?" If not for the Covid-19 pandemic, which forced an unexpected slowdown, it seemed the government had no intention of hitting the brakes. The lockdown, in its own way, became a moment to catch our collective breath amid the whirlwind.

What if the critics and naysayers were right? What if these reforms and actions were not good for the nation and were instead accelerating country's downfall at an unprecedented speed? To be honest, I was scared to some extent. In 2020, with Covid restrictions in force in Germany, where I was based at that time, life had slowed to a standstill. Gyms were closed, sports complexes shut down, and I was confined to working from home, eating at home, and occasionally going for a run or a cycling trip. I had more free time than I knew what to do with.

With little else to occupy me, I turned to reading and writing. I read voraciously—every notification, policy, law, and act introduced by the Modi government since 2014. I delved into e-books on Indian history, politics, and reforms, consuming whatever I could get my hands on.

The more I read, the more I wrote, and the more I wrote, the more my blog gained recognition and appreciation. As my writing evolved, so did my understanding of the policies and reforms taking shape in India.

What struck me the most was the realization that these changes were not entirely unique to India. My years abroad during this transformative decade gave me a distinct vantage point. Many of the policies mirrored initiatives already implemented in the West. The parallels were undeniable, and they offered a new perspective on India’s trajectory—one that blended apprehension with intrigue.

Why and how are the social "institutions" in the West fundamentally different from those in India? How does the collective mindset in India diverge from the individualistic approach in the West? How do concepts like individualism and feminism in India contrast with their interpretations in Western societies? In what ways does the "ideology" prevalent in Western countries align or differ from the principles driving Modi's India? What lessons can be drawn from German Denazification, and how might they parallel Modi's efforts in shaping India's "identity"? What are the differences in citizenship laws across the globe, and how does India's approach stand out? How do the thoroughly regulated and seamlessly managed borders of Europe compare to the contentious, poorly demarcated, and often unregulated borders of India? What explains the stark differences in resilience to threats between the West and India—their respective "immunities" to challenges? Why did the Second World War and the Cold War push the West into an era of unprecedented "innovation," while the multiple wars India fought post-independence failed to yield similar progress? From HAL Marut to HAL Tejas, what lessons can be drawn from India's journey in defense technology? And how does something as seemingly simple as a Swiss chocolate encapsulate "industrialization," showcasing the precision and efficiency India has yet to achieve? Meanwhile, why are India and Indians still entrenched in issues like MSP and diminishing returns, struggling to break free from outdated paradigms?

This book, *The Seven 'I's of Modi's India*, is a natural progression of the journey I unintentionally embarked on during the Covid lockdown—a journey of questioning, exploration, and reflection. It is my attempt to address some of the profound questions that arose as I delved deeper into India's policies, reforms, and its evolving identity. Unlike the restrictive two-thousand-word limit on my blog posts, this book provides a vast canvas of eighty thousand words to delve into the nuances and complexities of what I observed and experienced.

In today's AI-driven era, where algorithmic recommendations reinforce biases and filter out conflicting ideas, grasping an objective sense of reality has become increasingly challenging. The echo chambers created by these systems not only limit diverse perspectives but also deepen existing divisions, making it imperative to critically evaluate the information we consume and the narratives we accept. This challenge of fragmented realities mirrors the larger contradictions faced by nations as they evolve. Together, let's step back, see the entire elephant, and critically examine the journey of a nation navigating its contradictions with remarkable resilience. As you turn the pages of this book, join me in a deeper exploration of these thought-provoking questions. We begin with the most visible and tangible aspect of transformation: Infrastructure. It offers a striking contrast to the structures I observed upon moving to Europe, highlighting both the promise and the challenges that define India's journey

INFRASTRUCTURE

"Raajaa panthaanam karayet sarvaartha-siddhaye"
–Book II, Chapter 4, Arthashastra

"Investing in infrastructure is a key responsibility of the state, as it benefits all citizens and contributes to the overall development of the nation."

The Beginning

Traveling abroad for the first time was a mix of excitement and apprehension. Navigating through Munich and Bremen airports initially felt familiar, as the structured layouts and clear signage resembled those of airports back home in Delhi, Bangalore, Mumbai, or Pune. Airports, I realized, share a universal design language that eases navigation for travelers worldwide.

However, stepping outside Bremen Airport into an entirely new environment brought the reality of traveling abroad into sharp focus. My first task was to find a way to the Bremen *Hauptbahnhof* (train station). Having learned that *Straßenbahn* 6, a tram, would take me there, I faced a small but significant challenge—how do trams work? Do I need to purchase the tickets in advance, like for a metro, or can they be bought onboard, like a bus? Though a minor concern, I wanted to avoid starting my journey with an awkward mistake.

Using my basic German—picked up during eight months of classes in Bangalore—I deciphered the signs and located a *Fahrkartenautomaten*, a ticket machine. Successfully buying a ticket felt like a small win, boosting my confidence as I ventured into the unknown.

The tram arrived promptly, and with no immediate ticket checks, I boarded and found a seat. The journey took about 20-25 minutes, and I couldn't help but notice how seamlessly trams integrated into the city's urban landscape. Tracks ran alongside roads, effortlessly accommodating cars, cyclists, and pedestrians. Reaching the train station, I was struck by its surroundings. It was more than a transit hub; cinemas, restaurants, salons, food stalls, and even a gym surrounded the station. Later, during winter this vibrant space transformed into a Christmas market, further reinforcing its role as a community focal point.

Inside the station, the atmosphere was equally bustling. Shops, coffee outlets, and even a supermarket created a multi-functional space that reminded me more of a modern mall, like Shipra Mall, than the utilitarian railway stations common in India. The experience was unexpectedly pleasant, emphasizing convenience and accessibility.

Finding my train to Bremerhaven, the RE8 departing from platform 5, was straightforward thanks to the large display right at the entrance- it was difficult to miss the display. Dragging my heavy luggage, I was relieved to find an elevator—a small but welcome detail. The platform displayed "*RE8: 13 Minuten*" on a digital screen, hanging from the ceiling. Adjusting my watch to the local time, I marveled at the precision promised by such details and thought to myself, if the train will actually show up in the next thirteen minutes. True to schedule, the train arrived slightly earlier than expected, accompanied by a clear, albeit partially incomprehensible, German announcement. Despite successfully completing A1 and A2 levels in German, I barely understood a word. All I caught was "*Der Zug….* (The Train)" The rest? Music!

The train itself was an eye-opener. Its interiors resembled those of an airplane, with rows of two and three seats on either side of the aisle and occasional table arrangements ideal for families or groups. I was especially intrigued by its double-decker design, offering expansive views of Germany's picturesque countryside through its large, tinted windows. Even bicycles had their dedicated compartments, although an additional ticket was required—a detail that underscored the system's thoughtful planning.

The journey felt more like a flight than a train ride, with its quiet, clean interiors and smooth motion. Watching the rolling fields, wind turbines, and quaint villages go by was a serene and memorable introduction to the country. Arriving at Bremerhaven train station, I noted once again the absence of ticket checks—a sign of the trust and efficiency that seemed to define the system.

My journey wasn't over yet. The final leg required a bus ride to a temporary bed-and-breakfast where I'd stay until my student accommodation became available. Bremerhaven's station, though smaller than Bremen's, followed the same multi-purpose design ethos, offering shops, restaurants, and ample seating. Boarding a bus that resembled a centipede, with its articulated design, was another new experience. With just one driver and no conductor, the system ran seamlessly, reflecting the self-reliant and organized culture of German public transport.

This wasn't unique to Bremen or Bremerhaven. During subsequent travels across Europe and the UK, I found public transport systems that were efficient and intuitive. Amsterdam, for instance, offered iconic trams weaving through narrow streets and canals, while bicycles dominated the roads. The city's emphasis on cycling infrastructure—dedicated lanes and abundant bike parking—was striking. In contrast, Berlin's U-Bahn and S-Bahn systems felt industrial and precise, forming the backbone of its public transport. Minimalist underground stations emphasized functionality over aesthetics, reinforcing Berlin's no-nonsense approach. London's Tube, which I had imagined as some futuristic transport system using capsules like structures being hurled from point A to point B at supersonic speeds, turned out to be a straightforward metro network named for its cylindrical tunnels. Though less glamorous than expected, it underscored the importance of connectivity in urban planning.

Reflecting on these systems highlighted both the progress and challenges of public transport in India. Delhi's metro, which serves over four million daily passengers, is a testament to efficiency and scale, yet the city struggles under the weight of a population exceeding 30 million. London, with just 9 million people, utilizes multiple means of transportation—Tube, buses, Docklands Light Railway (DLR), Overground trains, trams, river buses, and cycling lanes. Of course Delhi while relying only on Metro and buses will appear way more congested. Bangalore's reliance on buses and an underdeveloped metro network for its 12 million commuters further illustrates the gap in local public transportation in the city. Despite beginning construction in 2007, the city's metro covers only two lines and 65 stations as of 2024—an entire generation has witnessed its slow progress.

By the time I reached the B&B, it was already quite late and I was left with no energy. It did not take much time before I dozed off. The next day, I headed to the university to finalize the formalities—submitting my original documents and getting a student ID, or in this case, a semester ticket. Fortunately, the place I was staying at was just a short walk from the international students' office.

I left around 10:30 AM, casually strolling through the streets. As I passed *Theodor Heuss Platz*, I spotted a small statue surrounded by vibrant flowers—a charming little photo spot. A few minutes later, I walked by a cinema, a casino, and a restaurant, eventually standing next to a building labeled *Haus V*. I remembered from the university brochure that one of my classes would be held there. But as I kept walking, something felt odd—when did I actually enter the university? Was the cinema, casino, and bar part of the campus? There was no distinct boundary or a grand gate marking the entrance. The campus buildings, library, international office, and student union (*StuCa*) blended seamlessly with the regular cityscape.

This open, borderless concept was new to me and honestly a bit disorienting. In my mind, universities had walls and clear separations from the outside world. Yet here, I could walk into most buildings, including the library, without anyone asking for an ID.

By 11:00 AM, I arrived at the international office. I submitted my original documents—German language certification (at least A2 level), GRE, IELTS, and a few others. After verification, I was officially registered and was provided with my semester ticket. It cost 240 euros, covering admin fees, exam fees, and unlimited student travel within the city and nearby places like Bremen and Hamburg. One of the perks of being a student in Germany is the discount on nearly everything—travel, health insurance, even restaurants. But once you graduate, the cost of living practically doubles overnight.

The lady at the international office suggested a temporary accommodation at Seemannsheim until my student hostel was available by April the 1st. She jotted down the address, pointed towards the street, and said it was about a 15-minute walk. In Germany, walking a couple of kilometers is normal, but I wasn't used to it, so I opted for the bus. Conveniently, the stop was next to *Haus K*, making it feel like the bus stop was practically a part of the campus.

International students had the option to pair with a local buddy—someone to help with settling into daily life. My buddy was a lifesaver, guiding me through city council registration at the *Buergeramt*. Apparently, registering your address within two weeks of moving is mandatory for everyone. Once that was done, I felt ready to dive into my studies. Well, almost.

I still needed one thing—a bicycle!

My buddy insisted I get a bike (a bicycle and not a motorbike; back home a bike meant a motorbike and a cycle meant a bicycle), explaining that it was the best way to explore the city. Most German students I met owned bikes, and cycling seemed to be woven into the culture. I soon realized this wasn't just the case in Germany but across Europe and even the UK. The infrastructure supported cycling everywhere—trains had bike coaches, buses accommodated bikes, and cars had optional racks to carry bikes. It was common for people to drive or take the train to far-off places and then cycle around to explore. Cycling wasn't just convenient, it was budget-friendly. Public transport is great but expensive, and for students, even with discounts, costs can pile up.

A bike became essential when I finally moved to my student hostel on April 1st, 2015. *Hochschule* Bremerhaven had two hostels—one in the city center at *An Der Allee* (10 minutes from the university) and another at *Adolf Butenandt Strasse*, 6 km away. I was assigned the latter. Both hostels had the essentials—24/7 electricity, water, internet (Wi-Fi and Ethernet), bathrooms, in-built kitchens, and communal washing machines. A bicycle shed was available too. Basic services like electricity, water, internet, and proper toilets are so standard in Europe that anyone hardly thought about them. Even during spontaneous motorbike trips, I never worried about finding accommodation with basic amenities.

Initially, the 6 km ride from Adolf Butenandt Strasse felt far, but with a bike, it became a manageable 20-minute commute. Over time, cycling became my main mode of transport. Today, I always consider commute times when moving, aiming for a 30-minute bike ride—short enough to avoid exhaustion but long enough for a decent cardio-workout. Plus, it's far cheaper. For context, taking the train to work costs 5 pounds daily in Portsmouth, where I live today, adding up to 880 pounds annually—essentially a month's rent! Cycling, on the other hand, is free, faster during peak hours, and lets me indulge in more chocolate and cake guilt-free.

Back in India, I cycled as a kid but stopped after high school. In smaller towns, bicycles were either for children or adults who couldn't afford scooters, motorbikes or four wheelers. It wasn't just a mindset issue— proper infrastructure was also and is still missing. In Europe, I could often zone out while cycling and still reach the destination in one piece, without a single scratch. In India, cycling lanes are rare, and the roads feel unsafe.

European and UK cities prioritize cyclists—there are dedicated lanes, underpasses, and bike-only bridges. If I had to rank cycling infrastructure, the Netherlands and Germany would lead, followed by the UK. One issue with the UK is that bike lanes often merge with regular roads, which isn't as safe. In Germany, this rarely happens.

Creating bike lanes isn't just about painting lines on roads. It requires thoughtful city planning—redesigning streets, creating seamless networks, and ensuring secure bike parking. Bike theft is a real issue. A friend once left his bike outside the gym overnight, only to return and find just the frame locked—the wheels had been stolen. The lesson? Lock your bike well or bring it inside.

Cycling became more than just a commute for me—it turned into a lifestyle. In a country like Germany, where cycling is second nature, it's hard not to embrace it fully.

The first two semesters passed in a blur, packed with coursework and intense learning, leaving me little time to explore Germany. Since I planned to stay and work in Germany after graduation, sightseeing didn't feel urgent. While many of my classmates had already begun exploring the country, I decided to focus on academics for the time being. The final semester of my "Embedded Systems Design" course was a thesis semester. Students had the option of completing an unpaid thesis with the university or pursuing a paid thesis with a relevant company. Occasionally, the university itself offered paid thesis opportunities or part-time work to students.

Three classmates from northern India, who lived in the same student housing as I did, became close friends over time. When I secured a paid thesis with Mentor Automotive, a subsidiary of Mentor Graphics, I decided it was time to explore not only Germany but also the rest of Europe. With my student visa, which allowed travel to 16 Schengen countries without additional paperwork, the possibilities felt endless.

When I mentioned my travel plans to my friends, they shared that they were planning a trip to Paris over the Easter holiday. They planned to leave on Wednesday, so I took two days off from work to join them. Easter in Europe is celebrated widely, and with both Friday and Monday as bank holidays, it created a six-day weekend. It seemed like the perfect opportunity for my first European adventure.

Once we all highlighted our preferred destinations and places we wanted to see, one of my friends meticulously planned the itinerary, ensuring we made the most of the long weekend. Our journey would include two full days in Paris and a day each in Frankfurt, Brussels, Cologne, and Bonn. It was an ambitious schedule, but we were excited to see as much as possible.

Since I had moved to Villingen-Schwenningen, a small town 120 kilometers south of Stuttgart, for my thesis, we chose Frankfurt as our meeting point. My friends, who were based in Bremerhaven, adjusted their plans to meet me there. They would have flown out of Bremen if I hadn't joined, but Frankfurt worked better logistically for everyone.

For the first time, I travelled by an InterCity Express (ICE), Germany's high-speed train that reaches speeds of up to 320 km/h. During my earlier semesters, my student ticket allowed travel only by regional trains (RE and RS) or InterCity (IC) trains, but not the ICE. The experience of traveling at such high speeds was thrilling.

We all met at the Frankfurt Central Station, a sprawling and impressive hub that dwarfed Bremen's train station. After a quick meal at the station, we headed out to explore the city. Located along the river Main, Frankfurt—often called "*Frankfurt am Main*"—offered picturesque views with tourist attractions on both banks. We strolled along the river and visited landmarks like the Imperial Cathedral of Saint Bartholomew, the largest religious building in the city and a historic collegiate church.

The next day, we flew from Frankfurt Airport, operated by Fraport, to Paris. Our time in Paris was magical. We walked from the Louvre Museum to the Arc de Triomphe, a route often described as a must-experience. The grandeur of these landmarks exceeded our expectations. In the evening, we visited the iconic

Eiffel Tower, enjoying its stunning light shows and vibrant atmosphere.

Instead of flying back, we opted to travel by train, which allowed us to spend a day in Brussels. The Brussels Central Station itself was a masterpiece of architecture, with its glass ceilings and modern design elements. The city charmed us with its vibrant streets and historic landmarks.

From Brussels, we continued to Cologne, where we visited the Cologne Cathedral, the largest Gothic church in Northern Europe and the tallest twin-spired church in the world. The cathedral was packed with tourists, including many Indians and Chinese, who were busy capturing the beauty of the place in countless photographs. The structure's grandeur and historical significance left a lasting impression.

Our final destination was Bonn, where we visited the *Haus der Geschichte*, a museum dedicated to Germany's post-World War II history. We were amazed by how Germany, devastated by the war with over 75% of its buildings destroyed, had managed to rebuild itself into a global powerhouse within a few decades.

Bonn marked the end of our enriching trip. My friends headed back to Bremerhaven, and I returned to Villingen-Schwenningen. Sitting on the train, I reflected on the journey and realized that visiting five cities in five days was overwhelming. It would have been more enjoyable to dedicate more time to each city, a lesson I carried into future travels.

This was my first real experience exploring a developed, first-world country, and it left me elated. The trip sparked a newfound appreciation for the culture, history, and infrastructure of Europe.

The months following the trip were consumed by my thesis work. Meeting the objectives of my project was challenging but rewarding. I gained in-depth knowledge of embedded systems development, particularly FPGA development, often learning through trial and error. As the saying goes, "All's well that ends well," and my thesis concluded successfully.

Interestingly, in mid-2018, an independent publisher approached me with an offer to publish my thesis as a book. Initially skeptical, I dismissed the proposal, thinking it might be a scam. However, they followed up in December with more details. Since there were no upfront costs, and I stood to earn royalties, I decided to move forward. After some re-editing, the thesis was published in late 2019 under the title "Visualization of the Internal States of an FPGA." The book is now available on Amazon and other platforms, a milestone I'm incredibly proud of.

I wanted to celebrate this feast with my friends. With travel plans disrupted by COVID-19 restrictions, my friends and I shifted our focus to local exploration. I invited them to visit Villingen-Schwenningen and explore the nearby Black Forest. According to German regulations at the time, outdoor areas like parks were still accessible, allowing us to enjoy the region's natural beauty.

This experience, though different from our earlier adventures, reminded us of the joys of exploring and appreciating what's close to home. In hindsight, every journey, whether near or far, contributes to growth and creates memories that last a lifetime.

Statues and Vistas

While I was immersed in my thesis on "Visualization of the Internal States of an FPGA" and exploring Europe whenever I had the chance, controversies were brewing back home in India over several high-profile infrastructure projects.

In 2018, Prime Minister Narendra Modi inaugurated the world's tallest statue, the Statue of Unity, dedicated to Sardar Vallabhbhai Patel. Even before its unveiling, the project ignited heated debates. Critics, including writers, bloggers, news anchors, and politicians, argued that the estimated cost of three thousand crore rupees could have been allocated to more pressing needs such as hospitals, schools, or public welfare initiatives. Environmental activists raised concerns about the ecological impact of the statue's construction, particularly regarding the alteration of natural landscapes and potential harm to the local ecosystem. Additionally, some critics pointed to the displacement of local communities and tribes as another drawback, arguing that these populations were not adequately compensated or consulted. Others questioned the cultural and political motivations behind prioritizing Sardar Patel over other significant historical figures, sparking debates about inclusivity in national representation.

Skepticism also extended to its location, with claims that it was not tourist-friendly and would not attract sufficient visitors to justify the expense. Critics argued that the statue's remote placement in the Kevadia region of Gujarat made accessibility a challenge for international and domestic tourists alike. Concerns were raised about the limited infrastructure in the surrounding area, which, at the time of the statue's inauguration, lacked robust transportation links and adequate hospitality options.

The redevelopment of Central Vista in Delhi faced similar criticism, with concerns amplified by its launch during the COVID-19 pandemic. Environmentalists once again highlighted the potential ecological cost, including the removal of trees and the alteration of vital green spaces in an already congested city. Heritage conservationists raised alarms about the potential loss of architectural value in existing colonial-era structures, which symbolize India's historical transition from colonial rule to independence.

Many critics also questioned the timing and necessity of the project. They argued that during a health crisis, when funds and resources were critically needed for pandemic management, prioritizing such a large-scale development seemed misplaced. Funds, once again, the critics suggested, could have been better allocated to healthcare infrastructure, addressing underfunded hospitals, or bolstering the economy with targeted relief measures. Critics also expressed doubts about the need for a new Parliament building, arguing that the existing structure—a colonial-era icon—had historical and functional value that could have been preserved through renovation.

Proponents of the redevelopment pointed to insufficient space, outdated facilities, and modern legislative needs as justification for the project. However, opponents claimed these challenges could be resolved without constructing an entirely new structure. They viewed the initiative as a symbolic move to assert political dominance, especially in the face of urgent socio-economic challenges facing the nation.

Interestingly as well as surprisingly, the ambitious Bullet Train project faced similar criticism for its potential displacement of local populations, environmental impact, and perceived favoritism toward major corporate players. The term "Bullet Train" here refers to high-speed rail systems designed to travel at speeds exceeding 250 km/h, offering significantly reduced travel times and enhanced efficiency. Critics, once again, argued that the vast funds allocated to such ventures, estimated at Rs. 1.1 lakh crore, could be redirected to urgent priorities, including education and rural development. Calls for investments in modernizing schools, enhancing teacher salaries, and improving access to quality education in underserved areas were strong. Rural advocates also emphasized the need for better roads, irrigation systems, and clean water projects, arguing that these would yield more immediate and far-reaching benefits for millions.

These overlapping arguments—misallocation of resources, environmental concerns, and questions of elitist priorities—echoed across debates about infrastructure projects, highlighting a recurring tension between symbolic initiatives and tangible developmental needs. Interestingly, these same set of arguments—financial misallocation, environmental concerns, and elitist agendas—were repeated irrespective of the nature of the infrastructure project.

A recurring refrain in these debates was "India is too poor to pursue such projects." This narrative is far from reality. Post-World War II Germany offers a compelling counterpoint. After the war, more than 75% of Germany's infrastructure, including historic monuments and public buildings, lay in ruins. Despite facing poverty, hunger, and massive debris from bombings, Germany began rebuilding almost immediately. Divided into East and West Germany under foreign occupation, the country still managed to reconstruct itself, eventually becoming a global economic powerhouse. Their lesson: building infrastructure, even under challenging circumstances, lays the foundation for long-term prosperity. European countries, many of which face economic struggles today, still maintain infrastructure far superior to that of India. The stark difference underscores the importance of prioritizing public projects.

One of the common criticisms of these projects is the scale of expenditure. "Three thousand crores" may sound astronomical to individuals, but for a government, it's a fraction of its revenue. For example, the state of Maharashtra earns over three thousand crores in less than three months from taxes on alcohol alone. To offer another perspective, Reliance Industries contributes an average of twenty-eight thousand crores in Indian Rupees annually to the national exchequer, nine times the amount spent on the Statue of Unity.

Since independence, India has built only a handful monuments of national prestige; Lotus Temple designed by Iranian-American architect Fariborz Sahba in 1986; Akshardham by Vikram Lall in 2005; Vidhana Soudha by BR Manickam in 1956 stand out, but the list is sparse. The lack of iconic architecture raises the question: where has the money gone? Why hasn't India's post-independence era produced more world-class landmarks?

Traveling through Europe underscored the transformative impact of visionary infrastructure. If India aspires to transition into a developed state, leveraging the immense potential of infrastructure is non-negotiable. Visiting museums like Bonn's "*Haus der Geschichte*" illustrated how Germany, devastated by World War II, rebuilt itself through a focused commitment to industrialization, infrastructure development, and innovation. Countries like Greece, Portugal, and Spain, which have faced economic crises in recent years, have managed to maintain public infrastructure that significantly enhances the quality of life.

Greece, for example, has transformed its tourism infrastructure into a key economic driver. Despite its debt crisis, the country boasts well-maintained roads connecting its islands and mainland, modernized airports like Athens International, and an efficient public transport system in major cities. The Greek islands are further supported by an extensive ferry network, catering to millions of international tourists annually.

Similarly, Spain's focus on tourism infrastructure is evident in its world-class high-speed rail network (AVE), which connects major cities like Madrid, Barcelona, and Seville, making travel seamless for both residents and tourists. Iconic landmarks like the Sagrada Família in Barcelona and Alhambra in Granada benefit from surrounding infrastructure that enhances accessibility and visitor experience.

Portugal, while smaller in scale, has also optimized its urban transport systems to support its growing tourism sector. Cities like Lisbon and Porto feature efficient metro networks and historic trams that not only serve residents but have become tourist attractions in their own right. The modernization of airports such as Lisbon Humberto Delgado Airport and sustainable urban designs, including pedestrian-friendly zones and cycling paths, further elevate the country's appeal to global travelers.

These examples highlight how visionary planning and sustained investments in tourism-related infrastructure not only support long-term economic recovery but also enhance a nation's global reputation and quality of life.

If Germany's IC and ICE trains can revolutionize travel for Germans, improving efficiency and connectivity, then why shouldn't India's Bullet Train project offer similar benefits? Currently, India's first Bullet Train project, the Mumbai-Ahmedabad High-Speed Rail Corridor, is under construction and expected to significantly reduce travel time between the two cities from over six hours to just two hours. Beyond travel time reduction, the Bullet Train is expected to stimulate regional economic growth by enhancing connectivity, creating thousands of jobs during its construction phase, and boosting industries such as real estate and tourism along its route. With proper planning and execution, such high-speed rail systems can create ripple effects that elevate infrastructure standards and set a precedent for sustainable and modern public transport in India.

My visit to Paris reinforced the importance of thoughtful planning and bold ambition. Imagine walking from the Louvre Museum to the Arc de Triomphe—it's more than just a stroll; it's an experience that leaves a lasting impression. In contrast, a similar walk from Rashtrapati Bhavan to India Gate in Delhi doesn't quite evoke the same sense of grandeur, even though both locations share similar architectural inspirations. Designed by Edwin Lutyens and Herbert Baker, Delhi's Central Vista was heavily influenced by Washington's Capitol Complex and Paris' Champs-Élysées. But the Indian version feels disjointed, often due to years of poor city planning and fragmented construction. What could have been a cohesive symbol of national pride ends up falling short of its full potential.

The gaps in planning and execution have financial consequences that cannot be ignored. For instance, the Indian government spends over a thousand crores annually on rent for office spaces to accommodate central ministries. This recurring expense highlights the inefficiencies in current infrastructure planning. Investing in integrated infrastructure could not only eliminate these inefficiencies but also significantly enhance the public experience by centralizing operations and creating more functional spaces.

Similarly, iconic projects like the Statue of Unity serve as more than just architectural achievements; they can become drivers of tourism and symbols of national pride. The Statue of Unity, despite initial criticism, has spurred local economic activity and attracted over 2.8 million visitors in its first year alone, generating revenue of approximately Rs. 80 crore. This influx has also boosted surrounding infrastructure, including the development of over 20 hotels, improved transport links, and additional attractions such as jungle safaris and light shows. Its success prompts the question: If France can transform the Eiffel Tower, which generates an estimated 434 million Euros annually from tourism, into a global icon, why can't India create similarly impactful landmarks? Developing such projects strategically could help elevate India's global image while simultaneously providing tangible economic benefits.

One remarkable aspect of the Statue of Unity project was its swift execution. The foundation for the statue was laid in 2013 by then Chief Minister Narendra Modi, and it was inaugurated by him as Prime Minister within just five years. This achievement stands as a clear example of efficient project management and effective governance. It's a stark contrast to other projects in India, like the infamous signature bridge that took an incredible twenty years to construct and was still incomplete at the time of its inauguration.

Criticizing large-scale infrastructure projects without acknowledging their potential long-term benefits diminishes the country's ability to progress. These initiatives are far more than mere expenditures; they represent strategic investments in a nation's future. Bold, visionary projects have the power to elevate India's global standing and transform the quality of life for its citizens. To shed the outdated label of a "third world country," India must focus on innovative and forward-looking infrastructure that meets modern needs while fostering national pride and economic growth.

Ram Mandir

The recent construction of the Ram Temple in Ayodhya had reignited familiar debates. A section of society echoed arguments previously made against projects like the Statue of Unity, Central Vista, or the Bullet Train. Critics argued, "India is poor; we should prioritize hospitals and other essential public services over temples." Concerns about the potential impact on local communities and resource allocation also resurfaced. However, a far stronger criticism emerged specific to the temple—that it is communal in nature. Opponents claimed that such constructions, actively promoted by the government, undermine India's secular ethos and risk further polarizing the nation.

Whenever I visit a European city, I'm struck by how prominently cathedrals, churches, and abbeys stand as landmarks and major tourist attractions. The Cologne Cathedral in Germany or Notre-Dame in Paris—these sites aren't just places of worship; they're celebrated for their history, stunning architecture, and intricate art. Millions of people visit them every year, including Indians and non-Christians. These landmarks aren't just spiritual hubs—they've become vital parts of the city's culture and identity, seamlessly blending the sacred with the secular to boost tourism and fuel local economies. It's fascinating to see how they serve as both symbols of heritage and engines of economic activity. But when it comes to India's cultural landmarks like the Ram Mandir in Ayodhya or the Kashi Vishwanath Corridor, the narrative often takes a different turn. Instead of celebrating these spaces, the conversation shifts to skepticism or even accusations of communalism. This perspective really misses the bigger picture. Why can't a Mandir be just as significant for India as a church is in Europe? Temples like these can be powerful economic engines, attracting millions of pilgrims and tourists. They don't just hold spiritual value; they offer opportunities for fostering a deeper appreciation of India's rich cultural and architectural heritage. It's time to rethink how we view and leverage these iconic sites.

Europe has mastered the art of turning religious landmarks into cultural assets. Cathedrals and abbeys are more than spiritual hubs; they're economic powerhouses that attract tourists and boost local economies. Now, imagine if India embraced a similar mindset with its own landmarks. Sites like the Ram Mandir or Kashi Vishwanath Corridor have untapped potential to go beyond their spiritual roles, driving economic growth and fostering a sense of national pride. The parallels are clear, and the opportunity is massive.

Religious tourism has a tangible and far-reaching economic impact. Pilgrims and tourists traveling to sites like the Ram Temple rely on various modes of transportation—flights, trains, buses, and taxis—pouring money into these industries and keeping them dynamic. Their journeys also involve staying in local accommodations, from hotels to guesthouses, which directly supports the hospitality sector. While visiting, they dine at local restaurants, sample street food, and shop for souvenirs ranging from handcrafted items to locally produced goods. This cycle not only injects money into local businesses but also promotes regional craftsmanship and culture.

The ripple effect doesn't stop there. Increased tourism spurs demand for better infrastructure, such as roads, rail connectivity, and public facilities, which benefits both visitors and local residents. It also creates a variety of jobs—from tour guides and hotel staff to small-scale vendors—and raises wages in the area. This ecosystem of consumerism and development builds a foundation for sustainable economic growth. And it's not unique to temples; a "museum," would do the same, showcasing the universal appeal of cultural landmarks.

Even in the Middle East, predominantly Islamic countries also capitalize on religious tourism, turning mosques into major attractions. Sites like the Sheikh Zayed Grand Mosque in Abu Dhabi draw millions of visitors each year, showcasing breathtaking architecture and cultural heritage. Adding to this, the construction of a BAPS Hindu Mandir in Abu Dhabi highlights the UAE's strategic efforts to embrace cultural diversity and broaden its appeal to global tourists. Beyond religious sites, the UAE leverages a mix of cultural and sporting events—like hosting the Indian Premier League (IPL) even without playing cricket and global expos—to drive tourism, stimulate economic growth, and establish itself as a hub for international engagement.

Christmas Market

Europe also provides a compelling case for the economic benefits of cultural celebrations. My first Christmas in Bremerhaven was nothing short of magical. By mid-November, the city center came alive with vibrant lights, a festive atmosphere, and rows of beautifully decorated stalls selling everything from handcrafted apparel and unique accessories to artisanal chocolates. Food vendors added to the sensory delight, offering a variety of local delicacies that extended well beyond the familiar currywurst or bratwurst.

For the first time, I got to experience German street food in its festive glory. *Kartoffelpuffer*, which reminded me of Indian *aloo tikki* but crispier and deep-fried, became an instant favorite. Spicy *champignons*, served steaming hot, and *Glühwein*, a wonderfully aromatic spiced hot wine, perfectly captured the cozy, heartwarming spirit of the season.

These markets weren't just about food and gifts; they created an ecosystem that brought people together, showcasing how culture and commerce go hand in hand during the holiday season. Exactly like the religious sites, these Christmas markets are also powerful economic engines. They infuse local economies with vitality, boosting businesses, creating seasonal jobs, and drawing tourists from near and far. Beyond the stalls and festivities, these markets generate significant revenue for the hospitality industry, with visitors often booking hotels and dining at local restaurants. Different markets cultivate unique reputations, adding a layer of healthy competition among cities. For instance, Oldenburg's Christmas Market stands out as the pride of the region near Bremerhaven, drawing both locals and tourists for its charm and offerings. In southern Germany, Tübingen's market is a major attraction, famous for its unique blend of traditional crafts and modern experiences, pulling in visitors from across the area. Across the Channel in England, Winchester's Christmas Market is equally iconic, known for its stunning backdrop of Winchester Cathedral and its ability to attract crowds from nearby cities like Portsmouth and beyond. These markets demonstrate how cultural celebrations can double as significant economic drivers, revitalizing entire regions during the festive season.

State and city councils are at the heart of making these markets a success. They handle everything from issuing permits and allocating spaces to ensuring public safety, which is no small task given the scale and popularity of these events. For local businesses, artisans, and food vendors, these markets are a golden opportunity to boost sales and reach a wider audience. The vibrant atmosphere draws in crowds, while the markets themselves breathe new life into city centers, transforming them into bustling hubs of activity.

But none of this would be possible without robust infrastructure. Roads need to handle the increased traffic; reliable 24*7 electricity is essential to keep the festive lights glowing and stalls operational; and in today's connected world, strong internet connectivity ensures smooth communication and even supports modern payment systems like mobile wallets. Together, these elements create the backbone that allows these markets to thrive, showcasing the perfect interplay of cultural celebration and meticulous planning.

Projects like the Kashi Vishwanath Corridor beautifully illustrate how Modi's India is striking a balance between cultural preservation and modern development. Unfortunately, such initiatives often don't get the recognition they deserve, partly due to the polarizing nature of political discourse in the country. A project like the Kashi Vishwanath Corridor is not just about laying bricks and mortar; it's an engineering and cultural marvel.

To even begin a project of this scale, extensive research and planning are non-negotiable. Preserving ancient structures while ensuring they meet modern safety standards is no small feat. Engineers and artisans have to get creative, employing innovative techniques to maintain the structural integrity of these historical sites without compromising their authenticity. Every intricate carving, every corner of the architecture needs to align with historical records and archaeological findings. This involves meticulous research into original designs, materials, and construction techniques—and here's the kicker: traditional craftsmanship, a skill set that's dwindling with time, becomes absolutely crucial. Replicating intricate designs isn't just a task; it's an art form.

The project doesn't stop at restoration. It also tackles practical issues like traffic congestion with redesigned roads, improved intersections, and smarter traffic management systems. And let's not forget the tourists. The development includes amenities like information centers, souvenir shops, eateries, and accommodations, all designed to make the visitor experience seamless and enjoyable. Imagine walking through a space that blends the sacred with the modern, where history feels alive and accessible. That's the vision projects like this aim to achieve.

I hope similar development initiatives are extended to places like Mathura and Vrindavan. Narrow, crowded lanes and unorganized construction detract from the spiritual and cultural experience these sites can offer. Transforming these areas with organized, world-class architecture would not only improve visitor satisfaction but also increase footfall, driving further economic growth.

Mr. X

For someone living in India, it's natural to feel that the country's infrastructure projects and the accompanying debates are unique to its context. What struck me, however, was the mindset of some individuals who, despite having experienced life in developed countries, hold contradictory and often critical views about India's developmental progress.

One particular example that stands out for me is Mr. X, an Indian friend I went on my first Euro trip with while studying at Hochschule Bremerhaven. His perspectives seemed both intriguing and contradictory, offering a lens into how experiences abroad shape, or sometimes fail to shape, opinions about one's home country.

On my second day in Bremerhaven, I met him at the university bus stop. Among a sea of predominantly white faces, he stood out—a fellow Indian who, like me, seemed to be figuring things out. It felt like spotting a friendly face in a crowd of strangers, so I didn't hesitate. "You from India?" I asked, and he nodded, a hint of relief crossing his face. That opened the door to a quick, no-fuss introduction: "Hi, I'm Anant. And you?" "Mr. X," he replied. "Hindi?" I probed further, curious if we could share a common language. "Yes!" he said enthusiastically. "ESD?" I guessed, referring to the Embedded Systems Design program we were both likely part of. "Yes!!" came his equally excited response.

Just like that, I wasn't alone anymore. It felt like finding an anchor in an unfamiliar place. He didn't just stop at the introduction, though. Within minutes, he added me to a WhatsApp group for Indian students in Bremerhaven, which turned out to be an invaluable resource for navigating everything from classes to local grocery stores. From that moment, we started building a friendship that made adjusting to life abroad a little less daunting.

Within a week, we discovered a thriving Indian student community, though it was clear that people gravitated toward familiar linguistic groups. There was a Malayali group, a Tamil group, a Telugu group, a Kannada group, and a Gujarati group. Each group bonded over shared language, culture, and cuisine, creating a sense of home away from home. By default, my friends and I fell into the "rest" category—a melting pot of North Indians who didn't quite fit into the linguistic cliques.

Our small group reflected India's diversity. I was from Uttar Pradesh, Mr. X hailed from Jharkhand, while the other two were from Madhya Pradesh and Maharashtra. Despite coming from different states, we found common ground in our shared experiences of navigating a new country. Our conversations ranged from adjusting to German weather to finding the best place for Indian groceries. These interactions not only brought us closer but also highlighted the cultural richness we each brought to the table.

We all ended up in the same student hostel. Mr. X and I, being of the same age and with prior work experience in India, naturally bonded more closely, while the other two had come straight from their undergraduate studies and were younger than us.

Together, we explored Europe, including our first Euro trip to Paris. Mr. X experienced everything I did—from marveling at the 305 km/h high-speed trains (the equivalent of a "bullet train" in Indian terms) to being captivated by the grand churches and cathedrals. We shared the same sense of wonder, soaking in the history, efficiency, and grandeur that Europe had to offer. But as we traveled, I couldn't help but notice a curious inconsistency in his views when it came to India.

For instance, while he was amazed by the smooth operations and speed of Europe's high-speed trains, he dismissed the idea of bullet trains in India as unnecessary, arguing that they would only benefit the wealthy, like Adani or Ambani—an argument that doesn't hold up under scrutiny. India's bullet train project has the potential to revolutionize connectivity and foster regional development in ways that mirror Europe's success.

Similarly, Mr. X was visibly thrilled while climbing the Eiffel Tower, enthusiastically posing for pictures. Yet, he failed to recognize the economic and symbolic potential of India's Statue of Unity, which drew over 5 million visitors in 2023 and significantly boosted tourism in its region. It was baffling how he could see value in one landmark while dismissing the other.

The contradictions didn't end there. Mr. X admired the privatization of Frankfurt Airport which is owned and operated by a private company Fraport AG, acknowledging its role in improving efficiency and passenger experience. However, when Gautam Adani won contracts to operate six airports in India, he labeled it "dangerous privatization," ignoring the potential benefits such reforms could bring to India's aviation sector.

His double standards extended to cultural landmarks as well. He marveled at the beauty and historical significance of Europe's grand churches and cathedrals, recognizing them as cornerstones of cultural and architectural heritage. Yet, he dismissed the Ram Mandir project in India as a communal endeavor, failing to appreciate its cultural and historical relevance for millions of Indians.

Why this double standard? Why does Mr. X view similar developments as progressive and beneficial in Europe but regressive in India? Is it a case of holding India to a different standard, or is it a reflection of deeper biases? These questions linger with me, prompting me to critically evaluate how perspectives on development and progress are often shaped by context and preconceived notions.

The Crux: Building India

India's infrastructure has long been a symbol of its struggles and aspirations, but recent years have ushered in an era of unprecedented transformation under Modi's leadership. It's not that roads or highways weren't built in the past, but the pace and scale of construction today are truly extraordinary. Previously, infrastructure projects often spanned multiple government tenures, leaving them incomplete for decades. If timely execution had been the norm, seventy years post-independence would have sufficed to connect every village in India by road, rail and electric wires.

Semi-high-speed trains like Tejas Express and Vande Bharat Express have introduced world-class amenities and reduced travel times. The Amrit Bharat Station Scheme aims to upgrade 1300 stations, transforming hubs like Gomti Nagar, Gandhinagar Capital, and Rani Kamalapati into modern urban hubs akin to their European counterparts. Expressways such as the Delhi-Mumbai Expressway are revolutionizing connectivity, while metro systems now operate in over 20 cities, bringing transformative change to urban mobility. The rapid expansion of airports and ports has made travel across the nation more accessible and efficient for millions. Projects such as Udan, Bharatmala Pariyojana, PM Gram Sadak Yojana, and Sagarmala are no longer just blueprints but active steps toward making this vision a reality.

Travel and tourism, once overlooked as a driver of economic growth, have seen a remarkable transformation over the past decade, emerging as a vital sector for regional and national development. Modi's India is actively addressing this untapped opportunity by investing in ambitious projects such as the Statue of Unity, which has become a symbol of national pride and a major tourist attraction. Beyond generating revenue, such initiatives aim to bolster regional development, create jobs, and showcase India's rich cultural and historical heritage on the global stage.

The construction of the Ram Mandir in Ayodhya, along with the restoration of iconic temples like Kashi Vishwanath, Ujjain Mahakal, and Kedarnath, marks a significant shift in national priorities. India, once cautious about openly celebrating its cultural heritage, is now taking bold steps to preserve and revitalize it. At the same time, initiatives like the Smart Cities Mission and Mission Amrit Sarovar are redefining urban living, tackling pressing challenges such as housing shortages, inefficient waste management, and dwindling water resources.

In today's high-tech era, digital infrastructure holds immense significance. Initiatives like the Saubhagya Yojana, which aspires to achieve 100% electrification, and BharatNet, aimed at delivering high-speed internet through optical fiber to rural areas, are pivotal in bridging the digital divide and empowering underserved communities.

These ambitious initiatives reflect a vision for a modern, inclusive, and sustainable infrastructure network that connects communities, preserves cultural heritage, and addresses environmental challenges. By prioritizing connectivity, cultural rejuvenation, and environmental sustainability, Modi's India is steadily crafting a future where infrastructure serves as the backbone of national progress and resilience. Having spent a decade living abroad, I have come to deeply appreciate that robust infrastructure is not just a necessity—it is the very foundation upon which industrialization and innovation are built and thrive.

Despite these commendable strides, India's infrastructure development still grapples with the vast and complex demands of a rapidly growing and diverse nation. As the saying goes, "Rome wasn't built in a day," and neither will India's aspirations be fully realized overnight. The journey ahead demands unwavering resolve, sustained effort, and a commitment to ensuring that no corner of the nation is left behind.

INDUSTRIALIZATION

"Yatra vyavasaayah tatra dhanam upalabhyate"
–Book II, Chapter 16, Arthashastra

Where there is industrial enterprise, wealth is created.

Cocoa

Once I successfully completed my thesis at Mentor, it was time for my first visit back home. Zurich Airport, being relatively close to Villingen-Schwenningen, made taking the train to the airport and back the most convenient option. Since it was an overnight flight, I decided to take the earliest train to Zurich, giving myself a full day to explore the city. Instead of heading straight to the airport, I deboarded at Zurich train station. European train stations often provide excellent locker facilities, and this came in handy as I stored my luggage and set out to explore the city freely.

My plan was simple: get a feel for Zurich by wandering through its streets and reach the airport well in time. Without any particular destination in mind, I opened Google Maps and noticed *Zurichsee* (Lake Zurich) was just a short walk from the station. I decided to head in that direction and stroll along the waterfront. What struck me immediately was the world-class infrastructure and immaculate cleanliness—it was like stepping into a postcard or a meticulously tended backyard.

Though it was my first time in Switzerland, the place felt oddly familiar. Bollywood had firmly etched images of Switzerland into the minds of every 90s kid, and walking those streets brought a mix of nostalgia and curiosity. The scenery seemed to echo the iconic movie backdrops, making me feel like I was retracing cinematic footsteps. As I explored, the city revealed a unique charm that blended the magic of movies with the grounded beauty of real life, leaving me with an experience that was as unexpected as it was unforgettable.

During my stroll, I spotted a billboard advertising the *Schokoladen* Museum. The decision to visit didn't take long—I bought a ticket and started the tour.

How did Switzerland, a small, mountainous country in the heart of Europe, become the ultimate "chocolate country"?

This question lingered as I began the museum tour. What struck me immediately was that Switzerland doesn't grow cocoa. In fact, they import almost all of it, primarily from Ghana. Before the tour, I had a naive assumption that European countries grew some "special" cocoa that gave their chocolates their renowned taste. It turned out I couldn't have been more wrong. The secret lies not in nature, geography, or climate but in the Swiss mastery of production processes, innovation, and craftsmanship. Advanced machinery, meticulous techniques, and a relentless focus on quality have turned Swiss chocolate into a global phenomenon.

The self-paced tour was an eye-opening experience, blending history, technology, and craftsmanship into a seamless narrative. Guided by an audio companion, I embarked on a journey that began with a virtual tour of Ghana, vividly illustrating the lives of cocoa farmers and the intricate process of cultivating cocoa beans. The exhibit brought to life the challenges and dedication of these farmers, whose efforts form the backbone of the global chocolate industry.

From there, the tour transitioned to Switzerland's world-class production methods. The cutting-edge technology and high-performance machines used to process cocoa beans were nothing short of impressive. Each stage of the transformation was meticulously detailed, from the raw cocoa mass to the liquid chocolate and finally to the perfectly molded bars and intricate pralines that have become synonymous with Swiss excellence.

The museum placed a strong emphasis on research and innovation, with a dedicated section highlighting the Lindt Home of Chocolate's advanced research facility, aptly described as "the heart of our engineers and researchers." This was more than a manufacturing showcase; it was a tribute to the ingenuity and precision that have made Swiss chocolate a global benchmark.

The tour concluded with a delightful finale: a generous sampling of LINDOR chocolates in a variety of flavors. It wasn't just tasting– it was an immersive experience that underscored the culmination of Swiss expertise, leaving every visitor with a newfound appreciation for the art and science behind the world's favorite treat.

This insight wasn't confined to Switzerland alone. Most European chocolate producers adopt a similar model—sourcing raw cocoa primarily from countries like Ghana and leveraging advanced techniques, state-of-the-art machinery, and meticulous quality control to produce world-class chocolate products.

Switzerland exemplifies a model of economic success, driven by a combination of innovation, thriving high-value industries, and a comprehensive social safety net. Its economy is highly diversified, with key exports including luxury watches, advanced pharmaceuticals, and precision machinery, which collectively bolster its global standing. This industrial sophistication contributes to one of the highest GDP per capita figures globally, ensuring a consistently high standard of living for its citizens.

In stark contrast, Ghana, despite notable strides in some areas, continues to wrestle with significant challenges such as poverty, inequality, and a lack of robust infrastructure. The Ghanaian economy is heavily reliant on agriculture and mining, sectors that often suffer from price volatility and limited value addition. Furthermore, Ghana's dependence on foreign aid and external investment hampers its ability to achieve self-sustaining growth. This dichotomy underscores the profound economic disparities between industrialized nations and those still navigating the complexities of development.

The contrast between Switzerland and Ghana serves as a compelling example of the dynamics of global inequality. This disparity highlights the significant advantages industrialized economies gain through innovation, technology, and value-added production, compared to resource-based economies that remain dependent on exporting raw materials. Industrialized nations consistently achieve higher levels of wealth and development than their non-industrialized counterparts.

Even when we go back in time, colonial powers deliberately deindustrialized their colonies to maintain economic and political dominance. Colonies like India were coerced into producing and exporting raw materials, such as cotton, which were then processed using advanced technologies in the industrialized nations of Europe. These countries created high-value finished goods that were subsequently sold back to the colonies at inflated prices, further entrenching economic dependence and suppressing local industries. This system not only enriched the colonial powers but also stifled the economic growth of the colonies, leaving a legacy of inequality that persists to this day.

A striking example of this deindustrialization is India's once-thriving textile industry during British rule. India, once known for its rich textile heritage and skilled artisans, was forced to export raw cotton to Britain, where advanced textile mills transformed it into finished goods. These products were then sold back to India at inflated prices, systematically undermining local textile industries and driving countless weavers into poverty, particularly in regions like Bengal. The Manchester mills, fueled by the Industrial Revolution, rendered many Indian artisans redundant, creating widespread unemployment and deepening economic despair.

This economic exploitation played a significant role in contributing to devastating events like the Bengal famine, as the region's economy collapsed under colonial policies that prioritized British profits over local welfare. The consequences weren't just economic; they were cultural and social, stripping communities of their livelihoods and traditions.

Visionaries like Vinayak Savarkar recognized the gravity of this injustice. In response, movements like the Swadeshi Movement of 1906 emerged, encouraging Indians to boycott British goods and support indigenous production. Savarkar himself led symbolic acts of defiance, such as collecting British-made clothes and publicly burning them, galvanizing a spirit of resistance and self-reliance among the Indian populace. These actions marked an important chapter in India's struggle for economic independence, highlighting the intersection of industrialization, colonialism, and national identity.

Even after gaining independence in 1947, the scars of deindustrialization remained deeply entrenched in regions like West Bengal, which was once a beacon of industrial progress. Under British rule, the state had been systematically stripped of its industrial foundations, a legacy that proved difficult to overcome. Post-independence, the situation was compounded by political mismanagement and short-sighted policies. The rise of communist governance in West Bengal further stifled industrial revival by promoting labor-intensive sectors such as tea, jute, and paddy over modernization and diversification.

These policies created an environment where traditional industries dominated, but modern manufacturing and technology-driven enterprises struggled to establish themselves. For instance, outdated labor laws and restrictive trade union practices discouraged investments and innovation. The result was a stagnating economy unable to attract or sustain modern industries, pushing major corporations to relocate their operations to other states. This economic inertia not only curtailed West Bengal's growth but also cemented its dependence on legacy sectors that could not keep pace with a rapidly industrializing global economy.

Tata Motors serves as a notable example of West Bengal's economic stagnation and its failure to retain industrial investments. The company originally planned to establish a manufacturing facility in the state, but persistent political opposition, labor unrest, and bureaucratic hurdles forced it to relocate the project to Gujarat. This relocation marked a significant loss for West Bengal, not only in terms of potential employment but also in terms of industrial confidence.

Unfortunately, Tata Motors' exodus was not an isolated incident.

Several prominent companies, including Brooke Bond, Emami, Shrachi, Ispat, JK Tyres, Shaw Wallace, and Phillips India, also moved their operations out of West Bengal due to similar challenges. For Phillips India, the decision to shift operations began as early as the mid-1980s, reflecting a prolonged trend of industrial decline in the region. This pattern underscores the state's inability to adapt to modern industrial demands, leaving it heavily reliant on labor-intensive sectors and further eroding its once-thriving industrial base.

The stories of Switzerland, Ghana, and West Bengal highlight the critical role of industrialization in shaping economic destinies. Countries and regions that prioritize innovation, high-value industries, and effective governance are better positioned to achieve sustainable growth. Meanwhile, those that rely heavily on raw material exports often find themselves trapped in cycles of dependency and underdevelopment. By understanding these patterns, nations like India can work towards reclaiming their industrial heritage and building a more resilient and equitable economy.

Philips Town

In 2021, I rented a van to move from Villingen-Schwenningen to Eindhoven, where I was starting a new role as a senior firmware engineer with Philips Innovation Services. This transition offered me a glimpse into a completely different side of Philips. While I had always associated the brand with household products like light bulbs and electronics, I discovered that Philips is a leader in advanced medical research, including 3D live heart modeling and the production of high-tech medical equipment like CT scanners and MRI machines. The move marked the beginning of an exciting chapter, blending professional growth with a deeper appreciation for cutting-edge innovation.

After a seven-hour van ride, I arrived at *Gemmastraat*, my new home. Exhausted from the journey, I quickly drifted off to sleep. The next morning, I embraced my usual ritual when settling into a new place: taking my bicycle out to explore the neighborhood. Moving to a new city or country always brings exciting opportunities—better pay, personal growth, and exposure to different cultures—but it also comes with its fair share of challenges. Starting afresh meant scouting for a suitable place to live, finding a gym, locating sports facilities, and, perhaps most importantly, making new friends. Navigating the language barrier added another layer of complexity. A particularly amusing incident remains etched in my memory: I bought a liter of orange juice from a vending machine and another liter labeled *'Sinaasappel,'* confidently assuming it was apple juice. Imagine my surprise when I discovered '*Sinaasappel*' is Dutch for orange—leaving me staring at two liters of orange juice and questioning my linguistic assumptions! Thankfully, I didn't confuse it with "*Aardappel*," which once again doesn't have anything to do with apples and means potatoes! Moments like these reminded me that adapting to a new culture often involves a blend of humor, patience, and a willingness to learn.

I planned a short one-kilometer-radius loop around my apartment to get a better sense of the neighborhood. Cycling down *Boschdijk*, the main street, I noticed a mix of local conveniences—a pet care shop, a supermarket called Jumbo, cozy cafes, and even a Chinese takeout. Turning left, I stumbled upon a small park with an intriguing statue of Gerard Philips, shaped like a gate. Curious about its significance, I paused to look it up online. To my surprise, I discovered that Gerard Philips, along with his brother Anton, was one of the founding figures behind the company I was about to join. This little piece of history felt like a warm welcome to Eindhoven and a glimpse into its deep connection with Philips.

Another turn brought me to Strijp-S, a neighborhood that immediately distinguished itself from the rest of the city. Parking my bike, I stepped into what felt like a dynamic intersection of creativity and technology. The area buzzed with activity, hosting a vibrant mix of creative agencies, design studios, tech startups, art galleries, trendy restaurants, and co-working spaces. Every corner seemed alive, seamlessly blending Eindhoven's industrial past with its forward-thinking present.

Strijp-S, once a Philips industrial complex, has undergone an incredible transformation into a hub of culture and entrepreneurship. This reimagined space stands as a powerful example of how industrial history can be thoughtfully repurposed to shape contemporary urban landscapes. It not only functions as a center for innovation but also serves as a must-visit destination for anyone interested in technology, design, and culture.

Not only Strijp-S, Eindhoven's High Tech Campus exemplifies the city's commitment to innovation. Initially part of Philips, the campus has evolved into a world-leading innovation ecosystem, housing numerous tech companies and research institutes. Together, Strijp-S and the High Tech Campus showcase Eindhoven's unique ability to honor its industrial heritage while embracing a cutting-edge future.

Continuing my ride, I arrived at Philips Stadion, the home of PSV (*Philips Sport Vereniging*) Eindhoven, a football club steeped in history and tradition. The stadium radiated energy, and it was impossible to miss the excitement when a match was on, with crowds cheering and a festive atmosphere filling the air. Intrigued by the connection between Philips and PSV, I discovered that the club was initially founded as a recreational outlet for Philips employees, embodying the company's commitment to fostering community and well-being. The Philips Elftal played at the stadium from 1911 to 1913 when PSV took over. Remarkably, Philips continues to play a central role as the club's main sponsor, contributing €2.5 million annually. This enduring relationship highlights the deep-rooted pride Eindhoven's residents have in Philips, a sentiment that surfaced in nearly every conversation I had with the locals.

Reaching the city center, I came across an impressive underground bicycle parking facility with an innovative design: vertically stacked racks that allowed bikes to be securely locked while optimizing space. This clever infrastructure reflected Eindhoven's focus on practical, user-friendly urban planning. As I continued my walk, I stumbled upon the Philips Museum and monuments honoring Frits and Anton Philips. These landmarks underscored the deep historical and economic ties Philips shares with the city. Beyond their industrial achievements, the monuments symbolize the company's role in shaping Eindhoven's identity.

With just a brief cycling tour around my new neighborhood and through the city center, I immediately grasped why Eindhoven is affectionately called the Philips City. The influence of Philips is unmistakable, leaving an indelible mark on the city's character and identity.

After staying in Eindhoven for over a year, I realized, most businesses in Eindhoven are either directly or indirectly linked to Philips, forming a complex and dynamic network of suppliers, service providers, and spin-offs. Global leaders like ASML and NXP, originally rooted in Philips, exemplify the company's far-reaching influence and the city's transformation into a thriving tech and innovation hub.

In short, Philips industrialized Eindhoven by transforming it from a quiet, modest town into a vibrant industrial hub. Over time, the city's identity became intertwined with innovation, driven by Philips' pivotal role in fostering industrial growth, technological progress, and a knowledge-based economy, ultimately earning Eindhoven the nickname "Brainport."

I made an interesting observation in Eindhoven. The city's industrialization has had a remarkable impact on non-technical businesses like restaurants, fitness centers, etc. For instance, a barber in Eindhoven charges approximately €30 for a haircut, while in Bulandshahr, India— the small town I come from , with little or no visible industry—the same service costs around INR 60. (at the time of writing this, one Euro is equivalent to 89 rupees). The price difference is staggering, especially considering, more often than not, the haircut back home is better than what I get in Eindhoven. This stark contrast illustrates the Klondike effect, where industrial hubs like Eindhoven create significant purchasing power, driving income growth across all sectors—not only in technology but also in everyday services such as haircuts and dining. This phenomenon highlights the extensive influence of industrialization on local economies and lifestyles. What's particularly intriguing is how companies like Philips act as engines for this ripple effect. By establishing technical and specialized jobs, they stimulate demand for complementary services, ultimately enhancing the earning potential for professionals in unrelated field

This isn't unique to Eindhoven and Philips. Similar patterns are evident in industrialized cities worldwide. Take Bangalore, for example, often dubbed the "Silicon Valley of India." The city mirrors these dynamics, with wages and the cost of living significantly higher compared to smaller, non-industrial towns. Bangalore's burgeoning IT sector has spurred growth in hospitality, transportation, and retail, creating a diverse and interconnected economic ecosystem. Such concentrated innovation and enterprise highlight the transformative power of industrialization in uplifting entire communities and fostering economic diversity. The same haircut that cost €30 in Eindhoven and INR 60 in Bulandshahr, costs INR 250 in Bengaluru .

Eindhoven's transformation underscores the transformative power of industrialization in defining a region's economic trajectory. Imagine if Philips had been compelled to leave Eindhoven, as it was in West Bengal due to challenges like land acquisition protests or union strikes—issues commonly encountered in parts of India—the city's trajectory might have been dramatically altered. Rather than evolving into a high-tech innovation hub, Eindhoven would have remained a cluster of villages dependent on agriculture, struggling with subsistence farming, and organizing protests for Minimum Support Prices (MSP). Philips' presence didn't just build factories; it built an ecosystem of progress that reshaped the region's identity and future.

In India, industrialists often become targets of political rhetoric, with slogans like "Ambani is a thief" or "Adani is a thief" dominating public discourse. While these narratives may garner short-term political gains, they carry long-term consequences—deterring industrialization and hindering the nation's economic growth. This vilification fails to acknowledge the critical role industrialists play in driving economic progress and generating employment. Interestingly, the scrutiny faced by family-run businesses in India contrasts sharply with the success of similar enterprises abroad. For instance, Dassault Aviation, a family-run company that exported Rafale jets to India, highlights how entrepreneurial vision can underpin industrial and technological advancement. Embracing this perspective is essential for creating an environment conducive to innovation and sustainable development.

West Bengal experienced a sharp decline due to decades of political mismanagement, policy stagnation, and frequent labor unrest. This hostile environment forced major companies like Tata Motors, Brooke Bond, Philips India, etc. to relocate their operations to other states, stripping West Bengal of critical economic drivers. As a result, the state became overly reliant on agriculture and small-scale industries, struggling to recover its former industrial prominence.

Similarly, Kerala's economy, though praised for its focus on social welfare under the "Kerala Model," remains heavily dependent on remittances from its diaspora and lacks a strong industrial foundation. While remittances provide a steady inflow of foreign currency and help stabilize household incomes, they come with significant downsides. Overdependence on remittances often discourages the growth of local industries and entrepreneurship, as a substantial portion of the working-age population seeks employment abroad instead of contributing to the domestic economy. This reliance also makes the state vulnerable to external shocks, such as economic downturns or policy changes in host countries that can drastically reduce remittance flows.

The state's agrarian focus, while supporting local livelihoods, has not translated into significant economic growth or diversification. In comparison, thriving industrial economies like Gujarat demonstrate how strategic investment in industry can drive robust development, creating a more balanced and sustainable growth trajectory. The absence of a solid industrial backbone in states like West Bengal and Kerala highlights the importance of fostering industries that can generate employment, boost exports, and sustain long-term economic health. States like West Bengal and Kerala serve as stark examples of the consequences of neglecting industrialization.

Having said all that, communist and left-leaning politics is not the sole reason for deindustrialization in various states in India—poor and shortsighted policymaking has also played a significant role.

A prime example of this is the Freight Equalization Policy. What the British Raj did to India pre-independence in terms of suppressing local industries, the Indian government post-independence inadvertently replicated in states like Bihar and Jharkhand through this policy. The policy disrupted the natural economic advantage of resource-rich states and contributed to their industrial stagnation, a setback that would take decades to overcome.

Geo-Return

Implemented in 1952, the Freight Equalization Policy was intended to promote equitable industrial growth across India by subsidizing transportation costs for raw materials. In theory, this meant that industries could be established anywhere in the country, especially in coastal regions with access to trade routes, without bearing the financial burden of transporting raw materials from resource-rich regions. The government subsidized these costs, removing the natural advantage mineral-rich states like Bihar, Jharkhand, Chhattisgarh, and Odisha would have had due to their proximity to resources. However, instead of fostering balanced industrial development, this policy unintentionally hindered the industrial growth of these resource-rich states, diverting investment and opportunities elsewhere.

This policy led to significant deindustrialization in these resource-rich states while simultaneously promoting industrialization in others. The resulting disparity continues to shape socio-economic dynamics today. When politicians visit states like Tamil Nadu, Karnataka, or Andhra Pradesh and mock Bihar for its poverty, they often overlook the root cause—a policy enacted in 1952 that systematically disadvantaged these regions. Quite interestingly, some of these politicians actually belong to the political party and the family that enacted the policy in 1952.

Although India gained independence in 1947, states like Bihar remained trapped in a colonial-style economic framework. They were forced to export raw materials like coal and iron ore while importing finished goods, effectively stifling any opportunity for local industrial development. This policy ensured that the economic benefits of their natural resources flowed to other regions, leaving these states underdeveloped.

Even though the Freight Equalization Policy was phased out in 1993, the damage it caused was long-lasting. By the time the policy was phased out, the industrial vacuum in these states had allowed anti-social elements to thrive, further destabilizing the region; illegal mining, extortion, land mafia-sand mafia etc. etc. The lack of industrialization not only impeded economic growth but also exacerbated issues like unemployment, migration, and poor infrastructure, setting these states back by decades.

When I began working with Airbus Defence and Space (ADS) in Portsmouth, I had no idea that I would contribute to an Earth exploration satellite being developed for the European Space Agency (ESA). This allowed me an opportunity to delve into ESA's industrial policy and its cornerstone principle of Geo-return. ESA, an intergovernmental organization comprising approximately 22 sovereign member states, operates with a clear mandate outlined in the ESA Convention. One of its primary objectives is to enhance the global competitiveness of European industry while fostering the participation of small and medium-sized enterprises (SMEs) in ESA procurements. This approach not only ensures equitable involvement of member states but also promotes innovation and industrial growth across Europe.

It ensures that all Member States participate equitably in implementing European space programs and the associated development of space technology, proportional to their financial contributions. To achieve this, the Agency prioritizes granting opportunities to industries within member states, ensuring they have the maximum chance to contribute to technological projects.

From its inception, ESA and its preceding organizations have adhered to the principle of 'fair return,' a policy that has continuously evolved over time. Since the Council at Ministerial level in March 1997, ESA has established the rule that the ratio between a country's share in the weighted value of contracts and its financial contribution to the Agency must reach a specified percentage by the end of a given period. This ratio, known as the industrial return coefficient, ensures balanced participation and fosters industrial competitiveness across all member states.

One of the projects I worked on, ROSE-L (Radar Observing System for Europe in L-band), exemplified the policy of geo-return for me. This Earth-observing synthetic aperture radar (SAR) mission aims to monitor geohazards, track land use, agriculture, and forestry, provide high-resolution soil moisture data, and observe the Arctic and cryosphere. The contract for ROSE-L was established between ESA and TAS (Thales Alenia Space), an Italian company. However, ESA's geo-return policy necessitated collaboration with numerous companies across various countries, ensuring that the work extended beyond Italy. Airbus was tasked with constructing the radar instrument, while Thales Alenia Space managed most subsystem components. Airbus Defence and Space in Friedrichshafen, Germany, led an industrial consortium spanning nine countries for the radar instrument. Meanwhile, Airbus Defence and Space Ltd in Portsmouth, UK, handled the satellite payload, including the Digital Back End (where I contributed) and the Software Validation Facility. Thales Alenia Space contributed components like the Power Control and Distribution Unit (PCDU) and Solar Array Photovoltaic Assembly (PVA) from Belgium, a monitoring camera from Switzerland, and the Ka-band Transmission Assembly, Remote Interface Unit (RIU), and S-band Transponder from Spain. Additionally, Leonardo provided the Star Trackers, further showcasing the extensive multinational collaboration behind this mission.

Apart from the major companies like Airbus and Thales, there are a number of SMEs that are used for providing various components. For example, the PCB design and layout are done at Airbus however, a different SME was used to manufacture the PCB. Transmit and Receive modules are done by a different SME, so on and so forth. In short, ESA's strict adherence to the geo return policy means that a number of places within Europe get a chance to industrialize their cities by just one project.

Imagine if India had implemented a policy similar to ESA's Geo-return instead of the Freight Equalization Policy. States like Bihar and Jharkhand, with their abundant natural resources, could have evolved into industrial powerhouses, driving regional development and reducing disparities. The economic opportunities lost due to Freight Equalization could have been redirected into creating a balanced industrial ecosystem across states.

Moreover, cities like Bangalore, which are currently overburdened and congested due to concentrated industrialization and IT growth, might have seen more sustainable development if industries were more evenly distributed across India. With 28 states in the country, a policy ensuring equitable participation in critical sectors like Defence and Space could transform India into a highly industrialized nation, leveraging the unique strengths of each region. Such a vision could address unemployment, reduce migration pressures, foster localized growth, and most importantly reduce the deep chasm of economic inequality in various regions of the same country leading to a more balanced and prosperous economic landscape. Some say there are two Indias within India, a policy similar to ESA's geo-return can reduce the distance and the differences between those two Indias and maybe one day, they become one!

This is just one example of how a cohesive policy and clear vision have facilitated Europe's industrialization. However, the process of industrialization became central to major European nations long before the introduction of ESA's geo-return policy.

Rebuilding Germany

Ever since I set foot in Germany, I was preoccupied by a recurring question: how did a country that was utterly devastated by a world war, bombarded, and reduced to ruins, manage to rebuild itself so quickly and to such extraordinary standards? This curiosity grew stronger once I began living and working in Villingen-Schwenningen, a small city I had never heard of until I received an offer to join Mentor Automotive.

Before making the decision to move 800 kilometers across Germany—to a place literally on the other end of the country—I decided to ask a few German colleagues at the university about it. Simple questions like, "Do you know this place? Have you been there? What's the work culture like?" Their responses were surprising; they had no clue where Villingen-Schwenningen was. If Mentor Automotive hadn't been part of the globally recognized Mentor Graphics, I might not have taken the leap and made the move from Bremerhaven to Villingen-Schwenningen. But as it turned out, this decision offered me a deeper understanding of Germany's remarkable journey of rebuilding and progress.

Once I actually started living there, I discovered that Villingen-Schwenningen was home to a remarkable range of small engineering companies. These included firms specializing in metalworking, precision engineering, automotive parts manufacturing, biomedical engineering, and even cutting-edge electronics, IT, and software development. The diversity and vibrancy of the industrial landscape was truly impressive.

To be honest, people like myself envy those living in these small yet industrially vibrant cities, where individuals often don't have to leave their hometowns to find meaningful and well-paying jobs. Of course, they have the option to move elsewhere if they wish, but having the freedom to choose is a privilege that many take for granted. Unfortunately, this kind of autonomy remains a distant dream for young professionals in most Indian cities. Except for a handful of urban hubs like Bangalore, Hyderabad, Chennai, Noida, Greater Noida, Gurgaon, Mumbai, Delhi etc. local tech opportunities in smaller cities are scarce. For the majority of Indians, moving to a metropolitan city isn't a choice but a necessity driven by the lack of industrial and economic opportunities in their hometowns.

Fortunately for me, a test engineer, who became a close friend and retired during my tenure at Mentor Graphics, shared invaluable insights on my recurring question during one of our lunch conversations. He provided just the right hints that not only guided me toward finding answers to several lingering questions but also dispelled some deeply ingrained myths that I, along with many others, have held for years. His perspective was both enlightening and transformative, leaving a lasting impact on my understanding of history and economic recovery.

He explained that after WWII, various plans were considered to rebuild war-torn countries, with two major strategies emerging for Germany. Initially, in 1944, U.S. Secretary of the Treasury Henry Morgenthau Jr. proposed the Morgenthau Plan. This plan sought to eliminate Germany as a military threat by dismantling its industrial base, particularly in the Ruhr region, and transforming it into a predominantly pastoral and agrarian nation. The logic was simple– without industry, Germany could never wage war again. However, the plan's implementation quickly revealed its flaws. Deindustrialization threatened to plunge Germany into severe economic devastation, leading to mass starvation and widespread social instability. As a result, the plan was abandoned within a few years.

In 1947, U.S. Secretary of State George C. Marshall proposed an alternative approach, now famously known as the Marshall Plan. This strategy was the polar opposite of the Morgenthau Plan. Instead of deindustrializing Germany, the Marshall Plan aimed to re-industrialize the nation. The focus shifted toward rebuilding war-torn infrastructure, restoring factories, and reviving the economy. This dramatic pivot recognized that a stable and economically prosperous Germany was essential not only for its own recovery but also for the broader stability and security of Europe.

As per the plan, a significant amount of funds were to be made available to war torn countries, not only to the allied force countries but also to Germany and Soviet Union. It is indeed a myth that all the funds as per Marshal Plan went to Germany or rather West Germany at that time. In fact between 1948 to 1952 approximately $13 billion was sanctioned toward the European Recovery Program. The largest pie, roughly 26% i.e. around $3 billion went to the UK, 20% i.e. around $2.6 billion went to France, $1.5 billion went to Italy, 11% i.e. around $1.1 billion to West Germany, 8% to the Netherlands, 5% went to Greece, and so forth.

The Soviet Union and other communist bloc countries, such as East Germany, Romania, and Poland, refused to participate in the Marshall Plan due to ideological differences and geopolitical tensions with the West. This refusal significantly impacted their industrial trajectories, as these nations relied on centralized planning and limited integration into global markets. While some achieved modest industrial growth within the Soviet sphere, their industries often lagged behind those of the Marshall Plan recipients in terms of modernization, efficiency, and competitiveness. The long-term effects of this decision are evident today, as many of these countries continue to grapple with the economic consequences of outdated industrial infrastructures and a slower transition to market economies post-Cold War.

Another question that quickly popped up in my head was: if funding was made available to roughly 16 countries under the Marshall Plan, what did Germany do differently to achieve such remarkable results compared to others? My colleague, in his characteristic engaging manner, offered a comprehensive yet accessible explanation. He explained that the success stemmed largely from how the Marshall Plan was structured and executed.

Recipient nations convened in Paris to identify and deliberate on their specific needs and priorities. This collaboration led to the establishment of the Organization for European Economic Cooperation (OEEC), which coordinated closely with the Economic Cooperation Administration (ECA) in Washington, D.C., responsible for overseeing the recovery program. This setup ensured not only that aid was tailored to the distinct requirements of each nation but also that the distribution process was efficient and collaborative, creating a shared framework for rebuilding Europe. Germany's strategic approach within this framework was what ultimately set it apart.

The money contributed by the U.S. under the Marshall Plan included funds for loans but was primarily allocated (70 percent) towards purchasing commodities from U.S. suppliers. This arrangement was carefully designed to address the specific needs of recipient countries. For example, if one country requested fertilizers and another required machinery, those goods were supplied accordingly. However, there were critical conditions attached to these transactions.

Firstly, all goods, machinery, and other supplies had to be procured from American companies. This stipulation not only ensured the effective use of allocated funds but also boosted the industrial productivity of U.S. suppliers, creating a direct economic benefit for American businesses; killing two birds with the same stone. These transactions were conducted in dollars, drawing from the funds allocated to each recipient country.

Secondly, and more importantly, the goods were not distributed as gifts or handouts. Instead, a counterfund mechanism was established in each recipient country. Under this system, countries paid for the goods they received, not in a single lump sum but through installments, akin to EMIs for a large loan, in their local currencies. These locally accumulated funds were then reinvested within the recipient countries for various developmental and infrastructure projects, effectively creating a cycle of reinvestment and growth that supported long-term recovery and modernization.

The key difference lies in the 1953 London Agreement, which made Germany liable to repay a third of its debts to the U.S., while other countries benefited from goods provided as gifts or through significant loan waivers, absolving them from repayment. This obligation to repay instilled a sense of fiscal responsibility in Germany, compelling it to allocate funds strategically. Rather than treating the aid as free assistance, Germany channeled the money into providing loans to its own small and medium-sized enterprises (SMEs). This approach fostered entrepreneurship and industrial recovery, ensuring that the funds were utilized effectively to rebuild the economy. In essence, Germany embraced the philosophy of "no free meals," turning its repayment obligation into an opportunity for sustainable growth.

While my colleague explained it brilliantly, it took me some time and patience to fully grasp and appreciate the nuances of the plan. Over time, as I gradually understood its bits and pieces, I began to notice parallels with developments in India over the last decade.

The Modi government has, knowingly or unknowingly, adopted strategies reminiscent of those that successfully rebuilt nations like Germany. One prominent initiative is the flagship "Mudra Loan" program, which parallels the Marshall Plan in its emphasis on empowering people through financial support rather than direct handouts. Under the PM Mudra Yojana, individuals and groups eager to start or grow their businesses are offered loans instead of subsidies. As of now, over 46 crore loans totaling ₹27+ lakh crore have been disbursed.

MUDRA, or Micro Units Development & Refinance Agency Ltd, was established by the Government of India under PMMY to promote financial inclusiveness and support the development of micro-enterprises. This scheme primarily targets marginalized and socio-economically disadvantaged communities, helping millions fulfill their entrepreneurial dreams while fostering self-reliance and independence.

Mudra loans are structured into categories to meet varied entrepreneurial needs. The "*Shishu*" category provides loans up to ₹50,000, aimed at startups and small businesses needing initial funding. The "*Kishore*" category, covering loans from ₹50,000 to ₹5 lakh, supports businesses seeking expansion or consolidation.

The "*Tarun*" category offers loans above ₹5 lakh and up to ₹10 lakh, focusing on established businesses investing in growth. Lastly, "*Tarun Plus*" extends support with loans between ₹10 lakh and ₹20 lakh for high-growth enterprises needing substantial capital.

The Pradhan Mantri MUDRA Yojana (PMMY) has significantly advanced financial inclusion, empowering millions of entrepreneurs to turn their ideas into successful ventures. By fostering economic growth and instilling independence, the scheme lays the foundation for a more inclusive and resilient economy.

Moreover, Mudra loans have formalized large sections of India's informal economy. By integrating unorganized sectors into a structured financial framework, the scheme enhances transparency, facilitates access to formal credit, and enables sustainable growth. This transformation not only uplifts small businesses but also strengthens the broader economic ecosystem, contributing substantially to India's development.

Similarly, "Make in India" initiative, coupled with various Production Linked Incentives (PLIs), has brought a significant push to industrialization and manufacturing in India. These programs aim to attract investment, boost domestic production, and enhance India's position as a global manufacturing hub. By incentivizing sectors like electronics, pharmaceuticals, and automotive manufacturing, the government has created a framework that encourages innovation and strengthens the supply chain ecosystem, signaling a transformative era for India's industrial landscape.

Unfortunately, due to the prevailing political discourse, you might have heard claims in India along the lines of, "It's too late to invest in manufacturing; we cannot compete with China in this domain." While there is some truth to the notion that India is late to the game, the adage "better late than never" applies perfectly here.

Despite the current limitations, such as outdated manufacturing practices and the fact that "Make in India" often translates to mere "assembling" in many cases, progress is still achievable.

Industrial development is a gradual process—you crawl before you walk, and walk before you run. This is evident in the historical trajectories of many European nations, where industrialization evolved over decades through strategic planning, policy consistency, and incremental advancements. For instance, Germany's transformation post-WWII highlights how focused efforts on rebuilding infrastructure, supporting small and medium enterprises (SMEs), and fostering technological innovation led to its emergence as an industrial powerhouse. Similarly, the United Kingdom's Industrial Revolution did not occur overnight; it was the result of gradual investments in mechanization, infrastructure, and workforce education over years.

For India, a robust manufacturing base can be built with persistent policy support, targeted investments, and a commitment to fostering innovation. Emulating these proven approaches, India can systematically overcome its current limitations, paving the way for sustainable industrial growth and global competitiveness.

I sincerely hope the government stays resolute against negative political influences and maintains its focus on strengthening the MSME sector through substantial financial incentives and accessible loans, rather than succumbing to political pressures and resorting to handouts and freebies. Strategic support for MSMEs can act as a catalyst, bridging economic disparities and steering the nation toward sustainable industrial growth. By nurturing innovation, enhancing productivity, and creating employment opportunities, such measures will lay the foundation for a resilient and competitive economy.

While it is true that India is industrializing at an unprecedented pace, it also remains a fact that more than fifty percent of the active workforce is still engaged in sectors yielding diminishing returns. Agriculture and farming, although vital for food security and rural livelihoods, inherently offer lower productivity and limited potential for exponential growth compared to industries, manufacturing, technology, and innovation-driven sectors. These latter domains provide increasing returns, characterized by scalability, higher efficiency, and greater economic impact. Transitioning the workforce toward such high-yield sectors, while maintaining the importance of agriculture, is crucial for India to achieve sustainable and inclusive economic development.

Diminishing Returns

The Law of Diminishing Returns is a core economic concept that explains why, as successive units of a variable input (such as labor or fertilizer) are added to a fixed input (like land), the incremental productivity of the variable input eventually decreases. Initially, increasing inputs like water, fertilizer, or labor leads to significant gains in output. However, beyond a certain threshold, these inputs yield progressively smaller benefits and may even result in inefficiencies. In extreme cases, excessive inputs can reduce total productivity due to overcrowding, resource depletion, or environmental degradation.

This principle poses a significant challenge for small-scale farmers, who often operate with limited resources. When farmers attempt to maximize yields by increasing inputs, they often face escalating costs and diminishing returns, which erode profitability. This issue is compounded by external factors like volatile input prices, unpredictable weather, and environmental constraints, making sustainable farming practices critical for long-term viability.

Punjab provides a striking example of the Law of Diminishing Returns in action. Despite being one of the driest regions in India, with an average annual rainfall of just 649 mm, the state continues to cultivate water-intensive crops like paddy on a large scale. Currently, approximately 28 lakh hectares of land in Punjab are devoted to rice cultivation, with a staggering 73% of this area relying on groundwater irrigation. This unsustainable practice has led to rapid groundwater depletion. If current extraction rates persist, Punjab's groundwater reserves could be entirely exhausted within the next two decades.

The implications are severe. Farmers must dig deeper wells to access water, which not only increases energy consumption but also inflates operational costs. Electric and diesel pumps become less efficient as they operate at greater depths, further exacerbating the financial strain on farmers. This scenario traps them in a vicious cycle of rising expenses and diminishing profits, perfectly illustrating the concept of diminishing returns.

Moreover, the over extraction of groundwater has broader environmental repercussions. It disrupts the natural hydrological balance, reduces soil fertility, and increases the risks of desertification over time. These compounding challenges make it imperative for Punjab to reconsider its agricultural practices and adopt more sustainable crop choices to safeguard both its economy and ecology. Agriculture is a dynamic field influenced by a range of interdependent factors, including soil quality, seed performance, fertilizer costs, and unpredictable weather patterns. These factors often amplify the challenges posed by diminishing returns, where escalating inputs yield progressively smaller outputs. Without embracing innovative techniques or implementing structural reforms, agriculture risks devolving into an unsustainable endeavor, particularly in regions reliant on traditional methods.

Punjab's agricultural challenges are deeply rooted in policy frameworks, with the Minimum Support Price (MSP) mechanism being a significant factor. Introduced in the 1960s to address food scarcity, MSP was instrumental in ensuring national food security by incentivizing farmers to focus on crops like wheat and rice. This policy played a critical role in making India self-sufficient in grains, but over time, it has created an overreliance on monocropping. Continuous cultivation of wheat and rice has led to soil nutrient depletion, forcing farmers to depend heavily on chemical fertilizers and pesticides. This not only escalates input costs but also accelerates ecological degradation, such as soil erosion and water contamination.

India's agricultural landscape has undergone substantial changes since MSP's inception. The country now produces surplus grains, much of which goes to waste due to inadequate storage infrastructure. This overproduction has trapped farmers in a cycle of declining productivity and rising expenses. For instance, Punjab's agricultural GDP growth rate has stagnated at just 1.9% annually since 2004-05, significantly below the national average of 3.5%. This disparity highlights the pressing need for structural reforms to address the inefficiencies stemming from outdated policy frameworks and to promote diversification and sustainable farming practices.

In response to these systemic issues, the Modi government introduced a series of agricultural reforms in 2020, encapsulated in three farm bills:

1. *Farmers' Produce Trade and Commerce (Promotion and Facilitation) Bill, 2020:* This bill aimed to grant farmers the freedom to sell their produce outside government-regulated APMC (Agricultural Produce Market Committee) Mandis.
2. *Farmers (Empowerment and Protection) Agreement on Price Assurance and Farm Services Bill, 2020:* This bill established a legal framework for contract farming, enabling farmers to secure buyers before sowing their crops.
3. *Essential Commodities (Amendment) Act:* This bill restricted government intervention under the Essential Commodities Act to situations of extreme price volatility.

While the latter two bills were relatively uncontroversial, the first bill, aimed at dismantling the monopoly of APMC Mandis and reducing the influence of middlemen, ignited widespread opposition. Middlemen, or *arhatiyas*, who currently earn commissions of up to 8.5% in Mandis, strongly resisted the bill as it posed a direct threat to their livelihoods. This resistance was amplified by political opportunism and media narratives, which portrayed the reforms as an attack on farmers' rights. This framing overshadowed the bill's potential benefits, which included empowering farmers by providing them with direct access to broader markets, reducing dependency on intermediaries, and enabling greater autonomy in deciding where and how to sell their produce.

Farmers in all the countries I have visited so far enjoy the freedom to sell their produce directly to wholesalers, supermarkets, food processors, or even export companies. This freedom enables them to negotiate better prices, retain a larger share of their profits, and minimize reliance on intermediaries, who often claim a significant portion of their earnings. By eliminating middlemen, transactions become more transparent, providing farmers with greater control over their livelihoods and financial stability. Moreover, direct access to a variety of markets allows farmers to respond quickly to changing consumer demands. This adaptability not only boosts their profitability but also ensures the long-term sustainability of the agricultural sector. In essence, this model creates a mutually beneficial scenario for both producers and consumers, fostering an efficient and dynamic agricultural economy.

The chaos and unrest that unfolded in 2020 in India, fueled by political opportunism and deep-rooted resistance to change, escalated to a point where a democratically elected government with a clear majority was forced to roll back the farm bills. This represented a major setback for agricultural reform in the country—a missed opportunity to tackle systemic inefficiencies and provide farmers with broader market access and greater autonomy. Although India came tantalizingly close to achieving transformative change in its agricultural sector, the rollback highlighted the persistent challenges and deep divides that hinder the nation's progress toward comprehensive agricultural modernization.

The silver lining for small-scale Indian farmers is that, despite the setback of the farm bill rollback, the Indian Government is actively exploring strategies to address the excess supply of wheat and rice. By manipulating demand and encouraging crop diversification, the government aims to create temporary relief for overproduction issues while laying the groundwork for more balanced agricultural practices. This approach seeks to provide some immediate respite to farmers while addressing broader systemic challenges.

To tackle the ecological and economic inefficiencies caused by rice and wheat monocropping, the Indian government has pivoted toward promoting millets as a sustainable alternative. Referred to as "Shree Ann" or the "mother of all grains," millets are not only water-efficient but also nutritionally superior to conventional staple grains. These crops require significantly less water to grow, making them particularly well-suited for regions facing water scarcity. By launching targeted awareness campaigns and branding initiatives, the government aims to stimulate demand for millets, thereby encouraging farmers to diversify their crop choices.

As demand for millets increases, their market value is expected to rise, offering farmers a viable economic incentive to transition away from water-intensive crops like paddy. This strategic shift is poised to create a dual benefit: enhancing environmental sustainability by reducing groundwater depletion and fostering economic viability for farmers. The promotion of millets exemplifies a forward-looking approach to agricultural reform, aligning economic incentives with ecological stewardship.

Agriculture isn't the only sector where the government has made an attempt to strategically influence the supply side by manipulating demand. A similar demand-driven approach has been extended to renewable energy, signaling a commitment to a greener and more sustainable future. Policies offering financial incentives for electric vehicles (EVs) and imposing restrictions on renewing old, polluting vehicles reflect a balanced carrot-and-stick strategy to accelerate the transition to green technology. Additionally, subsidies for solar panel installations further reinforce efforts to promote sustainable energy practices.

These initiatives align seamlessly with global trends. For instance, in the UK, several private companies have implemented salary sacrifice schemes, making electric cars more affordable for employees. Moreover, electricity providers offer mechanisms for households to sell surplus solar energy back to the grid, creating an added economic incentive for adopting renewable energy solutions. By aligning economic incentives with environmental objectives, such measures not only encourage the adoption of green technologies but also lay a robust foundation for long-term sustainability across industries. This multidimensional strategy underscores the government's forward-thinking approach to balancing economic growth with ecological responsibility.

While Prime Minister Modi's leadership has spearheaded bold reforms, the real challenge lies in ensuring these initiatives endure and adapt beyond his tenure. Achieving true transformation in agriculture and other sectors requires systemic reforms and broad societal acceptance. Adam Smith, a Scottish economist, philosopher, and author widely regarded as the father of modern economics, articulated in "The Wealth of Nations" that economic progress is driven by self-interest. While Smith didn't explicitly state, "a baker does not produce bread out of kindness or generosity but out of greed," his principle implies that economic activities are driven by the desire to earn a living and generate profit. Applying this to Indian agriculture, it becomes evident that farmers, like any other professionals, are motivated by economic returns. As such, the romanticized notion of the farmer as "*annadata*," or the benevolent provider for the nation, must evolve.

Farming should be recognized as a profession—an entrepreneurial venture driven by market forces, innovation, and efficiency. Industrialists, too, will only invest in mechanizing agriculture when there are tangible returns.

To realize meaningful and sustainable change, Indian society must empower farmers with the tools, opportunities, and incentives that align with market dynamics. Shifting this perception is critical to addressing systemic inefficiencies and unlocking the full potential of India's agricultural sector.

In India, however, the rollback of the farm bills starkly highlighted the entrenched "*annadata*" syndrome—a deep-seated cultural idealization that often resists modernization and reform. This mindset continues to obstruct progress, preventing farming from being recognized as a professional enterprise. Until farming is reimagined as a business opportunity rather than a traditional vocation, systemic inefficiencies will persist, and true agricultural modernization will remain elusive.

While Punjab struggles with groundwater depletion on one end of the spectrum, Kerala faces a contrasting yet equally alarming crisis related to its abundant rainfall, averaging over 3000 mm annually. Paddy is a water-intensive crop, and while water scarcity in Punjab contributes to diminishing returns, Kerala faces the opposite issue—abundant water but declining paddy cultivation due to political and economic factors. In the 1970s, Kerala produced 13.76 Lakh Metric Tonnes (LMT) of rice, a figure that has now plummeted to less than 5.49 LMT.

Historically, Kerala was rich in wetlands, which covered 8.8 lakh hectares in the 1970s. By 2015, this area had drastically shrunk to just 1.96 lakh hectares and continues to diminish rapidly. This reduction has caused two significant problems. First, the state now meets only 15% of its domestic rice demand. The dominance of plantation crops like rubber and coffee, which constitute 82% of Kerala's agricultural output, has further compounded the issue.

While these crops are profitable, they are not edible staples. The reality is stark: you can't feed a population with rubber or coffee. With a requirement of at least 40 LMT of rice to sustain its population, Kerala is heavily dependent on imports to bridge this gap.

Second, the disappearance of wetlands has posed a critical environmental challenge, as these wetlands historically served as natural water reservoirs. For instance, a paddy field with an average water level of one foot can hold approximately 3 million liters of water per hectare. The loss of 7.7 lakh hectares of wetlands represents a staggering volume of water no longer retained, which has significantly reduced the state's natural water retention capacity. This depletion is a direct consequence of short-sighted agricultural policies aimed at short-term electoral gains without considering long-term impacts.

The vanishing wetlands have left Kerala increasingly vulnerable to frequent and devastating floods, as starkly demonstrated by the catastrophic events of 2018. The areas submerged during these floods were, in fact, traditional wetlands reclaiming their natural role as water catchments. This phenomenon is not merely a manifestation of "nature's fury" but a systemic failure stemming from unsustainable land use practices and overpopulation in a state already operating beyond its ecological limits. The loss of wetlands has disrupted the delicate balance of Kerala's hydrology, exacerbating the intensity and frequency of such disasters. Unauthorized colonies in low-lying areas being flooded is a recurring issue in several states. While it's convenient to attribute such incidents to climate change, the root causes often lie in poor urban planning, unregulated construction, and neglect of natural drainage systems.

Countries like the Netherlands offer exemplary models for effectively addressing environmental challenges, particularly those posed by rising sea levels and flooding. Situated largely below sea level, the country would have faced devastating submersion if it had relied solely on natural conditions. Instead, a combination of historical innovation—such as windmills and dykes—modern technological advancements like storm surge barriers, and proactive governance through integrated water management strategies has enabled the Netherlands not only to safeguard itself but also to emerge as a global leader in water management and flood control. This approach underscores the importance of foresight and adaptability in tackling environmental vulnerabilities.

Tulip Bulbs

Coming back to agriculture, farming practices in Western nations are markedly different from those in India, primarily due to their heavy reliance on advanced technology and efficiency-driven processes. Observing the chaotic state of Indian agriculture in 2020 sparked my curiosity about how farming systems in Europe operate.

During my stay in the Netherlands—a country renowned for its agricultural innovation—I gained valuable insights. At a tulip farm near Rotterdam, I was astonished by how much the operation resembled a high-tech factory. The farmer's role had evolved from traditional hands-on labor to managing sophisticated machines and systems, making the entire process almost unrecognizable when compared to conventional Indian methods.

This tulip farm utilized state-of-the-art technology to achieve precision and efficiency at every stage of cultivation. Planting machines meticulously positioned tulip bulbs at uniform depths and intervals, ensuring optimal growth conditions. Advanced harvesting equipment, such as bulb diggers and sorters, significantly streamlined the collection process, reducing labor intensity and improving productivity. The integration of GPS technology and drones further enhanced efficiency by optimizing planting patterns, fertilization schedules, and irrigation systems. Wireless sensors strategically placed across the fields continuously monitored essential parameters such as soil moisture, nutrient levels, and temperature. These real-time data streams were fed into advanced analytical software, which generated actionable insights. This allowed the farmer, also the owner of the farm, to proactively address potential issues and refine crop management practices. Each tulip was cultivated with unparalleled precision, showcasing the seamless fusion of agricultural expertise and cutting-edge technology.

Although tulips are a seasonal crop, they are cultivated year-round at this farm and many others across the Netherlands, thanks to the widespread implementation of advanced greenhouse technology. These structures create and maintain optimal growing conditions with highly sophisticated climate control systems that precisely regulate temperature, humidity, and light levels. The use of hydroponic systems—a soil-free cultivation method—further enhances resource efficiency by delivering nutrients directly to plant roots. Rainwater collected from greenhouse roofs undergoes a rigorous filtration and sterilization process using ultraviolet and ozone treatments before being enriched with nutrients and reused. This innovative closed-loop system not only minimizes water wastage but also supports sustainable farming practices. Additionally, tissue culture techniques are employed to produce large quantities of tulip bulbs with genetic uniformity and enhanced resistance to diseases. This method guarantees consistent quality across production batches while significantly minimizing the risks of crop failures.

At the end of the process, tulip bulbs were meticulously sorted, de-bulbed, cleaned, and bundled into bouquets at the end of a conveyor belt, ready for shipment. This remarkable integration of advanced technology has automated approximately 80% of tulip cultivation tasks, significantly reducing manual labor while enhancing productivity and precision. Automation lies at the core of Dutch tulip farming, transforming previously labor-intensive tasks into streamlined, highly efficient operations. Astonishingly, the farm functioned smoothly with only two full-time employees in addition to the owner, exemplifying the transformative power of automation.

After completing my guided tour of the farm and heading back to Eindhoven, my mind was overwhelmed with thoughts, racing in every direction. I was utterly astonished, struggling to process how agriculture and farming could exude such sophistication and finesse. The sight of those advanced machines and groundbreaking technology left me in awe, even when my daily nine-to-five immerses me in cutting-edge technologies and state-of-the-art labs. Yet, this experience redefined my perception, blending the rustic charm of farming with the elegance of modernity in a way I could never have imagined.

The Netherlands' advanced logistics and transportation infrastructure, including sophisticated cold-chain systems, ensures that tulips maintain their freshness and quality during transit, allowing vibrant, pristine flowers to reach global markets efficiently. This seamless supply chain underpins the country's dominance in the global flower market. By leveraging these innovations, Dutch tulip farmers maintain a year-round supply of premium-quality flowers, solidifying the Netherlands' leadership in sustainable, efficient, and cutting-edge agricultural practices.

The nation's ability to blend centuries-old horticultural expertise with state-of-the-art technology has revolutionized tulip farming, elevating profitability and setting a global benchmark for sustainability and competitiveness. The Dutch government's focus on agricultural research and innovation further strengthens the sector. Instead of relying on traditional subsidies like loan waivers or minimum support prices, policymakers prioritize investments in advanced technologies and sustainable methods. This visionary approach not only ensures the industry's global competitiveness but also promotes long-term environmental stewardship, offering an inspiring blueprint for countries aiming to modernize their agricultural sectors.

Comparing this to India, the disparity is stark.

Developed nations like the Netherlands achieved wealth and stability by steadily investing in industrial and agricultural efficiency over decades, leveraging innovation to transform their economies. India, on the other hand, often finds itself constrained by a political culture that prioritizes short-term electoral gains over meaningful, long-term reforms. Measures such as waiving farm loans address symptoms rather than the root causes of agricultural distress.

The opposition to India's Farm Bills exemplifies this mindset. Although many political parties had previously proposed similar reforms, they opposed these bills merely because they were introduced by a rival party. This short-sighted approach—"Let's destabilize the government, even at the expense of national progress"—continues to impede the adoption of transformative policies, ultimately undermining meaningful progress in the agricultural sector.

India's agricultural sector remains entrenched in outdated and inefficient systems. Reform efforts, including attempts to overhaul the minimum support price (MSP) system and introduce the Three Farm Bills, frequently encounter strong resistance from various stakeholders. Former Prime Minister Rajiv Gandhi aptly observed, "If the center spends one rupee for the poor, only fifteen paise reach them." This inefficiency, largely perpetuated by intermediaries, continues to hinder the sector's progress. Initiatives like Direct Benefit Transfers (DBT), enabled by the Jan Dhan Yojana, have demonstrated the potential to significantly improve outcomes by bypassing these intermediaries. These reforms ensure that resources reach the intended beneficiaries directly and more effectively. Despite such advancements, a large portion of Indian farmers remain trapped in antiquated systems that resist modernization and fail to support their long-term prosperity.

Over half of India's workforce remains engaged in agriculture, yet this sector contributes less than 20% to the GDP, underscoring a significant disparity in productivity. To address this imbalance, the focus should be on transitioning a substantial portion of this workforce to more productive sectors like manufacturing and industry. However, policies such as the exemption of agricultural income from taxation inadvertently incentivize remaining in agriculture rather than encouraging diversification into more productive sectors. This tax exemption, notably absent in developed countries like the UK, Germany, the Netherlands, the US, and Canada, adds complexity to the already unbalanced agricultural framework in India. By comparison, developed nations impose agricultural income taxes to ensure fairness in revenue generation and to discourage inefficient practices, thereby promoting a shift towards industrial and service sectors for economic growth. India's continuation of this policy highlights the need for a reassessment to align with global standards and encourage broader economic development. Ironically, some Canadian lobbies that opposed India's Farm Bills during the 2020 protests have already had similar reforms in their own country, where agricultural income is subject to taxation. This highlights the need for India to align its policies with global practices to foster economic diversification and improve agricultural efficiency.

India's agricultural sector stands at a pivotal moment in its history. The future demands a decisive shift towards reforms that emphasize efficiency, technological innovation, and global competitiveness. Clinging to outdated practices will only exacerbate existing inefficiencies and hinder progress. By drawing inspiration from global leaders like the Netherlands—renowned for its seamless integration of advanced technology and sustainable practices—India has the potential to modernize its agricultural landscape. This transformation could pave the way for a sector that is not only sustainable and productive but also aligned with the demands of a rapidly evolving global economy.

Unified Market

The Dutch flower business, even with state-of-the-art machines and processes, would have struggled without access to a large, unified market like the European Single Market.

Central to this success is the Aalsmeer Flower Auction, the world's largest, which streamlines transactions and connects Dutch growers with international buyers, ensuring a steady balance between supply and demand. The Single Market facilitates the seamless movement of tulips and other flowers across EU borders by eliminating tariffs, quotas, and administrative barriers, enabling high-volume trade with minimal friction. The integration of logistics systems across member states, combined with excellent transport infrastructure and the absence of border checks, minimizes delays—crucial for perishable goods like tulips. This allows Dutch tulips to efficiently reach key markets such as Germany, France, the UK, and Italy within hours. Advanced cold-chain infrastructure further preserves freshness during transit, ensuring top quality upon arrival.

The unified European market harmonizes regulations like Value Added Tax (VAT), ensuring consistency across the EU while allowing member states to set their rates within guidelines. The European Commission enforces these trade policies, fostering cohesion and efficiency among member states. This framework strengthens the EU's position as a globally competitive economic entity by balancing integration with state autonomy. Harmonized standards simplify compliance for tulip growers and exporters, enabling them to scale operations and expand their market reach. Furthermore, the free movement of people provides access to seasonal workers from neighboring countries, critical for labor-intensive tasks like harvesting and packing, which ensures cost management and peak-season efficiency.

This isn't unique to the flower business; it applies equally to industries like the German automotive sector. The removal of tariffs, quotas, and customs checks within the EU allows seamless trade for German car manufacturers. Components and finished vehicles move freely across borders, enabling efficient supply chains. For instance, German automakers export cars to major markets like France, Italy, and Spain without extra costs or bureaucratic hurdles.

The Single Market integrates supply chains across EU countries. German manufacturers source parts from Poland, the Czech Republic, and Hungary, benefiting from reduced production costs and just-in-time delivery. This integration supports cost-effective production while maintaining Germany's renowned high standards.

Additionally, the EU's unified market provides German carmakers access to over 450 million consumers, boosting sales opportunities for brands like Volkswagen, BMW, and Mercedes-Benz. Harmonized technical and safety standards reduce costs by enabling manufacturers to produce vehicles that meet a single set of regulations. This also simplifies exports beyond the EU, leveraging Europe's global reputation for quality.

The free movement of people within the EU allows German automakers to access a skilled, diverse workforce, especially for automotive hubs relying on expertise from neighboring countries. EU funding and research initiatives further support investments in technologies like electric vehicles (EVs) and autonomous driving. Cross-border collaboration accelerates innovation and fosters sustainable practices, keeping the industry competitive globally.

Finally, the single unified market ensures efficient logistics. Well-connected ports, rail networks, and highways form the backbone of automotive exports, ensuring timely deliveries worldwide. By leveraging this framework, German carmakers benefit from streamlined operations, economies of scale, and access to a vast consumer base, cementing their global leadership. The European Union's Single Unified Market stands as a testament to the success of economic integration and unification. The Schengen Agreement complements the Single Market by ensuring the free movement of people, further strengthening economic and social cohesion within the bloc.

In contrast, when I look at India prior to 2017, despite being one country, it was once fragmented by a labyrinth of indirect taxes and state-specific entry and exit taxes, which turned a unified market into smaller, isolated ones. This system involved a convoluted array of central and state taxes, including VAT, service tax, excise duty, CST, and so on. These overlapping taxes often created a cascading effect, where taxes were applied repeatedly on already-taxed goods and services, significantly inflating costs for businesses. Furthermore, state-specific regulations restricted the free flow of goods across state borders, leading to severe logistical inefficiencies and economic fragmentation.

The implementation of the Goods and Services Tax (GST) by the Modi Government in 2017 marked a watershed moment for India's economy, transforming it into a cohesive national market. GST replaced the tangle of indirect taxes with a single, streamlined system applied uniformly across the country. This framework comprises Central GST (CGST) and State GST (SGST) for intra-state transactions and Integrated GST (IGST) for inter-state trade. By standardizing tax rates on goods and services, GST resolved long-standing disparities between states, creating a more integrated and efficient marketplace.

One of the most significant impacts of GST was the elimination of entry taxes and state border checkposts, which significantly reduced transportation delays and lowered logistics costs by an estimated 20-30%. This reform encouraged businesses to centralize their warehousing and optimize supply chains, leading to improved operational efficiency and reduced overhead costs. India's GST achieved a seamless domestic unification within the structure of a single nation, streamlining internal trade and enhancing economic integration.

The Digital India initiative played a pivotal role in facilitating the implementation of GST by enabling the necessary technological infrastructure and promoting seamless digital connectivity. The Goods and Services Tax Network (GSTN) has played a transformative role in modernizing tax compliance in India, making it significantly more transparent and accessible. Through the GSTN portal, businesses can seamlessly register, file returns, and make tax payments online, thereby drastically reducing administrative complexities and paperwork. The introduction of the input tax credit (ITC) mechanism under GST ensures that businesses are taxed solely on the value they add, effectively eliminating the cascading tax effect that previously inflated costs. Furthermore, digital innovations such as e-way bills have revolutionized the monitoring of goods movement, enhancing regulatory oversight and significantly curbing tax evasion.

Brexit

The UK, despite being separated by the English Channel, benefited greatly from the unified Single European Market. When Brexit was first announced, I found myself questioning why Britain would choose such a path. Working in the automotive industry at the time, I could foresee significant downsides, and only downsides. Brexit disrupted the European Union's Single Market, introducing trade barriers, straining relationships between the UK and EU member states, and undermining previously seamless economic integration. The UK's exit from the EU Customs Union led to non-tariff barriers such as customs declarations, rules of origin checks, and increased regulatory compliance costs, all of which added complexity and cost to trade.

While the EU-UK Trade and Cooperation Agreement (TCA) ensured zero tariffs and quotas on most goods, administrative hurdles complicated the movement of automotive parts and finished vehicles between the UK and the EU. Just-in-time manufacturing, a cornerstone of the automotive industry, suffered from increased border checks, leading to delays and additional logistics expenses. Consequently, some automakers shifted operations or restructured supply chains to focus more on EU markets.

A major challenge for the automotive sector post-Brexit has been the risk of regulatory divergence between the UK and the EU. Previously, vehicles produced in the UK adhered to EU standards, ensuring easy access to European markets. Post-Brexit, the UK's autonomy to set its own regulations has introduced uncertainty for automakers, who now face the possibility of complying with multiple standards to access both markets.

The end of free movement for EU citizens has further strained the automotive sector, which heavily relies on skilled labor from across Europe. This shift exacerbated labor shortages, particularly in technical and manufacturing roles, and increased costs associated with hiring and training workers domestically. Additionally, Brexit has led to a decline in foreign direct investment (FDI) in the UK automotive industry. Notably, Honda closed its UK factories citing Brexit-related uncertainties, while other manufacturers, such as Nissan, scaled back investment plans or redirected resources to EU countries to mitigate potential trade disruptions.

However, once I moved to England and started living here, I began to see the rationale behind the challenging referendum. It was not as black and white as I had initially believed. Many people I met in the UK were from economically struggling Eastern European countries. While free movement allowed the UK to attract highly skilled European professionals, it also made it easier for a much larger number of unskilled or low-skilled workers to settle in the UK, creating socio-economic pressures for native Britons.

The end of free movement now allows the UK to implement an immigration system tailored to national priorities. This enables the government to focus on attracting highly skilled workers while better managing labor market demands. Additionally, the UK no longer contributes to the EU budget, potentially freeing up significant resources for domestic investment. These funds can be redirected to national priorities such as healthcare, infrastructure, and education.

Brexit also restored decision-making authority to the UK government and parliament, granting greater control over both domestic and international policies. This aligns with the priorities of many voters who sought to "take back control." The introduction of new trade barriers on imports presents an opportunity for the UK to encourage domestic industries, potentially boosting local employment and reducing reliance on EU supply chains. This could come handy with the UK government's push for greener policies, such as the ban on new petrol and diesel car sales by 2030, aligns with a global shift toward electric vehicles (EVs). Brexit offers an opportunity to incentivize domestic EV production and infrastructure development, positioning the UK as a leader in sustainable automotive innovation.

More importantly, Brexit allows the UK to pursue independent trade agreements with non-EU countries, marking a strategic shift in its global economic policies. The UK has actively sought to strengthen partnerships with nations like Japan, the US, and India, creating new opportunities for automotive exports, technological collaborations, and broader trade engagements.

In particular, the UK has deepened its engagement with India, leveraging historical ties and mutual economic interests. Post-Brexit, Britain has actively negotiated trade deals and partnerships with India, focusing on high-potential sectors such as technology, healthcare, education, and renewable energy. A key initiative in this effort is the Enhanced Trade Partnership (ETP), announced in 2021, which sets an ambitious target of doubling bilateral trade by 2030. Under the ETP, both countries have committed to reducing trade barriers in crucial industries such as medical devices, agriculture, and defense manufacturing.

Further strengthening this partnership, the Green Growth Equity Fund (GGEF), a joint initiative, supports substantial investments in renewable energy projects, particularly solar and wind energy, highlighting a shared commitment to climate change mitigation. The UK-India Innovation Partnership fosters collaboration in cutting-edge fields like artificial intelligence, digital health, and fintech, creating a platform for startups and enterprises to share expertise and develop scalable solutions.

The education sector has also seen significant collaboration, exemplified by the UK-India Education and Research Initiative (UKIERI), which expands student exchange programs and promotes co-funded research projects between the two nations. In healthcare, notable partnerships such as AstraZeneca's expanded operations in India reflect growing trade and investment ties, focusing on pharmaceuticals and vaccine innovation.

These agreements and partnerships underscore the UK's strategic pivot toward engaging with emerging markets like India to offset reduced access to EU markets. They reflect a shared vision for sustainable economic growth and mutual development. By diversifying its economic dependencies and forging deeper ties with India, the UK has positioned itself to tap into one of the world's fastest-growing economies, aligning its post-Brexit strategy with the global shift toward innovation and sustainability.

The Crux: Reindustrializing India

While the current geopolitical landscape supports India's development narrative—strengthened by its relationships with Europe, the UK, and the US—the reality remains that 21st-century India cannot sustain 50% of its population in 20th-century agricultural practices that yield diminishing returns. India's exports remain concentrated in textiles, chemicals, and low-value manufacturing, while the nation lags in high-tech exports, a hallmark of Western industrialized economies.

The year 2020 marked a pivotal moment when India came close to historic agricultural reforms with the introduction of three farm bills. However, political opportunism triumphed over common sense, leading to their repeal. For India to truly industrialize, the agricultural sector must embrace mechanization and modernization to align with global standards.

Over the last decade, Modi's India has made remarkable strides toward industrialization, underpinned by structural reforms and visionary initiatives. The introduction of GST unified the nation's fragmented tax system, transforming India into a seamless single market that has streamlined interstate trade and reduced logistical complexities. Initiatives like Make in India and Production Linked Incentives (PLI) have propelled domestic manufacturing, fostering global competitiveness in industries such as electronics, automotive, and pharmaceuticals.

The government's vision of developing 100 smart cities has integrated urbanization with industrial growth, while the aggressive rollout of 5G technology positions India as a leader in global digital connectivity. Schemes like Mudra Yojana have empowered small entrepreneurs by providing easy access to credit and formalizing significant portions of the informal economy, fostering grassroots-level industrial growth.

But there is still a long way to go. While the progress made so far is commendable, it represents only the first step in a much larger journey. Achieving comprehensive industrialization will demand not just sustained effort and resilience but a united dedication to embracing innovation, fostering inclusivity, and adapting to an ever-changing global landscape.

As I mentioned earlier, industrialization is not a sprint; it's a marathon! India cannot afford to stray, take a break, or stop.

INNOVATION

"Yukti-prayogena rajyam vardhate"
–Book II, Chapter 15, Arthashastra

"The kingdom grows through the application of strategy and innovation."

The Wars

Over the years, I've observed how different nations interpret the legacy of World War II in uniquely revealing ways. My German colleagues often avoided discussing the war or expressing pride in the *Vaterland*, while my English colleagues frequently emphasized British resilience and military triumphs. Despite these contrasting narratives, one shared perspective was the recognition of the extraordinary technological innovations driven by the desperate need to outpace the enemy. During those tumultuous years, scientists, engineers, and visionaries achieved groundbreaking advancements that revolutionized the future. Initially developed as tools of war, these innovations later transitioned into civilian applications, reshaping the modern world in profound and unexpected ways. As the saying goes, necessity is the mother of invention—and in wartime, staying ahead of the enemy was not just strategic but a matter of survival.

Take radar, for example. When the skies over Britain became a battleground, the Royal Air Force relied on radar's invisible eyes to detect incoming *Luftwaffe* bombers long before they crossed the Channel. The British Chain Home radar system was pivotal in the Battle of Britain, enabling early detection of German air raids. Similarly, sonar advancements revolutionized maritime warfare, allowing the tracking of submarines. Post-war, these technologies expanded their reach—radar became integral to weather forecasting, maritime navigation, and aviation.

During my time at Mentor Automotive, I witnessed radar, along with lidar and cameras, playing a critical role in sensor fusion for autonomous vehicles and advanced driver assistance systems. At Airbus, I saw how Synthetic Aperture Radar was used for Earth observation, further showcasing radar's versatility and far-reaching impact.

Another transformative example is computing and semiconductors. Brilliant minds like Alan Turing raced against time to crack the Enigma code in secretive labs such as Bletchley Park. Their efforts led to the creation of early computers like the British Colossus—vast machines humming with data and potential. The Cold War, with its technological arms race, accelerated semiconductor development, eventually leading to modern microchips and computing. The UK's investments in companies like ICL and Ferranti aimed to keep pace with US and Soviet advancements, while German firms like Siemens emerged as leaders in electronics and telecommunications. These once-room-sized machines have since evolved into the sleek laptops and smartphones we carry today. The semiconductor industry's rapid advancements in reducing size, weight, and power consumption while exponentially increasing transistor counts—trillions on a single chip—have made today's artificial intelligence and neural networks possible.

One innovation often leads to another. Cold War tensions spurred the development of stealth aircraft, such as the F-117 Nighthawk, which was engineered to evade enemy radar detection. The creation of radar technology paved the way for countermeasures like stealth technology, exemplifying the cycle of innovation driven by conflict. Similarly, jet engines revolutionized aviation during the war. The German Messerschmitt Me 262, the world's first jet-powered fighter, and the British Gloster Meteor showcased the era's technological leap. These advancements didn't end with the war; they became the foundation of modern commercial air travel. Britain's de Havilland Comet, though initially troubled, made way for designs like the Concorde and the Boeing 707, making the world smaller and more connected. Jet engine research continued into the Cold War, resulting in aircraft like the SR-71 Blackbird, capable of speeds over Mach 3.

Europe, battered but resilient, emerged from the war with a determination to rebuild and innovate. The UK leveraged its expertise in jet engines and radar to establish itself as a leader in commercial aviation and defense technology, driving projects like the Concorde and advanced aerospace manufacturing. Germany retooled its industries, transforming wartime engineering precision into automotive innovation with companies like Volkswagen and BMW leading the charge. France heavily invested in aerospace, spearheading the Ariane rocket program and positioning Europe as a key player in space exploration. These advancements laid the groundwork for Europe's economic resurgence and technological leadership in global industries.

Post-war Europe demonstrated how wartime innovations could serve as the foundation for peacetime prosperity. In Germany and the UK, the technological strides made during the war underpinned their recoveries and established them as leaders in sectors like automotive manufacturing, aviation, and space exploration. These lessons remind us of the dual-edged nature of innovation—born out of necessity yet capable of profoundly shaping the world.

HAL Marut

India's post-independence history has also been marked by numerous wars, including conflicts with Pakistan in 1947-48, 1965, 1971 (which culminated in the liberation of Bangladesh), and 1999, as well as with China in 1962. These wars, along with ongoing proxy conflicts with neighboring countries, have brought severe humanitarian consequences, such as mass casualties, genocides, and widespread displacement. However, unlike the technological advancements spurred by World War II and the Cold War, India's wartime experiences largely failed to drive significant homegrown technological innovations. To India, Pakistan has served a role akin to that of the Axis powers for the Allies or the Soviet Union for the United States—a persistent rival shaping strategic imperatives, but failing to trigger a transformative domestic technological revolution. Why? A question that needs to be answered.

India's journey toward developing indigenous fighter technology began with the HF-24 Marut, designed by Hindustan Aircraft

Limited (now Hindustan Aeronautics Limited) under the guidance of German engineer Kurt Tank in 1959. The prototype was successfully completed by 1961. Despite India's emphasis on import substitution industrialization during the pre-1991 era, the government exhibited limited confidence in homegrown innovations such as the Marut. Instead, preference was given to foreign-built fighters, including the Dassault Ouragan, Hawker Hunter, and Sukhoi Su-7. By 1982, the Marut fleet was declared "operationally unviable," despite its commendable performance during the 1971 war and its superior safety record when compared to other Indian Air Force (IAF) aircraft of the time.

The Marut's inability to achieve supersonic speeds was primarily due to the absence of a suitable engine. Despite this, the government refrained from investing in the development of an indigenous engine or attempting to reverse-engineer existing technologies. Instead, it opted for importing replacements, which only delayed the advancement of domestic aviation capabilities. Notably, offers from countries like France to collaborate on engine technology development in India were overlooked, further stifling potential growth. Allegations of poor coordination among the Ministry of Defense, the military, and industry exacerbated the situation, reinforcing the widespread perception that the government prioritized short-term procurement over long-term self-reliance.

Even in popular culture, the achievements of the HF-24 Marut were overlooked. An extremely popular and successful bollywood film *Border* (1997) depicted the Battle of Longewala but omitted Marut's crucial role, instead depicted British made Hawker Hunter fighter jets. This absence in the narrative exemplifies how the legacy of indigenous technology was underappreciated, failing to inspire national pride or encourage further innovation. This is very different in the West, especially in the UK and the US. People actually take pride in the technological advancements of their country, and movies are filled with examples showcasing national achievements, cutting-edge innovations, and futuristic visions.

Whether it's through blockbuster films or documentaries, there's a strong emphasis on portraying technology as a point of cultural pride and progress.

India's neglect of indigenous aviation stands in stark contrast to Britain's proactive approach to early setbacks in its aerospace industry. The de Havilland Comet, the world's first commercial jetliner, experienced catastrophic failures in the 1950s due to metal fatigue caused by its square-shaped windows. These failures resulted in several tragic incidents, including BOAC Flight 783, which crashed near India in May 1953, killing all 43 onboard; BOAC Flight 781, which exploded mid-air over the Mediterranean in January 1954, claiming 35 lives; and South African Airways Flight 201, which disintegrated mid-flight in April 1954, killing 21 people. Rather than abandoning the project, Britain grounded the fleet, conducted thorough investigations, and introduced critical design improvements, such as rounded windows and a stronger fuselage, to address the underlying issues.

Although the Comet ultimately lost out to competitors like the Boeing 707, its advancements left a lasting legacy by influencing modern jetliner designs and solidifying Britain's leadership in aerospace innovation. Future aircraft, such as the British Aerospace 146 and Concorde, benefited from the lessons learned during the Comet's development. The Comet story serves as a testament to the risks inherent in innovation and the resilience required to overcome setbacks—qualities that stand in stark contrast to India's reluctance to invest in and improve upon the HF-24 Marut.

India's indigenous aviation story was exemplified by the HAL Tejas program, which began in 1969 with the aim of developing a fighter jet centered around a "proven engine." However, decades later, the Tejas continues to rely significantly on imported systems, such as the Israel Aerospace Industries/ELTA EL/M-2032 radar, an Elbit helmet-mounted cueing system, a British-made Martin-Baker ejection seat, and an American General Electric F404 afterburning turbofan engine. Moreover, many of its weapons systems, like the GSh-23 23 mm cannon, originate from Russia.

This heavy dependence on foreign components not only diminishes the Tejas' export potential but also subjects its international sales to geopolitical constraints, such as the U.S. effectively exercising veto power over deals with certain nations. Compounding this challenge, the Tejas lags behind global advancements, particularly as fifth-generation fighter jets set new industry standards. The Kaveri engine project, envisioned to create an indigenous powerplant for the Tejas, was ultimately abandoned in 2014 after repeated failures. This decision underscores systemic inefficiencies and a lack of sustained commitment to achieving self-reliance in defense technology.

The transition from designing the HAL Marut, a first-generation fighter jet, to the HAL Tejas, a fourth-generation jet, represents an ambitious yet incomplete technological leap that failed to address critical developmental stages. Developing successive variants of the Marut could have laid a strong foundation for progressively advanced designs, fostering gradual yet sustainable growth in India's indigenous aviation expertise. Unfortunately, India missed these opportunities due to the lack of continuous investment, inadequate ecosystem building, and an absence of effective mechanisms for knowledge transfer. These systemic deficiencies not only stymied the evolution of domestic aviation capabilities but also entrenched a persistent dependence on foreign technologies, undermining the long-term objective of achieving self-reliance in defense manufacturing.

Moreover, political corruption and a preference for kickbacks from defense deals significantly undermined efforts to invest in and prioritize domestic innovation. While World War II-era nations were compelled to innovate due to existential threats, India had the luxury of procuring ready-made solutions from foreign suppliers. This approach, though seemingly less risky in the short term, created a dependency that stifled the development of indigenous technologies and hindered the growth of a self-reliant defense ecosystem. By choosing immediate convenience over long-term capability building, India compromised its potential for sustained technological advancement.

India's struggles with indigenous aviation reflect a broader reluctance to embrace the risks and investments associated with technological innovation. The contrast between the Marut's neglect and the British response to the Comet's challenges highlights the missed opportunities in India's aviation history. Building a sustainable and innovative defense industry requires continuous effort, coordination, and a commitment to nurturing homegrown talent. Without these, India risks repeating its past mistakes, perpetually lagging behind global advancements.

The Space Race

World War II ignited a space race that continued to accelerate during the Cold War, fundamentally shaping modern aerospace and defense industries. The V-2 rocket, developed by Nazi Germany, laid the groundwork for both space exploration and intercontinental ballistic missiles (ICBMs). After the war, the U.S. leveraged Operation Paperclip to capture and recruit German scientists, including Wernher von Braun, whose expertise was instrumental in advancing U.S. ballistic missile programs and establishing its space exploration initiatives. The ensuing race to perfect ICBMs catalyzed significant advancements in rocketry, materials science, and precision guidance systems, laying the foundation for subsequent breakthroughs in space technology. The launch of Sputnik by the USSR in 1957 ignited the U.S. space program. This led to the creation of NASA and projects like Apollo, which landed humans on the Moon in 1969. Projects like Star Wars (SDI – Strategic Defense Initiative) further pushed laser technology, satellite defense, and surveillance systems.

While government agencies like NASA and the Soviet space program spearheaded the Cold War space race, private companies played an indispensable role in propelling space technology forward. Defense contractors, aerospace firms, and technology companies supplied the hardware, advanced materials, and groundbreaking innovations that were essential for the success of space exploration initiatives.

In the United States, companies like North American Aviation (later part of Boeing), Lockheed Martin, and Grumman (now Northrop Grumman) played a critical role in advancing space technology by designing and manufacturing essential components for spacecraft and rockets. North American Aviation was responsible for developing the command and service modules of the Apollo program, pivotal for ensuring astronauts' safe journey to and from the Moon. Grumman engineered the iconic Lunar Module, which enabled humanity's historic first steps on the lunar surface. Additionally, Rocketdyne, a division of North American Aviation, developed the powerful F-1 engines that powered the Saturn V rocket, a cornerstone of the Apollo program's success and a symbol of unparalleled engineering prowess.

The involvement of private industry significantly accelerated advancements in materials science, propulsion systems, and avionics, forming the bedrock for today's burgeoning commercial space ventures. The technological breakthroughs pioneered during the Cold War space race—from miniaturized electronics to advanced propulsion—continue to drive innovation in modern aerospace companies, enabling them to explore new frontiers in space exploration with greater efficiency and ambition.

While the United States and the Soviet Union dominated the early space race, European nations and private companies also made significant contributions. Individual countries established national space agencies, such as the United Kingdom's UKSA (United Kingdom Space Agency) and Germany's DLR (Deutsches Zentrum für Luft- und Raumfahrt). Additionally, the European Space Agency (ESA) emerged as a unified entity representing the collective ambitions of the European Union, fostering collaboration and innovation on a continent-wide scale.

The UK developed the Black Arrow rocket, which successfully launched satellites into orbit and marked a milestone in the nation's space capabilities. British Aerospace (now BAE Systems) and Rolls-Royce were instrumental in advancing satellite technology and propulsion systems. Rolls-Royce, in particular, harnessed its expertise in wartime jet technology to develop advanced engines for peaceful space exploration and aviation applications. France's Ariane program, spearheaded by Aérospatiale (now integrated into Airbus), solidified Europe's position as a global leader in commercial satellite launches. Ariane rockets became the backbone of European space activities, supporting numerous missions and fostering the continent's reputation for reliability and innovation in the aerospace sector. Germany also established itself as a key player in the space industry, with Daimler-Benz Aerospace (later merged into Airbus) playing a pivotal role in satellite manufacturing, launch vehicle development, and the creation of components for space stations. Leveraging its renowned expertise in engineering and precision manufacturing, Germany enabled Europe to achieve competitive parity in the commercial satellite deployment sector, effectively challenging the long-standing dominance of American and Soviet space programs.

The European Space Agency (ESA) has fostered close collaboration with private firms such as Airbus, Thales Alenia Space, and OHB SE, driving advancements in launch vehicles, telecommunications satellites, and deep space exploration technologies. OHB SE, a German company, has specialized in small satellite production, delivering cost-effective solutions for diverse space missions, thereby enhancing Europe's competitive edge in the global space sector. In the UK, Surrey Satellite Technology Ltd (SSTL) has been at the forefront of innovation, pioneering breakthroughs in small satellite technology and enabling more affordable access to space, which has significantly broadened the scope of commercial and scientific missions.

While working on a European Space Agency (ESA) project as the Firmware Lead for the instrument back end, I realized how far from straightforward the customer chain for the project was. While ESA was the final recipient of the instrument, for us at ADS, the immediate customer was Thales Alenia Space Italy (TAS-I). We supplied both the backend and frontend components of the instrument to TAS-I, which then handled integration and delivered the final product to ESA. Beyond this, over two dozen private companies were involved in manufacturing and developing various modules of the instrument, creating a highly intricate and collaborative supply chain.

This intricate network of vendors with diverse core competencies fosters an environment where startups, SMEs and private companies can thrive by innovating to meet the demands of projects driven by ESA. While ESA boasts a cadre of skilled engineers, their role is primarily to review designs rather than engage in the manufacturing or development of instruments themselves.

In stark contrast, until 2019, private companies in India were largely excluded from space exploration and related activities. Without sufficient demand, there was little incentive for private firms to develop the necessary expertise. Consequently, India was left with an underdeveloped ecosystem, stifling the growth of its domestic space industry.

The lack of a robust ecosystem has been a significant factor contributing to India's enduring issue of brain drain. This phenomenon presents a striking paradox: India boasts world-class institutions such as IITs, NITs, IISc, and other premier engineering colleges, all producing exceptional talent in fields like electronics and aerospace engineering. At the same time, the country is home to globally recognized organizations like ISRO, DRDO and

HAL. Yet, despite these assets, India has historically relied heavily on importing high-tech weapons and fighter jets while simultaneously exporting its engineering talent to other nations. This dichotomy highlights a systemic failure to harness domestic expertise and create opportunities that retain talent within the country.

Modi's India is steadily addressing long standing gaps in its space sector. ISRO now drives significantly more projects than ever before—a shift from merely "doing" projects to actively "driving" them—thanks in large part to the establishment of the Indian National Space Promotion and Authorization Centre (IN-SPACe) in 2020 and the Indian Space Association (ISpA) in 2021. These organizations were created to foster collaborative development within India's private space industry.

According to recent press releases and media reports, these initiatives have already begun to show positive results. The number of tech startups in India has surged in recent years, reflecting the country's growing contribution to the global space economy. In its first 60 years, ISRO contributed less than 2%—or under $8 billion—to the global space economy. But projections indicate that, over the next decade, this share could climb to $100 billion, or roughly 10% of the global market. It's worth noting that $100 billion is considered a conservative estimate, primarily derived from developments in the last three years.

Before 2014, India had only one startup focused on space technology; today, more than 140 such startups collaborate with ISRO, with over 100 of them founded in just the past three years. Unlike other tech ventures, space sector startups face higher entry costs. However, India's recent reforms and institutional support are lowering these barriers and fueling continued growth in this critical domain.

Technology Overlap

On March 27, 2019, Prime Minister Narendra Modi addressed the nation to announce the successful execution of "Mission Shakti," during which India conducted an Anti-Satellite (ASAT) missile test. In his address, the prime minister emphasized that India had become the fourth country to acquire such a capability, following the United States, Russia, and China. He highlighted that the mission was completed using an indigenously developed ASAT missile, showcasing India's advanced technological capabilities. The prime minister reassured the global community that this capability was not targeted at any nation and reiterated India's commitment to preventing the weaponization of space. He clarified that the test complied with international laws and treaty obligations and reaffirmed that India's space program is focused on national security, economic development, and technological progress.

This one speech, forced Pakistan to reevaluate its nuclear strategy and had to move past its "nukes aren't for showcase" rhetoric. But to understand and appreciate the significance of ASAT, we'll have to get a little background — ASAT technology has applications beyond military purposes, particularly in space sustainability, debris mitigation, and scientific research. For example, ASAT systems can be adapted to remove defunct satellites or large debris by using kinetic projectiles or interceptors to deorbit them safely, ensuring they burn up upon reentry. Ground-based lasers, initially developed for ASAT purposes, can apply photon pressure to adjust the trajectories of space debris without destroying it. Additionally, ASAT interceptors can be used to deorbit aging or malfunctioning satellites, mitigating hazards to operational spacecraft. Such technologies can also assist in the controlled deorbiting of satellites at the end of their operational lifespans. ASAT systems are also used in testing interceptors, sensors, and missile defense technologies, which enhance space situational awareness and refine tracking systems. These developments contribute to monitoring space traffic and predicting satellite collisions, with data often shared among international agencies to prevent accidents.

Several non-military initiatives utilize ASAT-like technology. For instance, Japan and the European Space Agency (ESA) have launched debris removal projects. A Japanese private company, Astroscale, focuses on capturing defunct satellites and deorbiting them in a controlled manner, effectively using satellite interception for peaceful purposes. Similarly, ESA's ClearSpace-1 mission, scheduled for 2025, aims to capture and deorbit space debris using technologies derived from ASAT systems.

The interesting point is that Anti-Satellite (ASAT) and Anti-Ballistic Missile (ABM) systems share significant technological overlap; both are designed to intercept and neutralize high-speed targets in space or near-space environments. ABM systems detect, intercept, and destroy incoming ballistic missiles before they reach their targets, offering protection against nuclear warheads, conventional missiles, and other projectiles. These systems are crucial for national security.

Despite their different objectives—targeting satellites versus missiles—ASAT and ABM technologies share common features in tracking, targeting, and interception capabilities. For instance, an ABM system can be adapted to function as an ASAT system. Historical examples highlight this overlap. The Soviet Galosh ABM system, while not explicitly designed as an ASAT, had the capability to target satellites in orbits similar to Intercontinental Ballistic Missiles (ICBMs). Similarly, the U.S. miniature homing vehicle ASAT originated from designs intended for midcourse ballistic missile defense.

India's ASAT system exemplifies this overlap. During the Mission Shakti test, the radar, data, and communication networks of India's DRDO-designed ballistic missile defense (BMD) system were employed to track the satellite interception. The missile used in the ASAT test was specifically developed by a team of 150 scientists over two years, following approval in 2016. According to Dr. Avinash Chander, former Chief of DRDO, there had been no formal ASAT program earlier, and the missile was adapted from the existing booster and kill vehicle of the BMD program.

India's ASAT test validated the effectiveness of its BMD system. The test also holds broader significance for Phase II of India's BMD program, which aims to intercept longer-range missiles at higher altitudes. While ASAT systems have specific applications, a fully deployed BMD system has more significant strategic implications, especially in altering the balance of deterrence in Asia.

Ashton B. Carter, an American physicist, public policy expert, and government official who served as the 25th United States Secretary of Defense under President Barack Obama from February 2015 to January 2017, in his journal article "The Relationship of ASAT and BMD," presents a hypothetical scenario that highlights the overlap between ASAT and ABM systems.

He says – "*The United States deploys an ASAT system consisting of fifty land based missiles carrying infrared homing vehicles. The Soviets worry that these fifty interceptors can be used against missile warheads along with the satellites. Fifty warheads is a small fraction of a Soviet arsenal of thousands, however, the US, in case of a nuclear war, could defend a handful of targets (with strategic importance) selected by the Soviets -- for example a few airfields capable of servicing US command posts and bombers, a ground command post, etc. This would be a substantial annoyance for Soviet planners, since they would have to use not one but several warheads for each selected target so as to be confident of destroying the target.*"

In short, he suggests that an ASAT system deployed by one nation could be perceived as a threat to missile warheads, leading adversaries to reconsider their strategic options. This scenario mirrors the strategic calculus in South Asia, particularly concerning India and Pakistan.

Over the last several decades, Pakistan's nuclear policy has evolved from "minimum credible deterrence" to "full spectrum deterrence," indicating a reliance on nuclear weapons for strategic leverage. With a growing stockpile of nuclear warheads and delivery systems like the Shaheen III missile, capable of reaching India's Andaman and Nicobar Islands, Pakistan has lowered its nuclear-use threshold. This has historically limited India's conventional military responses, as seen in conflicts like Kargil. However, India's ASAT capability, combined with its BMD system, forces Pakistan to reevaluate its nuclear strategy. The hypothetical scenario described by Carter applies directly: Pakistan now faces uncertainty about whether its missile strikes could be intercepted, undermining its doctrine of nuclear coercion.

India's ASAT test represents a significant milestone in the regional security landscape. It demonstrates India's technological self-reliance and strengthens its defensive posture. Moreover, it reshapes strategic dynamics in South Asia, challenging the nuclear blackmail tactics of adversaries and enhancing India's capacity to ensure national security and stability.

The technology overlap is not just limited to space and defence. Today, a lot of us actually carry in our hands what once was highly confidential military technology.

Hey Siri!

When I began working at Mentor Automotive as a thesis student, there was an American colleague in my team. He was only a few years older than me but had extensive experience working with various startups in the U.S. He was in Germany for a six-months project and was an ardent admirer of the innovative culture in the U.S., particularly in Silicon Valley. He would frequently emphasize how technological advancements in the U.S. outpaced those in other countries.

In 2017, Samsung had just released its voice assistant, Bixby, with the Samsung Galaxy S8. My colleague, aiming to make his point, gave me a brief timeline of the voice assistants available in the market at that time. He mentioned that Bixby was introduced in 2017 by Samsung, preceded by Google Assistant in 2016, which leveraged Google's expansive data infrastructure for advanced contextual understanding. Before these, Amazon's Alexa was launched in November 2014, shortly after Microsoft's Cortana in April of the same year. The journey of the voice assistants of course began with Apple's Siri, which made its debut in 2011.

This sequence reinforced his assertion that the U.S. was leading the global race in tech innovation. In addition to that, he also shared some interesting background information that I hadn't been aware of.

He presented a compelling point that sparked significant reflection and deeper understanding. He explained that Siri was not solely the product of Apple's internal research and development efforts. Its origins lay in a project called CALO (Cognitive Assistant that Learns and Organizes), part of DARPA's (Defense Advanced Research Projects Agency) Personalized Assistant that Learns (PAL) program. The PAL initiative aimed to create an AI assistant capable of learning from user interactions.

DARPA, established in 1958 in response to the Soviet Union's launch of Sputnik, was tasked with ensuring that the United States remained at the forefront of military and technological advancements. Over the years, DARPA has been responsible for groundbreaking innovations like ARPANET, autonomous vehicles, and stealth aircraft—all of which have had significant civilian applications. CALO's goal was to develop software that could adapt and learn in a way that mimicked human cognition. It was designed to manage emails, schedule meetings, and understand context, becoming more efficient over time. The project represented a major shift in AI development, emphasizing personalization and user-centric design.

The CALO initiative integrated advances in speech recognition, natural language understanding, and machine learning. Over 300 researchers from top universities and private institutions collaborated to create a system capable of anticipating user needs and offering relevant assistance. Early AI research was often funded by military institutions to develop smarter systems that could process large volumes of data and automate complex tasks. CALO's innovations in contextual awareness and machine learning became the foundation for Siri's ability to handle intricate queries and provide accurate responses.

In 2010, Apple acquired the startup that had commercialized CALO, transferring military-developed AI technology into the hands of consumers. The following year, Siri was launched, revolutionizing how users interacted with their devices.

Once my colleague completed his narration, I reflected on how, if something similar had occurred in India, it might have been framed as the government selling its tech secrets, knowledge, and assets to its allies in the private sector. Fortunately, in the American context, such developments led to technological breakthroughs like the voice assistants we now carry in our pockets.

Siri is far from the only civilian technology rooted in military research and development. Several other transformative technologies share similar origins.

The internet, for example, began as ARPANET, a Cold War-era initiative by the U.S. Department of Defense. ARPANET was designed as a decentralized communication network resilient to nuclear attacks. This innovation laid the foundation for the modern internet, fundamentally transforming global connectivity.

GPS technology, now essential for mapping and navigation, also originated from defense research. The U.S. Department of Defense developed the Global Positioning System in the 1970s to improve missile accuracy and support military navigation. It wasn't until the 1990s that GPS became widely accessible for civilian use, revolutionizing navigation in everyday life.

Capacitive touchscreens, a cornerstone of today's user interfaces, also have their roots in military research. Early touchscreen technology was developed in the 1960s for radar and air traffic control systems. Advances in materials science and military-funded electronics research eventually made possible the responsive and durable screens we rely on today.

Satellite imaging and spy plane cameras, such as those used in the U-2 reconnaissance program, pushed the boundaries of photographic technology. The miniaturization and sensor improvements originally developed for military applications later transitioned to consumer-grade cameras, enabling smartphones to capture remarkably detailed images.

These examples illustrate the profound influence of military research on civilian technology, underscoring the interconnected nature of innovation across domains.

Startups

Innovation and research are not limited to scenarios of war or survival. There are countless ways to create an environment conducive to progress. This became clearer to me during my time at Mentor Automotive, a transformative experience that unfolded unexpected stories about the origins of innovation. After completing my thesis at Mentor Automotive, I was thrilled to join the team as a full-time employee. Yet, a question lingered in my mind: why didn't Mentor Automotive appear on Google Maps under its own name, instead showing up as XSe or XS Embedded Systems? One day, during a coffee break, I decided to ask one of the project managers about it. Though we only exchanged occasional pleasantries before, he was eager to share the story behind the company's history and suggested we discuss it further over lunch the next day.

Excited yet apprehensive, I realized I'd never eaten sushi before, the cuisine he had proposed. That evening, with help from a friend, I learned how to use chopsticks during a sushi dinner, transforming my nervousness into curiosity and confidence.

The following day, as we walked to the sushi bar, the project manager began sharing his story. He explained that the area surrounding our office in Villingen-Schwenningen was once dominated by Thomson Consumer Electronics, one of the world's leading electronics manufacturers. Thomson Multimedia later emerged, focusing on digital technologies such as DVDs, high-definition televisions, and digital networks. Concurrently, Becker GmbH, another company in the area, became a key supplier of car entertainment and navigation systems for luxury automakers like Mercedes-Benz and BMW. In 1995, Harman International acquired Becker GmbH, forming Harman Becker.

The roots of XS Embedded Systems trace back to six ambitious employees who worked at Harman Becker. These individuals, with decades of collective experience, decided to venture out on their own in 2010. They founded XS Embedded Systems to provide cutting-edge embedded solutions to top automotive clients. Despite their expertise, financial challenges arose, leading to the company's acquisition by Mentor Graphics in 2014. Mentor Automotive, as it became known, thrived under this umbrella until Siemens acquired Mentor Graphics in 2017. This transition spurred yet another wave of entrepreneurial activity, as some employees left to establish startups like AOX Technologies.

Such stories aren't unique to Villingen-Schwenningen. When I moved to Eindhoven, Netherlands, in 2021, I observed a similar pattern. Known as the "Philips city," Eindhoven's economy is deeply tied to the legacy of Philips. Companies like ASML and NXP, which split from Philips, have grown into global leaders in their respective fields—ASML dominates in photolithography machines for semiconductor manufacturing, and NXP is a global leader in semiconductor solutions. Additionally, Philips' legacy is intricately connected to companies like Signify, which focuses on lighting solutions, and FEI Company, specializing in electron microscopy. Startups in Eindhoven often trace their origins to Philips' alumni or ecosystems, supplying components, services, or innovative technologies that complement Philips' extensive industrial network.

A consistent theme among successful startups is the founders' deep industry experience. These entrepreneurs identify gaps within their respective fields and develop innovative solutions tailored to address them. In stark contrast, startups in India are associated with young graduates just out of university. Therefore, a significant proportion of Indian startups seem to replicate existing business models without adding significant value, often earning the label of "Me-Too" startups. For instance, many food delivery services, e-commerce platforms, and app-based solutions fail to innovate beyond the offerings of established market leaders. Consequently, they struggle to sustain themselves once initial funding diminishes, as they lack differentiation and fail to meet unique market needs.

For example, I could assemble a team to create a web hosting service, food delivery app, e-commerce platform, or social media messenger. However, without innovation, such ventures are destined to fail—reinventing the wheel rather than offering something genuinely new. Why would users prefer my app over WhatsApp for texting, Amazon for shopping, or other market-leading apps? This absence of innovation is a primary reason why nearly 90% of startups in India fail. Many such startups secure initial funding at inflated valuations but later collapse under competitive pressure. Once the funding stops, they quickly fold, offering no substantive value over existing competitors. With virtually no entry barriers—in other words, minimal obstacles to entering the market—these ventures struggle to differentiate themselves. Entry barriers in technological startups could include factors such as access to cutting-edge technology, significant research and development costs, skilled talent pools, intellectual property protections, and high initial capital requirements. For instance, developing artificial intelligence or machine learning algorithms often demands advanced infrastructure and expertise that are not easily accessible to all. Similarly, creating semiconductors or other high-tech components requires not just technical knowledge but also substantial investment in specialized equipment. These barriers serve as filters, allowing only startups with significant innovation and capability to thrive.

Additionally, in India, the terms "startups" and "small businesses" are often used interchangeably. While all startups are small businesses, not all small businesses qualify as startups. For example, selling chai (tea) or panipuri and building a franchise for these businesses would be considered traditional ventures, not startups—unless they involve some form of technological disruption. If you've followed the news, you'd recognize several startups that rose meteorically, only to fall just as steeply due to these fundamental shortcomings. Reason - no innovation!

This lack of innovation often stems from founders' limited industry experience. Startups and small businesses are conflated, encompassing ventures ranging from chai stalls to local franchises that lack disruptive potential. True innovation requires a deep understanding of existing solutions and the ability to identify areas for improvement. Achieving this for young graduates demands a robust ecosystem of collaboration between universities and industries. Universities must actively bridge the gap between academic research and real-world applications, enabling future entrepreneurs to create transformative solutions rather than reinventing the wheel.

University Industry Collaboration

In 2008, during my third year of BTech, I developed a keen interest in embedded systems design and decided to pursue a career in FPGA (Field Programmable Gate Arrays) development. As I explored this domain further, I realized that FPGAs are primarily used in Research and Development projects for creating prototypes and proof-of-concept designs. They also find applications in highly specialized areas with low production volumes, such as industrial control systems, advanced test equipment, and military technologies. This niche focus made FPGA development a highly specialized skill, but it also meant that job opportunities were relatively limited.

To expand my knowledge and skill set, I enrolled in a six-month embedded systems course at an institute called CDAC. However, despite completing both – my BTech and the specialized course, my understanding of FPGAs and Embedded Systems Design remained confined to academic concepts, with little or no exposure to real-world industry practices. I lacked insight into current trends and practical applications in the field.

This disconnect between academic training and industry requirements is a widespread issue in most engineering colleges and universities in India, excluding elite institutions like the IITs and NITs. The majority of universities, which produce approximately 90% of the country's engineering graduates, often fail to bridge this gap effectively. As a result, graduates frequently find themselves ill-prepared to meet the demands of modern industries, highlighting a systemic flaw in engineering education.

When I began studying in Germany, my experience was markedly different. The university maintained strong partnerships with several private companies in the region, creating numerous opportunities for students to engage directly with industry. Many of these collaborations involved projects initiated by companies but carried out by students, often with financial compensation. This allowed students to gain practical experience while earning part-time income. In Europe, part-time work is a common practice among students, who typically finance their own expenses. This reflects a cultural emphasis on individual responsibility and independence, contrasting with the norm in India, where students often pursue personal freedom while relying on their parents to cover their expenses.

One key enabler for these live projects is the involvement of professors and technical staff who possess significant professional experience in the industry. These individuals act as a vital bridge between the academic environment and the industry, facilitating collaboration and ensuring students gain practical, real-world insights. This was particularly striking to me because, back home in India, professors, lecturers, and technical staff at universities often lack any prior industry experience. While they may be highly knowledgeable and academically accomplished, their understanding of industry practices and requirements is often limited, leaving a gap in preparing students for real-world challenges. At my university in India, some students graduated and immediately started teaching at the same institution, while others pursued postgraduate studies before taking up teaching roles.

Apart from live projects, universities in Germany also provide structured opportunities for internships. Many of my classmates participated in internships with companies across the country, referred to as a "practical semester." This approach actively encourages students to engage with the industry as an integral part of their academic curriculum. In some cases, the dual education system—which combines academic study with practical work experience—is a cornerstone of higher education. In this system, students split their time between attending classes and working in industry positions, allowing them to gain hands-on experience and develop skills directly relevant to employers.

However, unlike in India, universities in Europe or the UK put minimal effort into securing final placements for students. In India, a university's reputation often hinges on the percentage of final-year students placed in companies and the salary packages they secure. While this system offers immediate job opportunities, it does not necessarily ensure that students possess the practical skills and adaptability required by employers in diverse sectors. In contrast, universities in the West focus more on equipping students with industry-relevant skills and practical exposure, leaving the responsibility of employability and career readiness largely to the students.

I used to wonder why private companies in the West would even want to pay for internships. Reflecting on my own experience as a student intern with Mentor Automotive, I realized I wasn't of much immediate help to the company. Despite this, they invested time and resources in me—paying a monthly stipend, allowing access to company resources, and providing the invaluable opportunity to work alongside highly experienced FPGA developers.

Years later, when I became a team manager responsible for recruiting and managing project resources, I understood the rationale behind such investments. For example, when tasked with recruiting an intern for the firmware team, I was explicitly asked to consider whether the candidate would be a good fit for a full-time role after their internship. A six-month internship provides far more insight into a candidate's capabilities, work ethic, and alignment with the department's vision than a one-time interview ever could. As a result, many interns transition into full-time roles within the same organization.

Additionally, I learned that in some Western countries, governments incentivize internships through tax benefits for companies. Unfortunately, the situation in India is starkly different. Instead of fostering partnerships between universities and private companies, the government often imposes financial burdens on corporations under the guise of corporate social responsibility.

This short-term approach undermines the potential for long-term collaboration and skill development, further widening the gap between academia and industry.

Students in the West, even before graduating, gain substantial exposure to industry practices and are well-informed about current developments in the professional world. They have a clear understanding of "what exists" in terms of technology, innovations, and career pathways, which equips them with practical insights and a competitive edge.

Many students in India talk about dropping out of college, inspired by a few popular tech entrepreneurs in the west who succeeded in inducing technological disruptions after leaving formal education. However, they often overlook a critical factor: the exposure and opportunities these dropouts had even before leaving college. This level of early industry engagement is something a significant portion of Indian graduates only experience once they enter the workforce in core tech roles.

Take Mark Zuckerberg, for example. The co-founder and CEO of Meta (formerly Facebook) dropped out of college, but not before completing an internship at Microsoft's Product Development Group during the summer of 2004 while he was still a student. Similarly, Steve Jobs, another famous college dropout and the co-founder of Apple Inc., interned at Atari, a pioneering video game company, in the summer of 1974. At just 18 years old, Jobs worked as a computer technician, designing circuit boards for Atari's popular arcade game Breakout. During this time, he collaborated with Steve Wozniak, who would later become his business partner and co-founder of Apple.

These examples illustrate that the success of such individuals was not merely a result of dropping out but rather the result of leveraging significant industry exposure and building networks early on. This foundational experience set the stage for their future innovations and business ventures—a nuance that is often overlooked in the Indian context.

To be fair, there weren't many high-tech companies operating in India at the time, with the notable exception of information technology-enabled services and software development. Companies developing advanced technologies, such as electronic control units for automobiles or high-tech MRI and CT scan machines like those produced by Philips, were virtually nonexistent. Most research and development in areas like FPGA development was concentrated in the public sector. For instance, in the space sector, ISRO (Indian Space Research Organization) handled most of the research activities, while in defense, DRDO (Defence Research and Development Organization) was, and still is, the principal body driving innovation. Other sectors, such as automotive and healthcare, were even less developed.

I specifically highlight space, automotive, and healthcare because I have worked in these industries and can directly compare their state in India with that of Europe (including the UK). What struck me the most was the paradox in India's education system: nearly every engineering college in the country offered courses in Electronics Engineering, yet after completing a four-year bachelor's degree, very few graduates managed to work as electronics engineers. Instead, most ended up in IT or software roles, largely due to the lack of opportunities in core electronics fields.

At the same time, Europe and the UK were actively seeking skilled professionals to work in the electronics industry. These countries went to great lengths to adapt their policies, making it highly attractive for individuals like me to stay and contribute to their economies. For instance, the embedded systems course I pursued for my Master's program in Germany was entirely taught in English, unlike most other courses, which were still taught in German. Furthermore, the program had no tuition fees, significantly lowering the financial barriers for international students.

Even after completing my studies, when I applied for full-time employment, I was not required to demonstrate proficiency in German for roles related to Embedded Systems or FPGA development. However, my Indian and Chinese peers who applied for roles outside these niches often had to invest considerable effort in learning German to improve their employability.

The Netherlands, in particular, attracts engineers worldwide with its highly appealing 30% ruling. According to this policy, foreign workers living outside the Dutch border (at least 150 kilometers away) qualify for a significant tax break—only 70% of their annual salary is taxed, with the first 30% being tax-exempt. This tax incentive dramatically increases take-home pay, especially compared to the flat 49.5% tax on Box 1 income (employment income) that others are required to pay. Such measures make these countries highly desirable destinations for skilled professionals and encourage a steady inflow of talent to bolster their industries.

Products and Services

One notable difference I observed while working in Europe is the region's strong focus on product development as opposed to a primary reliance on providing services. Products and services play distinct roles in driving technological innovation, with each offering unique benefits in terms of impact, scalability, and sustainability.

Product innovation involves the creation of tangible or digital goods that solve specific problems or address unmet needs. Examples range from software applications and electronic devices to medical equipment. A key advantage of product-based innovation is its scalability. Successful products can be mass-produced or distributed globally, exponentially expanding their market reach with relatively low incremental costs. For example, companies like Apple, Tesla, Philips, Siemens, and ASML are all leaders in product innovation, investing heavily in R&D to develop groundbreaking technologies. Siemens, for instance, excels in industrial automation and medical devices, while ASML dominates the market for photolithography machines critical to semiconductor manufacturing. Such innovations not only set industry benchmarks but also drive technological progress by integrating advanced features, cutting-edge materials, and sophisticated designs.

Service innovation, on the other hand, focuses on delivering intangible offerings like IT solutions, consultancy, and customer support. India has been a global leader in service-based industries, particularly in IT and Business Process Outsourcing (BPO), with companies like Infosys, TCS, and Wipro dominating international markets. Service-based models are often easier to establish and expand, leveraging human resources and existing technologies.

While services drive economic growth, they typically lack the scalability and high profit margins associated with product-based innovation. Moreover, service innovation often emphasizes operational efficiency over transformative technological advancements. For example, many Indian IT firms excel in outsourcing and software development but rely on technologies developed by global product-focused companies instead of originating them.

The most successful companies integrate products and services to create ecosystems that complement one another. For instance, Apple pairs its hardware products with services like iCloud and the App Store, while Tesla supports its electric vehicles with charging networks and energy solutions. In India, achieving a balance between product and service innovation is crucial for sustained economic and technological growth.

India's ecosystem for product-based startups is still maturing. While there are notable exceptions like Bharat Biotech (Covaxin) and Ola Electric, high costs associated with prototyping, manufacturing, and securing intellectual property remain significant barriers. To unlock its potential, India must invest in R&D, enhance manufacturing capabilities, and implement policies that support entrepreneurship in both hardware and software sectors.

Interestingly, England, once a global leader in industrialization and technological innovation after World War II, has shifted its economic focus over the decades. Historically, the country led advancements in automotive engineering, aerospace, and consumer electronics, with companies like Rolls-Royce and British Aerospace symbolizing its technological prowess. Today, however, England has transitioned into a service-based economy, with financial services dominating its landscape. London's emergence as a global financial hub has attracted talent and investment but has come at the expense of industrial and product-based innovation. This shift has resulted in reduced investments in R&D and manufacturing, eroding the country's competitive edge in product development. While sectors like pharmaceuticals, represented by companies such as GlaxoSmithKline and AstraZeneca, continue to thrive, the broader decline in industrial manufacturing has long-term implications. For example, iconic British automotive brands like Mini and Jaguar Land Rover are now owned by foreign companies such as BMW and Tata Motors.

Product innovation often exerts significant downward pressure on service-related costs. For instance, advancements in the airline industry, such as fuel-efficient engines and lightweight materials, have substantially reduced operational expenses, enabling airlines to offer more competitive ticket prices. Similarly, the rise of the internet and online booking systems has transformed ticketing, enhancing efficiency and convenience for passengers while eliminating intermediaries. However, these innovations have also compressed profit margins for service providers, prompting cost-cutting measures that often affect employee wages in the service sector as businesses strive to stay profitable. These examples underscore a persistent challenge: while product innovation boosts efficiency and enhances consumer satisfaction, it frequently compels service-oriented businesses to rapidly adapt to shifting market dynamics, sometimes at the expense of profitability and employee well-being.

This dynamic is evident in the stark contrast between service providers like Air India, which often face financial difficulties, and aircraft manufacturers like Boeing or Airbus, which consistently remain profitable. Innovations in aircraft technology have enabled manufacturers to deliver highly efficient products, but the benefits of these advancements are not evenly distributed across the value chain. Airlines, caught in highly competitive markets, are compelled to pass on cost savings to consumers, further squeezing their already narrow profit margins.

While services have significantly contributed to India's economic growth, they must be complemented by a robust product innovation ecosystem to ensure long-term sustainability and global competitiveness. By addressing barriers to product development and fostering collaboration between product and service sectors, India can unlock its potential as a global tech powerhouse, drawing lessons from both its domestic challenges and international examples like England's evolution.

The key is product innovation and not just product manufacturing. It is also true that once a technology matures, manufacturing technically mature products often yields diminishing returns after a certain point. This occurs when most possible innovations or efficiency improvements have already been realized, making further advancements less impactful. Additionally, market saturation and intense competition can drive down prices, reducing profitability for manufacturers.

For example, the smartphone industry illustrates this phenomenon. In its early years, breakthroughs like touchscreens, high-resolution cameras, and app ecosystems drove rapid growth and profitability. However, as these features became standard across brands, innovation slowed, and differentiation became more challenging. Manufacturers now face intense price competition, and even flagship models see only incremental improvements year-over-year, reducing returns on investment in research and development.

From 2010 to 2015, Samsung consistently invested upwards of $9 billion annually in R&D, while Apple's spending grew from $1.8 billion to $8.1 billion in the same period. In contrast, HTC struggled to allocate comparable resources, limiting its ability to compete in an industry increasingly driven by high-value innovation. Over time, HTC failed to maintain differentiation and market share, leading to declining sales and significant financial losses. I chose 2010 to 2015 because it represents the peak years for HTC, a smartphone company that once dominated the market with innovative designs and features. During this period, HTC was still a significant player in the smartphone industry, making a comparison with competitors like Apple and Samsung meaningful. In later years, HTC's market presence diminished substantially, making such comparisons less relevant.

HTC's decline highlights how even early leaders in a technically mature industry can suffer due to diminishing returns, intense competition, and insufficient investment in innovation. As a result, businesses may struggle to justify significant investments in innovation for such products, shifting their focus to newer, high-growth opportunities instead.

An interesting current example is Apple's decision to manufacture iPhones in India while retaining its innovation and R&D efforts in the United States. This highlights a growing trend where manufacturing is decentralized to leverage cost advantages, but high-value innovation remains concentrated in developed economies. For India, this move boosts local industrial growth, job creation, and the country's global supply chain relevance. However, the innovation gap remains significant, underscoring the challenge for emerging economies to transition from manufacturing hubs to centers of technological innovation.

The Crux: The missing ecosystem

Over the last decade, Modi's India has undergone an incredible transformation in fostering an ecosystem for innovation. This has been achieved through policy reforms and actively encouraging private sector participation. For example, the introduction of INSpace and ISPA to welcome private players into the space sector is a groundbreaking move. Initiatives like the Atal Innovation Mission (AIM), launched by NITI Aayog, aim to promote innovation and entrepreneurship in academic institutions by establishing Atal Tinkering Labs (ATLs) and Incubation Centers. These efforts have bridged the gap between universities and industries, giving students hands-on exposure to cutting-edge technologies and real-world innovation challenges.

The introduction of the National Institutional Ranking Framework (NIRF) by the Ministry of Education has further emphasized research output and industry collaboration. Universities are increasingly focused on collaborative projects to boost their rankings, which has naturally led to stronger industry partnerships. Through campaigns like Startup India and international startup challenges in collaboration with countries like Israel, the government has successfully turned "startup" into a buzzword in India. Once, government jobs were the ultimate aspiration for the youth, but now entrepreneurship has taken center stage.

In addition, incentives such as tax exemptions, the Fund of Funds, and the Credit Guarantee Fund have made it easier for startups to access credit. Simplified regulations have encouraged universities and industries to work together, especially in areas like technology, entrepreneurship, and research. These efforts have had a visible impact. The number of startups in India has skyrocketed from around 350 in 2014 to over 90,000 in 2023, including more than 100 Unicorns—startups valued at over $1 billion. The space sector has also witnessed a significant increase in startup activity.

It's time for India to shed its tag as merely a global IT service provider and leap into a high-tech revolution. With Atmanirbhar Bharat as the ultimate goal, innovation must lead the way forward.

IMMUNITY

"Rakshanam eva raajya-shaasanam apekshate."
–Book II, Chapter 1, Arthashastra

"The primary duty of governance is to ensure protection."

Threats

The immune system is like a body's personal security team—always on high alert, using its intricate network to detect and neutralize potential threats such as pathogens before they can cause harm. This sophisticated system comprises cells, tissues, and organs working seamlessly to fight infections, remove dead cells, and even hunt down rogue cancer cells. Key players in this team include the thymus, spleen, lymph nodes, stem cells, white blood cells, antibodies, and more. Together, they create immunity—the body's remarkable natural defense mechanism.

In much the same way, countries have their own version of an immune system to safeguard against a range of threats. National defenses, such as military forces, intelligence agencies, border control and diplomacy act like the body's immune cells, identifying and neutralizing external dangers like war and terrorism. Internal threats, on the other hand, are comparable to autoimmune disorders—issues like poverty, corruption, social unrest, and weakened law enforcement can destabilize a nation from within, much like a body turning against itself.

Just as personal fitness boosts immunity, a robust economy fortifies nations against financial crises and political instability. For example, during the 2008 global financial crisis, countries with stronger economies, like Germany, were able to provide stimulus packages and sustain public welfare, while weaker economies faced severe instability and unrest. The Covid pandemic highlighted the ability of resilient economies to adapt and recover from unprecedented challenges, emphasizing the critical role of flexibility and preparedness in overcoming crises, in contrast to the struggles faced by fragile economies.

Similar to how people adapt to new diseases with vaccines and improved hygiene, nations must continually evolve their defenses to counter emerging threats. This could mean investing in cutting-edge technology for cybersecurity, strengthening global alliances for coordinated responses, or enhancing education and infrastructure to build resilience against internal and external challenges. Recognizing vulnerabilities and addressing them is crucial—not just for survival but for thriving in a rapidly changing world.

Technological threats are the new frontier. In today's digital age, cyberattacks and data breaches function like viruses, making cybersecurity the essential vaccine of the modern era. The world seems more precarious than ever, grappling with uncertainties on multiple fronts. The COVID-19 pandemic, ongoing conflicts like Russia-Ukraine and Israel-Palestine, illegal migration, and economic downturns are testing the resilience of nations globally. It's as if the world is in a perpetual flu season, and no country is entirely immune.

Exactly like people have better immunity due to genetics, certain nations naturally possess stronger defenses because of geography. The U.S., for example, benefits from the vast protective barriers of the Pacific and Atlantic Oceans, which make it difficult for external threats to reach its shores. In contrast, India shares a 3,323-kilometer border with Pakistan and a 4,096-kilometer stretch with Bangladesh, making infiltration comparatively easier and sometimes even a simple crossing on foot. A terrorist could simply walk across India's borders, whereas targeting the U.S. typically requires crossing entire oceans. The U.K. finds itself in a middle ground. Its island geography offers a reasonable buffer, but it isn't as isolated as the U.S. Similarly, European nations benefit from barriers like the Mediterranean Sea, which complicates infiltration but doesn't make it impossible. Moreover, an external threat to reach, say for example Germany, the threat has to pass through a number of other European countries.

Geography even influenced the spread of COVID-19. Some regions, like parts of the Sahara, recorded minimal cases due to factors like dry air, sparse populations, and pre-existing antibodies—an invisible shield of sorts. Conversely, densely populated urban centers like New York City, Delhi, or London, etc. with high human interaction and reliance on public transportation, faced significant outbreaks, highlighting how geography can exacerbate the spread of infectious diseases.

CoronaVirus

The pandemic not only tested the immunity of the entire planet but also left a lasting impact on how we work, reshaping industries, accelerating digital transformation, and highlighting the vulnerabilities of various sectors. While healthcare systems were stretched to their limits, remote work revolutionized the tech and service industries, and supply chains adapted to new realities, often relying on automation and technology for resilience.

By the end of 2019, I was working hard on the development of my first IP (Intellectual Property) Core while working at Mentor Automotive. The IP was supposed to be showcased at the Nuremberg Auto Expo in February 2020. I was putting whatever I had got in me to complete this activity; completely unaware of the fact that this IP would never reach the expo, not because it won't be completed in time but because the people won't be allowed to travel to the expo to demonstrate. The company issued a notification banning business travel until further notice due to the spreading coronavirus in the last week of January. Many companies pulled out of the expo. But guess who didn't cancel? The delegates from China! Of course, the healthy ones!

By mid-March, we were all asked to work from home. Office visits required senior management approval—a tedious process that often delayed critical tasks and created bottlenecks in productivity and innovation, particularly for hardware-dependent projects. Office occupancy was restricted by strict time slots. Our work involved electronic hardware, PCBs, and FPGAs for ADAS (Advanced Driver Assistance Systems) and autonomous vehicle projects (cameras, LIDARs, and RADARs). While firmware/software development could be handled from home—writing and simulating code. However, debugging and integrating on actual hardware required office visits.

Since we weren't in the automation business, there were no remote automation policies, forcing everyone to rely on ingenuity and adaptability. Team members crafted creative solutions to overcome these challenges, showcasing an impressive spirit of resourcefulness during an unprecedented time. How do you switch on/off an evaluation kit from home? That was my first hurdle. IoT to the rescue—an extension cord controllable via the internet. Problem solved!

Another issue involved sensor fusion with four camera sensors feeding input to the IP. Even if the board was powered on, the cameras showed the same image each time; I wasn't there to move the cameras and see if the frames changed as expected. If every pixel remains static, how do I know it's working? I tried pointing them at windows, hoping for movement. But during lockdown? No chance. The solution? Rotating table fans! I placed two near the first and third camera sensors, creating enough movement to capture changes. The office was full of these makeshift setups. If and when I visited, I found handwritten notes like "Please do not move; testing ongoing." I had one for my own little setup.

Programming FPGAs remotely (usually done via USB/JTAG) became another challenge. By the end of the year, we had automated several processes, transforming challenges into opportunities. In the early lockdown phase, these obstacles felt like engineering puzzles—and engineers thrive on a good puzzle! For some, the process turned work into an engaging and enjoyable endeavor, blending creativity with problem-solving. And of course, for every missed deadline we had covid to blame - enough time for experimentation without accountability!

However, not everyone shared this enthusiasm, as the constraints and uncertainties of the pandemic created stress and frustration for many. Countless jobs don't offer the luxury of working from home. For example, gym receptionists, taxi drivers, shopkeepers, and bartenders were among the hardest hit, with many losing their jobs entirely. According to a report by the International Labour Organization, millions of jobs in the service and informal sectors were wiped out globally during the pandemic, highlighting the stark disparity between those who could work remotely and those who couldn't. Others, like supermarket clerks and healthcare workers, had to keep going, increasing their risk.

Picture standing behind a supermarket counter, exposed to a constant flow of customers, each interaction amplifying the risk of virus transmission—a stark reminder of the vulnerability frontline workers faced during the pandemic. As I mentioned earlier, Covid didn't hit everyone the same way. Different locations, professions, and social statuses meant wildly different experiences, shaping both the response to and recovery from the pandemic. Densely populated areas faced greater risks, often requiring stricter lockdowns and more robust healthcare interventions. Conversely, rural and less populated regions experienced fewer cases but often lacked the medical infrastructure to handle outbreaks effectively. High population density is probably why India's lockdown was stricter than Germany's.

In Germany, there was no blanket ban on going outside of the house. You could walk around, and local buses still continued providing services (though with fewer passengers—sometimes just 5-6 people per bus). With sports complexes shut down and squash courts remaining off-limits even after outdoor tennis courts reopened, it was a stark reminder of how the pandemic restricted many aspects of daily life. The rationale? Confined areas were more susceptible to the virus. During that time, running became my only way to stay active and avoid turning into a couch potato.

This contrasts sharply with India's stricter lockdown measures, which included complete bans on movement in many areas to contain the virus. While Germany's approach preserved a sense of normalcy, India's strict measures arguably reduced the virus's spread in densely populated regions, though they came at a significant social and economic cost.

After waiting for almost a year, uncertain about when the chaos would settle and eager to reunite with my family, I finally decided to plan a trip back home. This journey allowed me to witness firsthand the stark contrasts between how India and Europe managed the crisis, ranging from logistical preparedness to the cultural nuances that defined their responses to such unprecedented challenges. Throughout the pandemic, the Government of India initiated and continued Vande Bharat Missions, a series of repatriation flights that enabled Indians to travel to and from other countries amidst global restrictions.

Travel required paperwork, registrations, and—most importantly—an RT-PCR test. In my small city of Villingen-Schwenningen, rapid tests were everywhere—15-minute results. But RT-PCR tests? Not so easy. They were subsidized for health reasons but expensive for travel. One place offered the test—for 240 Euros! That was insane. Near Frankfurt Airport, tests ranged from 69 Euros (results available in 12-24 hours) to 149 Euros (results available in less than 5 hours). The airport had a complete menu card of different tests available. The cheapest option worked if only I lived in or near Frankfurt. But I lived four hours away. Staying overnight added costs, making the expensive test more practical. Eventually, I found a place in Tübingen offering the test for 60 Euros with results in 12-24 hours. A 50-minute drive, problem solved.

At Frankfurt Airport, plenty of people struggled with RT-PCR tests—some waited for results, others presented fake ones (and got caught). This made me anxious about Delhi. But surprisingly, Delhi Airport was super organized. Tests were affordable (INR

800) and quick. My mom usually picks me up from the airport. Before boarding my flight in Germany, I had asked her to leave late, assuming there would be delays. To my surprise, when I landed in Delhi, I was out of the airport—immigration, baggage, and all—in just 40 minutes.

The return from India was smooth too. Lab technicians visited home on motorbikes, donned PPE kits, took samples, and left. Results came the next day. The Delhi airport was more crowded but efficient. Sure, some people tried fake results, but their reactions varied. In Germany, people were apologetic—"I'm sorry, but I don't want to miss my flight." In India, the tone was more aggressive—"It's not my fault! Will you pay for my flight? The system is broken!" (with some colorful language). It's funny—Indians abroad are often more polite than at home.

It looked like India was absorbing the crisis much better than many western countries. One significant factor? Family. In countries like Germany, the Netherlands, and the UK, social life after work often revolves around bars, restaurants, sports centers, and other public venues. When I moved to these countries, I joined meetups to make friends. I was quite surprised to see a large number of locals attending those meetups. They've lived in those cities their whole lives, then why do they need meetups? That's the difference. In India, family time is the default. I never scheduled dinner with my parents—I just eat at home - I lived with them! This cultural norm fosters strong familial bonds, which acted as an emotional cushion during the pandemic. But here, people schedule dinners with family like they do with friends. When Covid hit, no bars, no meetups—people who relied on these felt the impact. Depression, loneliness, and stress shot up. India's family structure absorbed much of this emotional strain. For people like myself, who were away from home, video calls that often lasted for hours came to rescue. Sometimes, the phone was just on, and everyone did their own thing without talking. It felt like I wasn't alone. People crave connection—if they can't go out, they'll find new ways. I never thought I'd play online Ludo before 2020, I hated ludo. But there I was, reconnecting with family and friends. Thanks to technology, I felt at home.

At the very least, Covid taught us that hugging and kissing everyone might not be the best greeting! Namaste might just save us!

In hindsight, while the pandemic brought its share of hardships, it not only fast-tracked India's development in critical areas but also validated some of Modi government's flagship programs. One of the standout successes during this period was the validation of the government's JAM trinity: Jan Dhan Yojana, Aadhaar, and Mobile connectivity.

For years, the Modi government had been pushing for financial inclusion through Jan Dhan accounts, and during Covid, this initiative proved its worth. Direct Benefit Transfers (DBT) became a lifeline for millions, ensuring that financial aid reached people directly, bypassing the often-tedious layers of bureaucracy. Free rations distributed through the public distribution system ensured that even the most vulnerable families had food on the table throughout the year. The efficiency with which these benefits were rolled out showcased how digital infrastructure could bridge gaps and provide timely relief during a crisis. Over 80 crore people benefited from free ration schemes under the Pradhan Mantri Garib Kalyan Anna Yojana, highlighting the reach and scale of the initiative.

Beyond welfare, Covid also accelerated India's position in the pharmaceutical and healthcare sectors. Faced with the monumental task of vaccinating over a billion people, the country rose to the challenge. The development and mass production of vaccines like Covaxin and Covishield put India on the global map, not just as a consumer but as a leading producer and exporter of vaccines. The sheer scale of the vaccination drive was staggering. Crores of Indians were vaccinated within months, thanks to coordinated efforts at the national and state levels. Over 220 crore vaccine doses were administered by mid-2023, a figure that dwarfed many Western countries' efforts. When compared to other nations, India's vaccination drive stood out for its scale and efficiency, enabled by the CoWIN platform, while initiatives like Vaccine Maitri showcased a commitment to global health, unlike some countries that prioritized only their populations. These efforts reflect India's capacity to adapt, innovate, and lead on the global stage, shaping a future that is not only digitally empowered but also inclusive and self-sustaining.

One significant distinction in how the COVID situation was managed between India and the West lay in the approach to vaccine rollout and reception. In India, the government emphasized public awareness and voluntary participation. In contrast, many Western countries implemented mandates or restrictions tied to vaccine certification, which often felt more coercive than collaborative. In many western countries, like Germany and the Netherlands, getting vaccinated felt more like an obligation than a choice. If I wanted to sit inside a restaurant, grab a drink at a bar, or watch a movie in a theater, I needed to show either a proof of vaccination, or a recent negative test, or proof of recovery from COVID-19. Each country had its own name for this requirement. The Netherlands called it the "COVID passport" or "vaccine certificate"; France called it the "health pass"; and Germany rolled out the "3G rule" (Geimpft, Genesen, Getestet - Vaccinated, Recovered, Tested).

At first, I wasn't super eager to get the vaccine, but I ended up getting one simply because life became inconvenient without it. In India, though, things felt different. The government didn't really force people's hands in the same way. Instead, they leaned into convincing the public, appealing to their sense of responsibility rather than creating barriers. It felt more in line with the spirit of democracy – letting people make their own informed choices. I think a big part of why this worked was having a leader like Prime Minister Modi, who has a huge following and knows how to connect with the masses. When he spoke about the importance of vaccines, people listened. The ministers including Prime Minister himself played a crucial role in engaging with citizens throughout the pandemic. PM Modi's regular addresses to the nation, often referred to as "Mann Ki Baat," served to reassure the public and keep them informed. Ministers frequently held press conferences, town halls, and virtual interactions, addressing concerns directly and providing updates on vaccination drives, lockdown measures, and economic relief packages. This consistent communication built a sense of trust and unity, reinforcing the idea that the government was actively working to mitigate the crisis. Grassroots outreach by local leaders and health workers further amplified these efforts, ensuring that even remote villages were part of the national effort. The Rashtriya Swayamsevak Sangh played a noteworthy role in the vaccination drive, actively supporting logistical efforts and community outreach to ensure wider coverage and accessibility.

India's success in vaccine rollout was notable for its speed and efficiency, often surpassing that of many Western nations. The CoWIN platform allowed seamless online registration, real-time tracking of vaccinations, and easy availability of slots. This digital approach minimized logistical delays and confusion, ensuring that India could vaccinate millions daily. In contrast, Western nations often struggled with appointment backlogs and fragmented systems, highlighting the efficiency of India's centralized strategy. When I finally did decide to get the vaccine in the Netherlands, I still had to wait for a couple of months to get the appointment. India's ability to coordinate vaccinations at scale was a testament to its growing digital capabilities and focus on technological innovation. This experience underscored the resilience and adaptability of India's pharmaceutical industry. It wasn't just about meeting domestic demand; India also stepped in to supply vaccines to neighboring countries and even nations in Africa and South America, reinforcing its reputation as the "pharmacy of the world." Initiatives like Vaccine Maitri, where India provided over 250 million doses to more than 100 countries, highlighted the nation's soft power and commitment to global health.

Additionally, the rapid rollout of 5G and expansion of high-speed internet played a crucial role in India's pandemic response. With remote work, online education, and telemedicine becoming necessities, India's growing digital infrastructure ensured connectivity across urban and rural areas in distinct ways. In urban regions, the rapid rollout of 5G enabled seamless remote work, enhanced streaming quality for OTT platforms, and bolstered e-commerce growth. In contrast, rural areas benefited significantly from improved internet access, which facilitated telemedicine services and online education, bridging gaps in healthcare and learning resources that had long been inaccessible. areas. Companies like Jio spearheaded the 5G rollout, rapidly expanding network coverage and making high-speed internet accessible to millions. This expansion allowed schools to continue online, small businesses to thrive, and patients in remote areas to access telemedicine services, reducing the burden on urban healthcare systems. OTT Platforms in India flourished as a result of which the quality of web series improved greatly. More importantly, with good quality content on OTT platforms, the quality of the conventional cinema in India improved greatly.

Big online retailers expanded, they could reach the areas where people would otherwise stick to physical shops. By imposing restrictions on movement, the consumers were left with the only option of online shopping. This was enough to overcome the deterrents for online shopping: “can I trust the online retailers?” or even “how to buy online?”. Now when Covid is hardly mentioned in day to day lives, how many of those customers went back to shopping in person? If I take my own example. I never got groceries online before covid, but today I can’t imagine myself getting groceries from the market (this includes fresh fruits and vegetables). The ease and convenience of purchase, no queues, the logistics - nothing to worry about. Everything is just a click away!

Covid, despite its devastation, catalyzed growth in sectors that had long been overlooked or underdeveloped. The push for digital healthcare, increased funding in medical research, and the growth of telemedicine were byproducts of the pandemic that continue to thrive post-Covid. India's telemedicine platform, eSanjeevani, recorded over 10 crore consultations by late 2023, demonstrating the rapid adoption of digital healthcare solutions. The Indian government quickly recognized the need to ramp up domestic production of PPE kits. Government initiatives and incentives encouraged domestic manufacturers to shift production towards PPE, resulting in India becoming one of the largest producers globally within months.

The JAM trinity, the mass vaccination drives, the expansion of 5G, and the growth of the pharmaceutical industry are not just milestones but stepping stones towards a more resilient and self-reliant India.

Border Control

A virus isn't the only unwelcome visitor to a country. Sometimes, it's people—crossing borders without permission, slipping into a nation the way a virus sneaks into a body. You'd think spotting and stopping someone crossing a border would be easier than detecting an invisible, microscopic virus. But in reality, that's not always the case. Illegal migration brings its own set of challenges. One of the biggest– Border control. As I mentioned earlier geography plays a huge role in how easily a country can manage illegal migration. For instance, natural barriers like oceans and mountain ranges can act as formidable deterrents, as seen with the rugged terrain of the US-Mexico border; if someone wants to sneak into the UK, they'd need to cross the English Channel—usually in small boats. Europe? It often involves crossing multiple countries or the Mediterranean Sea.

Now, let's flip to India. No need for boats —just walk across the long and porous borders.

And despite Europe and the UK having better natural barriers, their borders are far more tightly regulated than India's.

During my stay in the Netherlands for a year, one of the most enriching things I did, which greatly enhanced my exploration and understanding of Europe, was buying a motorcycle. Motorcycle riding in Europe is notably different from how it is in India, at least from my perspective. It's not just about wearing a helmet and gloves; complete bike gear is essential. The process almost feels like preparing for a MotoGP event. However, once you hit the motorway, the need for such gear becomes evident. Riding a 1000cc motorbike on a motorway without proper protective gear is not just risky but tantamount to courting disaster, and it is also freezing cold.

Motorbike ride-outs to some of the remotest places in Europe revealed that the borders between European countries are meticulously marked. Wherever I traveled, the borders were clearly identified, even though no border forces were patrolling them. It was straightforward to ride from Eindhoven to cities like Brussels, Bruges, or Antwerp, and I could immediately recognize when I had crossed into Belgium due to the prominent signs and markings. Even in remote, desolate areas far from civilization, these markings were consistently present, ensuring you always knew which country you were in.

Some borders have even been transformed into tourist attractions, such as "*Drielandenpunt*"—the Three Country Point for the Netherlands, Belgium, and Germany. While it's simply a spot with three flags and not much else, it serves as a symbolic location. I found it a bit underwhelming on my first visit after riding over 100 miles, expecting something more elaborate. On a subsequent ride with friends to *Dreiländereck*, the three-country point for Belgium, the Netherlands, and Germany, I managed my expectations and appreciated the simplicity of the experience. I was pleasantly surprised by how seamless and efficient it was to enter England via the EuroTunnel on my motorbike. This memorable experience occurred during my longest solo journey, which took me from the Netherlands through Belgium and France, and ultimately to England.

It is notable that Europe, despite its open borders and decades of peace among neighboring nations, has consistently maintained clearly defined and well-marked boundaries. In contrast, India, despite enduring multiple wars and border tensions, has historically neglected to adequately demarcate and regulate its borders. For much of its post-independence history, India did not prioritize developing infrastructure along its borders. This lack of focus is perhaps best illustrated by a former prime minister's remark about the Aksai Chin region: "When not even a needle grows there, why should we be worried about that piece of land?" This comment, made during a parliamentary debate in 1961 about the Sino-Indian border conflict, had sparked a sharp response from parliamentarian Mahavir Tyagi. Pointing to his own bald head, Tyagi retorted, "Nothing grows here either. Should I lose it?" This exchange highlighted the stark differences in opinions regarding the significance of barren territories and underscored the broader debate over national priorities and border security. Consequently, vast stretches of borderland remained underdeveloped and poorly managed for decades.

The recent skirmishes with China can largely be attributed to India's abrupt focus on infrastructure development in previously neglected border areas. For decades, the Indian side experienced little to no progress in these regions. When the Modi government initiated projects such as roads and tunnels, it disrupted the long-standing status quo, prompting a reaction from China. Given the inertia of the previous seventy years, such changes inevitably heightened tensions.

Having said that, India's historical neglect of its borders with China could, to some extent, be rationalized by viewing China as a relatively stable neighbor compared to the more volatile dynamics along the borders with Pakistan and Bangladesh. However, it remains perplexing that even these two more contentious borders were not effectively monitored or regulated, despite recurrent and significant provocations.

In the last ten years, India has significantly shifted its focus toward building essential infrastructure along its borders. The government has actively worked to address long-standing border issues that had been neglected for decades, leading to a complex web of challenges. This renewed emphasis underscores a recognition of the vital role borders play, not merely as physical demarcations but as powerful symbols of sovereignty, security, and national identity.

A great example of the government regulating India's borders is the 2015 resolution of the India-Bangladesh enclave issue. The enclaves are small pockets of land from one country inside the other. And then, there are third-order enclaves, say for example – Bangladesh land inside India, with a smaller Indian enclave inside that Bangladeshi enclave. The India-Bangladesh border isn't just tricky—it's almost comical. Managing these borders was a logistical nightmare.

This wasn't a new issue either—India and Bangladesh agreed to settle the enclave problem back in 1974. Managing these enclaves presented logistical challenges such as determining territorial boundaries, relocating residents, and ensuring that essential services were provided to people transitioning from one country's jurisdiction to another. But despite the agreement between Prime Minister Indira Gandhi and Sheikh Mujibur Rahman, it wasn't resolved until 2015. Under the deal, ratified on June 6, 2015, India received 51 Bangladeshi enclaves (covering 7,110 acres), while Bangladesh got 111 Indian enclaves (covering 17,160 acres). By this time, there were already second- and third-generation families living in these enclaves. The delay caused pain for countless souls. Over the past decade, Modi's India has become increasingly conscious of border security and regulation. This effort not only demonstrated India's commitment to addressing border anomalies but also highlighted the challenges posed by porous borders in regulating illegal migration.

Another factor in migration? Weather. Geography isn't just about land—it's also about climate. Extreme temperatures, whether scorching hot or freezing cold, act as natural deterrents. In the Middle East or northern Europe, illegal migrants can't just set up camps. For example, extreme cold in countries like Germany or Sweden makes it nearly impossible to survive in a tent during winter, requiring migrants to seek formal housing. Try living in a tent under a bridge in England during winter—it's a death sentence. But in Delhi? Thousands of Rohingyas settle in and around the city because the weather, while unpleasant, won't kill them. I once watched a TV series where a housing company was sued because someone died from pneumonia after the heating in their building broke. I thought it was just a dramatic plot device—until I lived through my first German winter. Turns out, it's more than possible. In fact, earlier this year, the heating in my office broke, and we were all told to work from home until it was fixed. That's why illegal migrants can't hide in northern Europe. They need housing and heating, making them easier to track. But in India? Tents and flyovers work just fine. The reality is, controlling migration isn't just about policies or border walls. Geography, climate, and history all play a part.

Even after such conditions the UK struggles controlling rampant illegal immigration, one of the top five priorities for the former British Prime Minister Rishi Sunak in 2023 was curbing the influx of small boats carrying migrants to the UK. According to the UK Home Office, 45,755 people crossed the Channel in small boats in 2022. To stay politically correct, the Home Office calls them "irregular migrants" instead of "illegal migrants." But here's the thing— 45,000 is just the number of people traced. The real number could be much higher as those small boats aren't the only way people sneak in.

As I write this, the UK government is pushing forward with the controversial "Rwandan asylum plan." The idea? Send these migrants to Rwanda, a "safe" third country. There's been plenty of debate about whether the plan is ethical or even legal. There's even a court case going on. But despite that, the deal is moving forward. In fact, the UK has already paid £240 million as part of a five-year agreement with Rwanda. The facility set to host these asylum seekers has an interesting backstory. It was once a refuge for survivors of Rwanda's 1994 genocide, where around 800,000 people were slaughtered by ethnic Hutu extremists targeting the Tutsi minority. The facility sits in Kigali's upscale Kagugu suburb, with some rooms offering a view of the presidential palace. The hostel's managing director, describes the place as having fifty double rooms—enough to house at least a hundred people. He mentioned that Qurans and prayer mats have been placed in each room, expecting most arrivals to be Muslim migrants from the Middle East. Most of these migrants—around 80%—came from Islamic countries like Afghanistan, Iraq, Iran, Syria, and Albania. And the majority (38,522) were men.

While countries like the UK (GDP per capita: approximately $47,000) and other European nations, such as Germany (GDP per capita: approximately $50,000), actively address the socio-economic challenges posed by illegal migration. India (GDP per capita: approximately $2,300) on the other hand has quietly become home to millions of illegal migrants, including the Rohingyas fleeing persecution from Myanmar, Bangladeshis, and other vulnerable groups. Many of these migrants have found shelter in states like Assam, West Bengal, Delhi, and Jammu & Kashmir.

This influx of migrants has stirred up humanitarian concerns and sparked debates over national security, resource distribution, and cultural integration. Unlike global practices such as structured asylum programs in Western countries or work-permit systems in Gulf nations, India's approach has largely lacked formal policies to address the complexities of illegal migration. This absence often exacerbates the challenges of balancing humanitarian obligations with national security concerns.

The complexities surrounding this issue add layers to India's already diverse socio-economic landscape. Illegal migrants often settle in densely populated areas, where competition for essential resources like public services, housing, and jobs is fierce. This increased demand puts a strain on infrastructure that's already stretched thin, leading to overcrowded schools, hospitals, and a shortage of affordable housing. In regions like Assam, where over a million people were registered as illegal residents during the NRC (National Register of Citizens) exercise. These issues have led to growing political unrest. Local populations worry about political disenfranchisement and resource scarcity, further fueling the debate on migration and its socio-political consequences. These illegal migrants work as low-cost labor in sectors like construction and agriculture. With an increased supply of unskilled labor resulting from illegal migration, wages often experience downward pressure, destabilizing the economic security of native populations. This phenomenon reflects a classic example of supply and demand dynamics, where an oversupply of labor leads to reduced earning potential for workers. This phenomenon is not unique to India but a universal trend observed globally. For instance, debates around the U.S.-Mexico border have frequently highlighted similar economic concerns regarding wage suppression; the famous idea of a wall on the US Mexican border is a shining example.

Change in the demographics is another threat perceived. In 2015 when there was a heavy influx of Muslim refugees in Germany as a result of Chancellor Markel's decision, a common question was ubiquitous - "If there is a war in Syria, where are the women and children, why are only men migrating?" This was in response to a series of molestation, eve-teasing, and rape incidents reported during New Year's celebrations in various German cities. For example, in Cologne, over 1,200 complaints were filed, sparking widespread public outrage and raising concerns about the demographic changes brought by such migrations.

Illegal migration isn't just about people crossing borders; it often intertwines with human trafficking, cattle smuggling, drug running, weapons smuggling, and counterfeit currency operations. For instance, the porous India-Bangladesh border had become a hotspot for cattle smuggling, with thousands of cattle reportedly trafficked every year. Similarly, drug smuggling along this border remains a persistent issue, with authorities frequently seizing significant quantities of narcotics. This situation poses varied threats to different sections of society. While law-abiding, tax-paying citizens are concerned about the impact on law and order, many among the native underprivileged population view it as a direct threat to their survival, while others see it as a challenge to their culture and traditions.

NRC

After years of sidestepping the issue, Modi's India is finally addressing the challenge of illegal migration. Like it or not, illegal migrants are a reality—many have lived in the country for years and now consider it their home. The question remains: what comes next?

It is essential for any government to know who resides within its borders. Sound economic planning depends on reliable demographic data. Governments use population figures to determine investments in infrastructure, education, healthcare, and other necessities. For example, in the 1970s, India underestimated the pace of urban population growth, leading to insufficient infrastructure in cities like Mumbai. This oversight resulted in overcrowded slums and inadequate public services, underscoring the importance of accurate data. Without clear knowledge of the population's size and distribution, planning becomes a shot in the dark. Misjudged numbers can mean underfunded schools, hospitals, or roads—or worse, wasted resources on areas that don't need them.

The NRC, or National Register of Citizens, is a government initiative designed to document all legal citizens of India. It aims to provide a clear demographic overview, which can help in making smarter decisions about development and resource allocation. But the 2019-2020 push to roll out the NRC sparked massive protests. People took to the streets, shouting slogans like "The government has no right to ask for ID," or "We won't show our papers." The protests were fueled by fears of discrimination and exclusion, particularly among marginalized communities who worried they might not have the necessary documents to prove citizenship.

Social media lit up with hashtags like *#KagazNahiDikhaenge*. Celebrities and journalists—people who clearly had passports and other IDs—were leading the charge. Honestly, I found it a bit disturbing. As someone who's lived abroad, this whole debate felt unnecessary and ludicrous. In Germany, for example, when I applied for a student visa, I had to submit a pile of documents—certificates, mark sheets, proof of address, bank statements. And even then, my visa was valid for just three months. After arriving, I had to renew it for the duration of my studies, not a day longer, handing over the same stack of papers all over again. Later, when I switched to a work visa, my employer had to confirm that my job aligned with my education. At first, I thought it was a pain, but eventually, I realized that's just how things work in other countries as well. The same ordeal when I moved to the Netherlands and the same when I moved to the UK. The governments wanted to make sure everything was legit.

Living abroad made me realize that the Modi Government wasn't trying to create some Orwellian surveillance state. It was just catching up to basic systems that make governance smoother. When I lived in Germany, the UK, and the Netherlands, every time I moved, I had to let the authorities know - even if I moved within the same city. It wasn't just for immigrants—locals did it too.

Everyone has a unique ID that follows them across public services. That's just how organized societies function. Even little things, like paying for public TV in Germany, tie into this system—everyone contributes. When I moved for my thesis, I deregistered from Bremerhaven, assuming my obligations were complete. However, weeks later, I received a €450 bill for two years of unpaid TV fees. They tracked me through my old registration records, ensuring no obligations were missed. This meticulous tracking keeps census data accurate and public services well-funded. Far from being seen as intrusive, this level of accountability is considered normal and efficient.

So why is India's version, like Aadhar, seen as controversial? Unless somebody has some fishy ideas!!

The introduction of Aadhar in India—designed to streamline services by linking bank accounts, PAN numbers, properties, and gas connections—faced significant backlash from certain quarters. Critics argued that the government doesn't need to know details like individual earnings or the number of bank accounts people hold. However, such systems are quite common in developed countries. For instance, the UK's National Insurance Number connects citizens to taxes, healthcare, and social benefits.

Both systems share the goal of enhancing efficiency and reducing fraud, but Aadhar's integration with diverse digital platforms gives it a uniquely expansive role in India's governance. By curbing fraud in welfare schemes, Aadhar ensures subsidies reach the rightful beneficiaries, significantly boosting efficiency. Ironically, some Indians criticize their own government's initiatives while admiring similar practices abroad. They argue, "India's push for modernization through Aadhar and initiatives like NRC is an unnecessary breach of privacy," while accepting similar mechanisms as indispensable in Western democracies.

Far from prying into personal lives, digitalization and resource tracking through Aadhar aim to create efficient and transparent systems. As these initiatives mature, they promise smoother governance, economic growth, equitable resource distribution, and strengthened public trust.

Terrorism

Illegal migration is not the only consequence of weakened security; cross-border terror activities are another direct outcome. Living abroad has given me a deeper understanding of how terrorism's impact goes far beyond the immediate loss of life. It profoundly destabilizes societies by eroding trust in institutions, fracturing communal bonds, and undermining the collective sense of safety and stability. Unfortunately, this broader impact of terrorism is rarely discussed in India.

Back home, heading to a public place—whether it's an airport, a shopping mall, or a cinema—always involves navigating a security checkpoint. Bags are thoroughly inspected, metal detectors scan every entrant, and a security guard sizes you up before granting entry. Given the times we live in, such precautions are entirely justified. In a world fraught with uncertainties, you can never be too careful.

Turns out, that's not the case everywhere. I was genuinely surprised to find that in Europe and the UK, you can simply walk into an airport without anyone even glancing at you. In India, this would likely be perceived as a major lapse in security, given the history of terror attacks and the heightened vigilance ingrained in public life. The stark difference reflects not just the security environments but also the contrasting societal attitudes toward risk and preparedness. No ID checks at the entrance, no bag scans—just walk right in. Sure, there's a security check before boarding, but that's about it. Shopping malls, cinemas, metro stations, and even train and bus terminals maintain the same relaxed approach. Churches and cathedrals are equally open, with minimal visible security. The only time I ever noticed security forces was when a cop was writing a parking ticket or casually cruising by in their patrol car. The contrast couldn't be starker.

It really made me think—why is security so much more visible in India? Perhaps part of the reason Europe appears more relaxed is their success in tightening border security, which reduces the need for intense scrutiny at every nook and cranny within the country. Alternatively, it may be that terrorism isn't as immediate a concern for people in Europe. Conversations with friends and colleagues here often revolve around issues like LGBTQ+ rights, climate change, or economic challenges. Finding a suitable pronoun is a more pressing concern!

In India, however, terrorism—particularly cross-border terrorism—remains a dominant force shaping the national discourse. It's an inescapable reality, with Kashmir standing as a stark reminder of the heavy toll these ongoing tensions exact on the nation. Public spaces and transportation hubs have frequently been targeted, necessitating robust and visible security measures to counter persistent threats. Growing up in this environment, vigilance has become second nature, deeply ingrained a collective mindset where heightened security is seen not only as a necessity but as a fundamental aspect of daily life.

Growing up with constant news of terror attacks, it's clear how profoundly they shaped the psyche of Indian youth. These attacks systematically erode trust—trust in institutions, trust within communities, and even trust among fellow citizens. The 2001 Parliament attack was particularly harrowing, not merely because of the violence, but because it struck at the core of India's identity. Beyond the immediate tragedy, the attack sent shockwaves through the political and social fabric of the country, highlighting the vulnerability of its democratic institutions. Parliament represents the sovereignty, unity, and governance of India, making it a powerful symbol of the nation's democratic identity. Targeting it was a calculated attempt to destabilize these foundational pillars. The attack not only sought to disrupt governance but also aimed to instill fear and shake public confidence in the country's institutions. By striking at the heart of India's democracy, the perpetrators intended to erode the trust that binds its diverse communities and their faith in a unified national framework.

Moreover, the reactions of Indians to these incidents were often more disheartening than the gruesome and cowardly acts themselves. The masses, instead of demanding accountability, adjusted to living in a state of constant fear, with a resigned mindset of "we are lucky this didn't happen to us." Politicians, on the other hand, seemed more focused on balancing vote bank politics rather than addressing the root causes or ensuring justice. There are plenty of instances to quote. When Mumbai was rocked by twelve coordinated blasts in 1993, the then Chief Minister of Maharashtra, known as the Chanakya of Indian politics, deliberately claimed there were thirteen blasts, including one in a Muslim-majority area. This false statement was later admitted to be a calculated move aimed at preventing tensions by deflecting the narrative that the attacks were solely Islamic terror targeting Hindus in the aftermath of the 1992 Babri Masjid demolition. This was not a one off instance, in the aftermath of the 2008 Mumbai attacks, a senior politician from the Indian National Congress co-authored a controversial book titled *26/11 RSS Ki Saazish?*. The book attempted to link the attacks, which were perpetrated by the Pakistan-based Islamist group Lashkar-e-Taiba, to the RSS. This claim was widely criticized as baseless and politically motivated, given the lack of any evidence supporting such allegations. Critics viewed it as an attempt to discredit the RSS (*Rashtriya Swayamsevak Sangh*) and divert attention from the actual perpetrators, reflecting the deep polarization in Indian politics.

A significant shift has unfolded in recent years. Under Modi's leadership, India has taken a decidedly assertive stance on national security and foreign policy. Following the 2016 Uri terror attack, India conducted surgical strikes, marking a decisive break from its historically restrained approach. Similarly, after the 2019

Pulwama attack, India launched airstrikes, sending a clear message: this is no longer an India that confines itself to issuing statements and waiting for tensions to dissipate. The Modi government has been openly calling out Pakistan for harboring terrorism and taking bold actions such as revoking Pakistan's "Most Favored Nation" status to sever economic ties. This assertiveness extends beyond diplomacy and economics, to sports, particularly cricket. Over the past decade, India has refrained from playing any bilateral series with Pakistan and has avoided traveling to Pakistan for international tournaments. Most recently, India refused to visit Pakistan for the 2025 Champions Trophy, ensuring that matches against Pakistan are held only at neutral venues. This multi-faceted approach reflects a profound transformation in India's strategy, sending a powerful and unequivocal signal to the world.

A reaction like this isn't unprecedented on the global stage. When Russia invaded Ukraine in 2022, the international community responded with a wave of sanctions and diplomatic isolation. The US, the UK, the UN, and most European nations collectively imposed measures that transformed Russia into the most heavily sanctioned country in the world. Over 1,000 companies curtailed or completely ceased their operations in Russia, further amplifying the economic pressure. Before the invasion, Europe relied heavily on Russian oil and gas, with Russia serving as one of its largest and most critical energy suppliers. Europe made a decisive and unprecedented shift by reducing and ultimately ceasing imports of Russian oil and gas. This transformation was not without its challenges — European countries faced soaring energy costs, disruptions in supply chains, and the urgent need to find alternatives. Governments had to introduce subsidies and one-time payments to citizens to help mitigate the burden of rising energy costs, ensuring public support for these shifts.

Additionally, Russia faced widespread exclusion from global events, spanning from trade forums to sports competitions, and even ceremonial occasions like Queen Elizabeth's funeral. The

International Olympic Committee (IOC) went so far as to ban Russia and Belarus from participating in key events, including the Winter Paralympics and international football tournaments. India's diplomatic distancing from Pakistan reflects a similar strategy of leveraging international pressure to isolate and counter adversarial actions effectively.

Modi's India is unapologetic in its stance, reflecting an unwavering commitment to safeguarding national security and interests. Whether on the battlefield, in diplomatic negotiations, or even on cricket pitches, India's assertiveness is reshaping its global image. This transformation seems to be gradually restoring the trust eroded by years of terror attacks and political complacency. It signifies a renewed confidence in the country's institutions and, more importantly, a reclamation of the collective faith in the enduring idea of India.

Law and Order

It isn't that a country only faces external threats like border control issues, illegal migration, pandemics like COVID-19, or cross-border terrorism. Equally alarming are homegrown challenges, such as left-wing extremism—manifesting as Naxalism and Urban Naxalism, —and an inadequate law and order framework. These internal threats can be just as destabilizing and require systemic reforms, or a metaphorical "vaccination," to mitigate their impact. Crime transcends boundaries, affecting both urban and rural areas through theft, fraud, and assaults. While the West grapples with similar issues, the nuances differ. In the U.S., gun violence remains a persistent problem, whereas knife crime frequently dominates headlines in the UK. Although India's legal system often appears sluggish, the West also contends with challenges such as significant backlogs in U.S. courts and rising crime rates in European cities.

Vigilantism and mob lynching were widely reported during PM Modi's first tenure (2014-19), often linked to religious or caste-based tensions. The tragic reality is that this phenomenon is far from new. Long before it became a media buzzword, vigilante justice was deeply rooted in various parts of the country, fueled by issues ranging from cattle theft to child abductions to unverified rumors that spread faster than authorities could respond. Change the context slightly—switch "cattle" to "cow", replace "missing law and order" with "vigilantism" and profile the victim as a Muslim or a Dalit—and you've got a recipe for political propaganda; that's all you need. Leading up to the 2019 elections, incidents of mob lynching targeting Muslims dominated headlines, polarizing communities and overshadowing critical governance issues that demanded attention. But now Mob lynching is hardly a news headline. Does it mean the country got rid of it?

While mob lynching in India often garners significant media attention, the West is equally susceptible to mob violence. In the U.S., racially motivated violence has deep historical roots, with lynchings of African Americans in the 19th and 20th centuries paralleling incidents in rural India today, similar violence has been cited in various parts of Europe and the UK. The Capitol riots in the U.S. in 2021 highlighted how misinformation and collective anger can escalate into chaos. Similarly, vigilante groups in Europe have targeted immigrant communities, perpetuating cycles of violence.

Mob justice thrives on fear, ignorance, and herd mentality—a phenomenon prevalent in both India and the West. Though it manifests differently—racial violence, hate crimes, mass shootings in the West, and extremist vigilantism in India—the underlying triggers are alarmingly similar. Both societies struggle with distrust, rumors, and a misguided belief in "taking justice into one's own hands." These drivers—fear, ignorance, and herd behavior—are consistent across regions, spreading rapidly and often outpacing containment efforts. In India, social media often amplifies rumors, igniting lynchings, while in the West, extremist ideologies fuel violent actions. Regardless of geography or labels, the consequences—the pain, loss, and destruction—are universally devastating.

There are a few key differences, though. In India, the population is several times larger than that of Western countries, yet the number of law enforcement personnel remains disproportionately small. This stark imbalance exacerbates challenges in maintaining order and responding effectively to crises. Also, mob violence in the West often triggers swift inquiries, public outrage, and even legal reforms. For example, the George Floyd protests in the U.S. not only resulted in widespread demonstrations but also initiated nationwide discussions on police reform and systemic racism. In India, however, responses can sometimes feel delayed or entangled in political blame games.

Riots are also a universal expression of discontent, often fueled by social, economic, or political frustrations. India has witnessed many such instances, from politically charged protests to religious clashes. Similarly, the West is not immune to social unrest either. The 2020 Black Lives Matter protests in the U.S. and France's labor reform riots illustrate how deeply societal grievances can ignite widespread demonstrations. In the UK, the 2011 London riots, triggered by the police shooting of Mark Duggan, escalated into looting and violence across several cities, reflecting underlying social tensions. France's Yellow Vest protests, which began in 2018 as a response to fuel taxes, evolved into national riots highlighting economic inequality. Similar unrest occurred in the Netherlands during COVID-19 lockdowns, where protests turned violent and clashed with police. The 2023-24 Farmer Protests in France further emphasized discontent, with agricultural workers blocking roads and confronting authorities over economic policies. More recently, the UK experienced significant riots in 2024, driven by anti-immigration sentiments and concerns over radical extremism. These riots, centered in cities like London, Birmingham, and Manchester, were marked by vandalism and clashes with law enforcement, fueled by growing economic uncertainty and social divisions.

The common thread across these events lies in broader anxieties about identity, integration, and inequality, which transcend national borders and underscore the universal nature of unrest.

A key distinction lies in the operation of law enforcement. In the West, police forces benefit from superior resources, advanced technology, and rigorous training. Faster response times in urban areas, widespread use of body cams, and robust public accountability mechanisms significantly enhance their effectiveness. In contrast, India's law enforcement faces resource constraints, delayed responses, and corruption, which erode public trust and hinder justice. Addressing these systemic issues is crucial for India's progress. India today faces a monumental task in reforming its judiciary and law enforcement systems.

The use of surveillance technology, such as facial recognition and AI-driven crowd monitoring is one good example. During the 2019 Hong Kong protests, Chinese authorities employed AI-powered facial recognition to track protesters, which acted as a significant deterrent. Similarly, during the 2020 Black Lives Matter protests in the U.S., law enforcement agencies used tools like Clearview AI to monitor demonstrations and identify individuals involved in violent activities. In Europe, countries such as France and the UK have tested AI-based crowd management systems during large-scale events, enabling authorities to address potential unrest preemptively.

India has also begun adopting advanced surveillance technologies. For example, during the 2020 Delhi elections, facial recognition software was deployed to monitor crowds and identify individuals with criminal records or links to potential disturbances. However, India's implementation remains limited in scale and efficiency, often leading to delayed responses and allowing unrest to escalate. Bridging this gap requires substantial investments in resources, infrastructure, and training to achieve the level of effectiveness seen in Western nations.

While the push for AI, digital advancements, and a growing digital economy has many benefits, it also opens the door to a variety of new, unheard of before crimes - the cyber crimes – online frauds, scams, deep fakes, fake news, data theft and so on and so forth.

Much like India, Europe and the UK are also grappling with online scammers. I nearly fell victim to one myself while apartment hunting in Germany. I found an appealing listing where the "landlord," claiming to be abroad, promised to mail me the keys if I transferred the deposit and the first month's rent upfront. Having moved across countries and cities frequently, I was accustomed to transferring deposits upfront, so the request didn't strike me as particularly unusual. Although tempting, I fortunately recognized the red flags and avoided the scam. It is quite difficult to differentiate between an authentic correspondence and a scam; one has to be extra careful these days! A dear friend of mine wasn't as fortunate. After moving to a new country, he received what seemed like a legitimate request from his "bank" to open a new current account for parking his funds. Unfortunately, it turned out to be a sophisticated scam, and he lost a significant amount of money. While he has shown remarkable bravery and patience in pursuing legal recourse, the outcome still remains uncertain.

Interestingly, many of these scammers often have South Asian accents, underscoring the global nature of these operations. Back home, scammers are frequently perceived as sophisticated hackers. However, most scams rely on social engineering, which involves manipulating individuals rather than exploiting technical vulnerabilities. Social engineering preys on human psychology, using tactics that play on emotions such as fear, urgency, or trust, to deceive people into willingly sharing sensitive information. For example, a scammer might impersonate a bank representative to warn of "suspicious activity" on an account, pressuring the victim to provide credentials or make immediate payments. Similarly, phishing emails and messages, often disguised as official communication from trusted organizations, lure victims into clicking malicious links or sharing confidential details. For instance, if a link claims you are eligible for a million-dollar inheritance, it is almost certainly a scam. These schemes prey on the human tendency to trust or act impulsively, exploiting universal vulnerabilities in online interactions. The scripts used by scammers in India are strikingly similar to those employed in the West, highlighting the universal methods of such schemes.

In the grand scheme of things, it's tempting to believe that the West has all the solutions to cybercrime and the complexities of the digital landscape. However, a closer examination reveals cracks on both sides. News channels in the west frequently broadcast scam awareness programs, much like the initiatives run by Indian news channels. While the style of presentation may vary, the underlying methods and vulnerabilities exploited by scammers remain remarkably similar, highlighting the universal nature of these challenges.

Fake News

Fake news is also not just India's problem—it is a global challenge. In India, WhatsApp forwards and doctored videos have incited unrest, while in the West, deep fakes and misinformation campaigns have influenced elections. Deep fakes, in particular, represent the next frontier of misinformation. These AI-generated videos or images convincingly manipulate reality, often blurring the line between fact and fiction. In India, deep fakes have been used to spread political propaganda, targeting public figures to influence opinions or disrupt elections. In the West, they have been weaponized to impersonate leaders, spread disinformation during campaigns, and undermine public trust. The sophistication of deep fakes has made it increasingly difficult to distinguish them from authentic content, posing significant challenges for governments and media organizations globally. Although governments worldwide are beginning to recognize the threat, policy responses often lag behind the technology's swift advancement. The positive news? Awareness campaigns and AI-driven detection tools are gaining traction globally, providing a glimmer of hope in combating this pervasive issue.

Fake news often thrives on partial information, where one side of the story is amplified while the other is conveniently ignored, creating a polarized and distorted narrative. When coupled with sensationalist mainstream media, such content quickly escalates into a dangerous force capable of inciting riots, fueling arson, and even costing lives. The 2020 and 2024 US elections vividly illustrated the power of misinformation to shape public perception and influence outcomes. While the internet itself remains a neutral platform, social media has become increasingly aligned with particular ideologies, shedding any pretense of neutrality.

In India, efforts like PIB Fact Check, an initiative by the Press Information Bureau to verify and debunk misinformation related to government policies and announcements, are emerging to counter the spread of fake news. AI tools are being developed to detect deep fakes, and public awareness campaigns are ramping up. Comparatively, the West's response includes the EU's Digital Services Act and platforms like Facebook and Twitter partnering with independent fact-checkers during election seasons. However, the challenge remains enormous. The Indian government also collaborated with social media platforms during the pandemic to counter health-related misinformation, issuing alerts through SMS, WhatsApp, and Twitter. Initiatives like these, along with the emergence of dedicated fact-checking portals, are steps in the right direction.

One of the major reasons for the rise of fake news is the erosion of trust in mainstream media. These days, mainstream media in India resembles reality TV more than a reliable source of information. While tv news studios have become bigger and more extravagant, meaningful content has diminished. The fourth pillar of democracy has been faltering for years, but the advent of social media has made its weaknesses more glaring. News channels now prioritize sensational and controversial stories to grab attention, often at the expense of factual reporting. In their race to compete with social media, headlines have devolved into clickbait, sidelining journalistic integrity in favor of entertainment.

Bollywood was once notorious for borrowing liberally from the West. I remember the awkwardness of realizing, mid-conversation with my English friends at a restaurant, that the song that was playing in the background wasn't humming—"*Dil Mera Churaya Kyu*"—was actually "Last Christmas, I Gave You My Heart." Or discovering that "*Love Hua*" was a rendition of "Long Ago... High on a Mountain in Mexico." Now if any song or melody sounds vaguely familiar, I stay mum and avoid the embarrassment. This tendency to mimic seems to have extended to Hindi news channels as well. During the COVID-19 pandemic, I noticed some reports that felt suspiciously like translated versions of British news segments from a few days earlier. In the race to stay relevant and compete with social media, it's clear that originality is often left behind.

If only the news circulated on channels was authentic and complete, the space for fake news would have been much smaller. Partial information, as we know, leads to polarization. Unfortunately, the prevalence of misinformation has grown significantly. Issues like the Uniform Civil Code, Citizenship Amendment Act, National Register of Citizens, Bullet Train, Statue of Unity, Central Vista, Farm Bills, Covid Management, etc. all became victims of a whirlwind of rumors and distorted narratives.

The Covid pandemic, in particular, served as fertile ground for half-baked stories, conspiracy theories, and panic-driven social media campaigns. Media coverage often seemed more intent on stoking fear than offering balanced solutions. Managing perceptions appeared to take precedence over focusing on medical science. The deluge of content prioritized sensationalism over accuracy, leaving the public more confused than informed.

Some may recall how Indian news channels portrayed scenes of people in China allegedly dropping dead while walking on the streets due to the virus. Four years later, with the benefit of lived experience during the COVID pandemic, it is clear such dramatic portrayals were grossly exaggerated. Did healthy individuals truly collapse suddenly while walking? The reality proved far less sensational.

News channels back home vividly showcased the dire hospital conditions in Italy, with elderly patients lying outside medical facilities, accompanied by the haunting question: "If this is happening in the developed world, what will happen when COVID hits India?" While this was a valid concern, the coverage presented only half the story.

The full context reveals that Italy had been grappling with hospital bed shortages for years, well before the COVID-19 pandemic emerged in 2020. This issue was not unique to Italy; other European nations like Germany and the UK have also faced significant challenges in providing adequate healthcare facilities. For instance, healthcare crises in 2016 and 2018 exposed similar systemic issues in these countries. While COVID-19 undoubtedly worsened the situation, it was not the sole cause of the scenes showing patients in dire need of hospital beds. Additionally, these countries are more vulnerable to seasonal flu outbreaks, which contributed to the crisis highlighted by Indian media as related to COVID. It's worth noting that most people in these countries receive "flu jabs" annually before winter to mitigate such risks irrespective of the pandemic.

The real challenge lies in fostering critical thinking across the board. One major distinction between India and Europe or the UK is the vast difference in population size. In India, social media shares can amplify minor issues into major controversies at an unprecedented speed. The rapid availability of inexpensive internet and the swift shift of a large section of Indian society from the physical to the digital world left little time for adaptation. This transition occurred while the framework of rules and regulations was, and still is, evolving, exacerbating the challenges of managing misinformation and fostering digital literacy.

Data Protection

The lockdowns during the Covid-19 pandemic really pushed everyone online. With people stuck at home, scrolling endlessly through social media, binge-watching shows, and hopping on video calls became the norm. Platforms like TikTok exploded during this time. Before Covid, TikTok's parent company was bleeding money to promote the app, but once lockdowns hit, people flocked to it—both to create and consume content.

A new breed of influencers was born during this period. People who were not famous at all before the pandemic suddenly had millions of followers, rivaling even Bollywood celebrities in popularity and earnings. But with all this growth, serious concerns about data privacy started popping up. By June 2020, the Indian government banned TikTok, citing national security and privacy issues. It became clear that platforms like these could misuse the massive amounts of personal data they collected.

During the same time, several Chinese companies rolled out AI tools capable of doing everything from facial recognition to predicting flight delays. But the big question was—where were they getting all the data to train these models? Building AI isn't magic; it requires massive datasets. For example, if you want to teach an AI to tell cats from dogs, you need millions of labeled pictures of cats and dogs. This data trains the system to recognize patterns.

Now think about those millions of people lip-syncing to popular songs on social media. That data can be used to train AI to match lip movements with audio—leading to the rise of deep fakes. With enough data on different voices, words, and facial expressions, someone by using various AI Models, could possibly create a deep fake video of anyone delivering a speech they never gave. This is one of the many reasons why protecting data is so important. If countries or companies don't secure user data, they're opening the door to all sorts of exploitation—from identity theft to political interference.

It's not just TikTok or Covid-driven apps—pretty much all online platforms collect data. From online shopping sites to streaming services, they store metadata in massive data centers. Sometimes, these data centers aren't even in the same country as the users, which raises concerns about who can access that data and how secure it really is.

India has been dealing with data protection challenges for years. As a rapidly growing economy with millions of internet users, the country has been under pressure to come up with strong data privacy laws. A big milestone was the 2017 Supreme Court ruling in the case of Justice K.S. Puttaswamy v. Union of India, which officially recognized privacy as a fundamental right. This case laid the groundwork for India's data protection laws.

In 2019, the Indian government introduced the Personal Data Protection Bill (PDPB), which is heavily inspired by the EU's GDPR (General Data Protection Regulation). The bill aims to give users more control over their personal data, requiring companies to notify users about data breaches and letting individuals access, edit, or delete their data. It's a step in the right direction.

Europe has been ahead of the curve when it comes to data protection. The GDPR, which became law in 2018, is one of the strictest data privacy laws in the world. It forces businesses to get clear consent before collecting personal data and gives users the right to access, edit, and delete their information. If a company experiences a data breach, it's required to inform users right away. What's more, GDPR doesn't just apply to European companies—it applies to any company handling data from EU citizens, which has made it a gold standard worldwide.

The UK follows similar rules. Even after Brexit, the UK adopted GDPR principles through the Data Protection Act 2018. The Information Commissioner's Office (ICO) is responsible for making sure companies comply, ensuring that user rights are respected.

The biggest difference between India and the West (especially Europe and the UK) is how mature the legal frameworks are. The EU has been refining GDPR for years, while India is still in the early stages of rolling out its data protection laws. GDPR puts a lot of emphasis on transparency and holding businesses accountable, while India's evolving system is still balancing privacy with national security needs.

Another key difference is data localization. Under GDPR, data can move across borders if specific conditions are met, but India's PDPB has much stricter rules about keeping sensitive data within the country. This has sparked debate, as smaller businesses and startups might struggle with the cost of complying, and international companies could face logistical hurdles. Critics worry this might slow down innovation and make India a less attractive place to do business.

At the end of the day, data protection is crucial—whether you're in India or Europe. The approaches might differ, but the goal is the same: to safeguard personal data in an increasingly digital world. India's Personal Data Protection Bill is a big leap forward, but it still has some kinks to iron out to strike the right balance between security, privacy, and economic growth.

The Crux: Safe and Secure India

What is the value of investing billions in public infrastructure if it remains vulnerable to terrorism and vandalism? What is the purpose of developing transport systems like buses and trains if they are repeatedly destroyed during riots? Furthermore, how do infrastructure, industry, and innovation serve a nation if hunger remains a pressing issue for the majority? These questions underline the importance of a holistic approach to national resilience. While delayed, Modi's India has shown remarkable progress in addressing these issues over the past decade, focusing on strengthening immunity across social, economic, and security domains.

India has made significant strides in reducing cross-border terrorism through decisive and bold actions. Diplomatic measures, coupled with military responses such as surgical strikes and airstrikes, have transformed how India addresses terror threats. The modernization of armed forces, including the integration of advanced weaponry and indigenous defense production, ensures preparedness for external challenges. Enhanced border controls, advanced surveillance systems, and comprehensive fencing have further strengthened internal security, resulting in significant reductions in cattle smuggling and illegal migration.

Revoking Article 370 has played a pivotal role in stabilizing Jammu and Kashmir, reducing violence and fostering closer integration with the rest of the country. Domestically, violence associated with left-wing extremism has decreased by 52%, and insurgency-related unrest in the Northeast has dropped by 71%, enabling the removal of the Armed Forces Special Powers Act (AFSPA) from most areas. It is worth noting that the Naxal-affected states, often referred to as the Red Belt, are the same regions that underwent significant deindustrialization post-independence, largely due to policies like freight equalization, as discussed in the industrialization chapter. At the same time, these states were extensively exploited for their natural resources. Rapid industrialization and decreased corruption at the policy making level has been reducing leading to decreasing left-wing extremism in these states.

India has aggressively targeted inefficiencies perpetuated by bureaucracy, red tape, and middlemen. The PM Jan Dhan Yojana has brought over 50 crore citizens into the formal banking system, paving the way for financial inclusion. Direct benefit transfers totaling ₹34 lakh crore have revolutionized welfare distribution by minimizing corruption and delays. Since 2020, over 80 crore citizens have received free rations under the PM Garib Kalyan Anna Yojana, ensuring food security during critical periods.

While India has experienced destruction of public infrastructure due to violent protests, the government has responded decisively by imposing heavy reparations on those responsible. Confiscation of private assets has served as a deterrent, emphasizing accountability.

India's foreign policy over the last decade has played a vital role in safeguarding the nation's interests and enhancing its global standing. Through strategic alliances and active diplomacy, India has strengthened its ties with key global players, enabling mutual defense collaborations and technology sharing. Initiatives like the Quad partnership with the U.S., Japan, and Australia, and deeper engagement with neighboring countries through SAARC and BIMSTEC, have not only bolstered regional stability but also ensured India's interests are protected against external pressures. This proactive approach has helped secure critical resources, improved border management, and enhanced India's role as a responsible global player. India's global initiatives reflect its growing influence and commitment to international solidarity. Programs like Vaccine Maitri have enabled the delivery of over 30 crore COVID-19 vaccines and essential medicines to more than 100 countries. Domestically, the safe evacuation of over 1.5 crore citizens during emergencies showcases the government's proactive approach to safeguarding its people.

National immunity is not a one-time achievement but a continuous process of adaptation and strengthening. Cybersecurity, once a peripheral issue, has become a critical priority in safeguarding against the ever-evolving threat of cyberattacks. Strengthened digital defenses now play a crucial role in protecting national assets and sensitive information. Just as new viral mutations demand updated vaccines, emerging threats require constant innovation and flexibility in security measures. India's strategy for building immunity goes beyond addressing immediate challenges; it seeks to lay a resilient foundation for long-term stability and progress. Resilience is not a destination but a journey—one that requires nurturing, fortifying, and consistently refining to withstand the tests of time and the complexities of modern challenges. By integrating efforts in social welfare, national security, disaster preparedness, and global collaboration, India is constructing a robust framework to navigate future uncertainties. These measures promise a safer, stronger, and more prosperous future for its citizens as the nation continues to evolve and adapt.

IDEOLOGY

"Swabhimaanam sanskriti-shauryena vardhate"
–Book II, Chapter 16, Arthashastra

"Pride in one's heritage and culture strengthens national honor."

Political Ideology

Ever wondered why some countries thrive while others seem stuck in a loop of crisis? The answer often lies in their political ideology.

There are many ways to define ideology or political ideology, but here's how I see it:

A political ideology really does three things:

1. It interprets the current state of society or the country.
2. It defines an ideal state the country should aim for.
3. It lays out a plan to get from point 1 to point 2.

The third point, the action plan, is what makes government not just valuable but indispensable. Sure, individuals can work toward their own goals, but for a country that outlives its people, grows steadily, and doesn't just disappear after a few decades, you need a government with a solid, rational, and consistent political ideology. And how do we know if the ideology is good or rational? That's why having a democratically elected government matters so much. If the ruling ideology isn't backed by democratic support, it will definitely destroy a society.

When you compare countries with open, transparent governance to those run by authoritarian regimes, the difference is night and day. One of India's neighbors imposed the harshest lockdowns ever, strangling an entire province. Covid was everywhere, but democracies handled it differently—with more empathy. An authoritarian government (a one-party system often masquerades as democratic without truly embracing its principles) might make you a $20 trillion economy, but would you really want to live in Wuhan?

Another of India's neighbors, governed by military regimes that label themselves democratic, has long pursued the ambition of leading the Muslim ummah. However, the results of this endeavor have been far from promising, often reflecting internal instability and waning influence on the global stage.

History demonstrates that without the checks and balances provided by democracy, ideologies can easily spiral into dangerous extremes. Governance isn't just about achieving economic growth; it's fundamentally about safeguarding freedom and ensuring a high quality of life.

For a few decades before 2014, Indian politics felt like a ship drifting without direction. Coalition governments struggled to pass meaningful reforms, and corruption scandals dominated the headlines. From the 2G spectrum scam to the Commonwealth Games fiasco, the political scene was riddled with inefficiency and indecisiveness. Economic growth slowed, infrastructure projects stalled, and governance felt more reactive than proactive. Parties seemed more interested in survival and short-term appeasement than long-term planning. Leaders like Sardar Patel and Pt. Nehru had once guided the nation with clear ideologies and visions, but over time, opportunism replaced conviction. Even in today's Nehru-bashing era, where his flaws are dissected, one can't deny that there was a clear ideology in place—even if some decisions were questionable.

When the BJP came to power in 2014, ideology came roaring back to the forefront. Issues like Hindutva, nationalism, citizenship, uniform civil code etc. dominated the political discourse. Interestingly, many of these themes—nationalism, citizenship, and civil codes—aren't unique to India. Most developed democracies grapple with them in some form. Hindutva, of course, is uniquely Indian, but many issues associated with it—religious identity, cultural pride—find parallels elsewhere.

Hindutva & Hinduism

When I first moved to Germany for my master's, I stayed at a place called *'Seemannsheim,'* originally built for sailors but later opened to students and travelers. My student dorm wouldn't be available until 2nd April, but classes began on 15th March, so I needed a temporary stay. The international office recommended Seemannsheim.

It was a lively, friendly spot. The guy at the reception was around my age, and we became friends quickly. He worked part-time, so we'd hang out after his shifts, playing chess for hours. He'd bring beer, I'd have coffee, and we'd chat about life while I consistently beat him at chess.

I had endless questions about Germany—"What's traditional German food?" "Are there many vegetarians here?" "How do you celebrate Easter?"—just to name a few. He answered them all happily. In return, he asked about India—our festivals, food, and vegetarian recipes.

One day, he asked, "What is the caste system in India? Are lower castes treated like slaves?" The first part of the question was fine, but the mention of "slaves" threw me off.

He wasn't the only one. Over the past ten years, I've fielded countless such questions. Questions revolving around caste discrimination, reincarnations as cows, beef bans, mob lynchings, dowry, child marriage, menstruation taboos, etc. haven't left me alone. People who had never been to India—sometimes without ever even meeting an Indian—had these ideas and opinions. How did they form these views?

Turns out, their perceptions came from the media—articles, movies, columns. And often, the authors of these pieces were Indians themselves.

What I realized a little late in life is that Indians themselves are responsible for such a skewed perception of Hinduism. I'll never forget one instance at Istanbul airport. I saw a few Indian guys wearing white t-shirts that read: "Cows are safer than women in India." This was clearly political, but to the thousands of travelers passing by, it wasn't just a political statement—it shaped their entire perception of India. In the last ten years, I've seen Indian politicians visiting Europe and the UK, openly criticizing Hindutva and Hinduism for their own electoral gains. They forget that foreigners take these words at face value. Their view of India is shaped by what they hear in these speeches. A surprising number of negative articles about Hinduism in Western media are penned by Indians. Next time you see one, check the byline. Nine times out of ten, it's an Indian writer.

"Are you a practicing Hindu?" is a question I'm asked often. Simple, right? But explaining Hinduism to someone unfamiliar with Sanatan Dharma is anything but simple.

Hinduism doesn't fit into the neat religious templates used to describe Christianity, Islam, or Judaism. Even open-minded Westerners find it hard to grasp. Unlike monotheistic religions, Hinduism is polytheistic, with gods that defy Western expectations. How can a tree, a river, or the sun be a god? How can there be goddesses? How can human laws apply to divine beings?

We don't have a single book like the Bible or Quran. Instead, we have an ocean of texts—

Four Vedas- *Rig Veda*, *Yajur Veda*, *Sama Veda* and *Atharveda*; divided in four classes - *Samhitas* (Root Text), *Brahmana* (Interpretive Text), *Arnyaka* (Anchorite Text), *Upnishad* (Philosophical Text);

108 major *Upnishads* several other minor ones;
six streams– *Shiksha* (Phonetics) , *Kalpa* (Ritual) , *Vyakaran* (Grammar), *Nirukta* (Etymology), *Chanda* (Prosody) and *Jyotish* (Astrology);

6 up-vedas– *Ayur-Veda* (Health), *Dhanur-Veda* (Archery), *Sastrasastra* (Martial Arts), *Gandharva-Veda* (Music), *Sthapatya-Veda*(Architecture) and *Shilpa-Shastra* (Fine Arts);

3 *Dharma-Shastra* (Law Books) or secondary scriptures – *Manu Smriti*, *Yajnavalkya Smriti* and *Parasara Smriti;*

18 *Maha Puranas* - 1. *Brahma*, 2. *Padma*, 3. *Vishnu*, 4. *Siva*, 5. *Linga*, 6. *Garuda*, 7. *Narada* 8. *Bhagavata*, 9. *Agni* 10. *Skanda* 11. *Bhavishya* (*Kalki*), 12. *Brahma Vaivarta* 13. *Markandeya* 14. *Vamana* 15. *Varsha* 16. *Matsya* 17. *Kurma* and 18. *Brahmanda*;

18 *Upa Puranas – 1. Sanatkumara, 2. Narasimha, 3. Brihannaradiya, 4. Shiva Dharma, 5. Durvasa, 6. Kapila, 7. Vamana, 8. Aushanasa, 9. Brahmanda, 10. Varuna, 11. Kalika, 12. Maheshvara, 13. Samba, 14. Saura, 15. Parashara, 16. Maricha, 17. Bhargava, and 18. Aditya;*

2 *itihasas – Ramayana* and *Mahabharata* with supplementary literatures in the form of *Bhagavad Gita*, *Harivarhsa* and *Yoga-Vashishta*;

and other literatures in the form of *Kama-Sutra* (Erotics), *Artha-Sastra*(Politics and Economics), *BrihatSamhita* (Astrology), *Niti-Sastra* (Philosophy) and *Hitopdesh* (Good Counsel) etc. etc.

These are some that I am aware of, though there may be others I am clueless about. People follow different literary traditions, and while a few Hindus have explored some of these, the majority have barely scratched the surface.

And yet hinduism or *sanatan* in today's discourse is reduced to caste, cows, and mob lynchings

Of course, some people are genuinely curious and want to know or would at least try to make sense of the news headlines. One colleague, during excessive reporting on Beef bans and cows in India and in the west, asked if Hindus eat dogs or elephants or is it just the cows that are sacred and other animals can be eaten. I had never thought of it that way, but it made sense—most creatures hold religious significance in Hinduism, from rats to elephants, snakes to eagles everyone has its own religious significance, can't eat them, can't hurt them.

Beef and cows tend to get pulled into politics as a way to win over certain voters. If locals try to stop cattle smuggling or trafficking and things get violent, it's usually brushed off as a law-and-order issue—unless the BJP is in power. Then, it's often labeled as mob lynching in the name of Hinduism.

Food choices and how it's prepared aren't just controversial in India – the same debates play out across Europe and the UK, especially around halal and kosher meat. These are religious methods of slaughter – halal for Muslims and kosher for Jews – and they've sparked quite a bit of controversy over the years. Arguments keep popping up about whether halal and kosher slaughter follow animal welfare standards. Since both methods require the animal to be conscious at the time of slaughter, critics say it causes more suffering compared to the usual pre-stunning method. This has led to protests from animal rights groups, with calls for bans or tighter rules.

On the other side, religious communities argue that banning these practices infringes on their rights and traditions. In Belgium, for example, some regions banned unstunned slaughter in 2019, which caused major backlash from Jewish and Muslim communities who felt targeted. Similar bans have been introduced in Poland, Denmark, and Switzerland, all in the name of animal welfare. In France, the whole debate often ties into bigger issues around immigration and integration, making things even more heated.

In the UK, people have been arguing for years about whether meat should be labeled if it's been slaughtered in a halal or kosher way. Some schools and public institutions faced criticism for serving halal meat without informing parents, which stirred up debates around identity and religion. Protests outside slaughterhouses and supermarkets aren't uncommon, with far-right groups sometimes using the issue to rally support. Meanwhile, religious leaders continue to defend these practices, stressing that they balance animal welfare with religious obligations.

Back in India, the situation can feel pretty similar. Some people want the freedom to slaughter cattle openly in the middle of the road without expecting any backlash in the name of freedom, and if anyone speaks up, it's quickly framed as Hindutva trying to suppress minorities. Animal welfare takes a day off at such moments!

Having said that, there is one major difference. In Europe and the UK, I have not observed a single political party that explicitly relies on religion or a particular community to win elections, even though these countries have strong historical ties to Christianity. For instance, the Church of England plays a ceremonial and cultural role in the UK, with bishops holding seats in the House of Lords. Similarly, Christian principles and heritage have significantly shaped Germany's Christian Democratic Union (CDU), one of the country's leading political parties. In the Netherlands, Christian parties like the Christian Democratic Appeal (CDA) and ChristianUnion (CU) continue to exist, though their influence has declined in an increasingly secular society. Despite these historical and institutional associations with Christianity, political parties in these countries generally prioritize broader policy issues over explicitly aligning themselves with religious communities to secure votes.

In contrast, many political parties in India, especially the regional ones, often align themselves with specific religions, communities, or caste groups to secure votes—despite claiming to be secular. Constructive governance, which demands consistent effort and long-term strategies, takes a backseat as exploiting religious sentiments offers a quicker path to political gains. Bashing Hinduism is frequently used as a tool to consolidate vote bases, while the Muslim vote bank remains one of the most sought-after and contested demographics in Indian politics. This reliance on identity-based politics often leads to Hinduism becoming a focal point for criticism, making it a target for political narratives and media headlines. Given this political culture, had Christianity been the majority religion in India, similar stories of its exploitation for political purposes would likely have emerged.

Decolonization & De-mughalization

In the last ten years, one of the things that kept popping up in the news was the renaming of various places and streets. This really hit another level when Yogi Adityanath became the Chief Minister of Uttar Pradesh. Suddenly, Allahabad became Prayagraj, Faizabad turned into Ayodhya, and Mughalsarai Junction was renamed Deen Dayal Upadhyay Railway Station – and that's just the tip of an iceberg.

Interestingly, at the same time this was happening in India, I was living in Germany. This made me a little more aware of the whole name-changing thing. I noticed something similar had happened in Germany after World War II.

During my six years there, I never saw anything named after Adolf Hitler or anything that reeked of Nazi Germany. No street names, no cities, nothing. I thought maybe Hitler just didn't name things after himself – or maybe they had all been quietly changed or removed over the decades. But the more I asked around and looked into it, the clearer it became – this wasn't a coincidence. It was part of a deliberate effort to erase traces of Nazi ideology.

Places that once bore Hitler's name were systematically renamed. For example, Adolf-Hitler-Brücke became Westbrücke, and Adolf-Hitler-Platz was switched to Rathausplatz. The list goes on. This wasn't random – it was part of a larger process called "Denazification."

Denazification was all about removing Nazi ideology from German society. Denazification touched every part of society – the economy, culture, judiciary, government, and administration. Getting rid of signs, names, literature, and symbols was the first and the easiest step. Changing the mindset of the people was rather challenging. In order to achieve that, Germans were put through a kind of "democratic re-education." In 1946, they had to fill out questionnaires about their involvement with Nazism, and people were sorted into five categories of involvement or culpability:

1. Major Offenders – Life imprisonment or death sentence.
2. Offenders – Up to ten years in prison. This included Nazi supporters and beneficiaries.
3. Lesser Offenders – Probation of up to three years.
4. Followers – Restrictions on jobs, travel, and political freedoms.
5. Exonerated – No sanctions or punishments.

Denazification was seen as essential for rebuilding Germany and Europe. And looking at Germany today, it's hard to argue with the results. In fact, a 2014 BBC World Service Poll ranked Germany as the most popular country. I lived there for six years, and I can agree to that ranking.

Now, let's contrast that with India. After independence, nothing remotely close to this happened. One glaring example is the Babri Masjid and Ram Mandir dispute. The "Babri" in Babri Masjid is a direct reference to Babur and the Mughal Empire – a symbol of invasion, oppression, and foreign rule. Another example is the statue of King George V, that once stood at India Gate, symbolizing British colonial rule; symbolizing colonialism, slavery and persecution. I had to take one example from the Mughal era and one from the British Raj, had I not done that and just mentioned Babri Masjid some people would have deemed it islamophobic within a blink of an eye. The context is extremely important; it's not about the religion, it's about the ruler, the invader, the colonizer.

Both are gone now, but not because of any formal process. Babri Masjid was demolished by a mob in 1992, and King George V's statue was removed in 1968 after angry protests. These weren't proactive steps – they were reactions to public outrage. There was no structured effort at decolonization or “de-Mughalization,” which I think should have happened after 1947. Unfortunately, the ruling elite lacked the vision or political ideology to make it happen.

Modi's India has started filling in these gaps, introducing Indian symbols to replace colonial and Mughal remnants. The Ram Mandir is being built at the Babri site, and in 2022, Subhash Chandra Bose's statue was installed at India Gate's canopy.

Yet, even now, some people refuse to separate themselves from figures like Ghazni, Ghori, or Babur. They see everything through a religious lens and resist disassociating from foreign invaders. Honestly, a bit of “democratic re-education” wouldn't hurt this part of Indian society.

Beyond Denazification, Germany also embraced something called “Truth and Reconciliation.” In German, there's a word for it – *vergangenheitsbewältigung* – which means coming to terms with the past.

Reconciliation involves truth-telling, sharing historical narratives, and fostering dialogue to rebuild trust and mend relationships. Germany started paying reparations to Israel as early as 1953 – long before the country was even fully rebuilt. By 1965, the payments stopped at a state level, but individual payments are still being made to this day. Germany has transferred around sixty billion euros in reparations, with Israel being the biggest recipient. Even today, the German penal code prohibits the public denial of the Holocaust and the distribution of Nazi propaganda. This includes sharing images of swastikas, wearing an SS uniform, and supporting Hitler. The penalty for denying the Holocaust in Germany is up to five years in prison or a fine.

This is a major reason why Germans, despite sharing the same ancestry, religion, and skin color, have no problem disassociating from Hitler and the Nazis. Meanwhile, some Indians still hesitate to break ties with figures who once invaded and ruled over them.

Part of the problem lies in the narratives we've been fed. We're told the colonizers "helped" by reforming Hindu society, or that they "developed" India by building railways. We're taught that India gained independence purely through non-violence. It wasn't until I read Vikram Sampath's 'Savarkar: Echoes from a Forgotten Past' that I realized just how wrong that narrative was.

Savarkar and others like him shed blood, endured torture, and made unimaginable sacrifices. Non-violence wasn't the sole path to freedom – it's just the version of history we were taught. It's honestly a shame that it took seventy years for someone like Savarkar to get the recognition he deserved.

Another narrative I find disturbing is the idea that "Mughals were nice because they became us." Became part of India? How? Babur was born in Uzbekistan, lost battles in Fergana and Samarkand, and fled to India because he had nowhere else to go. He even traded his sister's safety for his own life. Babur built his empire here because he was in exile – not because he wanted to "become Indian." Can imposition of jizya tax on Hindus, Destruction of Temples, restricting Hindu religious practices and promoting the conversion of Hindus to Islam, etc. sound like becoming us?

It's like someone showing up at your house uninvited, eating your food, making you pay taxes on your own kitchen, and harassing your family. Then, a few generations later, your kids start praising this person because "they became part of the family." How would you feel about that?

Since we've already talked about the names, I found an interesting way to understand their significance. What's in a name, after all?

What's in the name?

When it was confirmed that I'd be moving to Portsmouth, England for my new job, two things immediately excited me: Indian food and cricket. I've covered cricket in another chapter, so let's stick to food for now. Knowing England's reputation for its Indian diaspora, I assumed Portsmouth would be teeming with Indian restaurants, stores, and vibrant cultural hubs. While still in Eindhoven, I decided to Google "Indian restaurants in Portsmouth." Unsurprisingly, a long list of options appeared: Desi Indian Cafe, T&J Mahal, Indian Cottage, and more. Among them, two names stood out immediately—Bombay Bay and the Gandhi Restaurant.

Even though I'd never been to Portsmouth, I already knew where I'd be having my first dinner. Since the Gandhi Restaurant was closer to my place, I decided to give it a try first. After a 15-16 minute walk, I finally spotted the restaurant. I walked in with excitement, anticipating a taste of authentic Indian food. The waiter showed me to a table, and soft instrumental music played in the background, evoking a sense of nostalgia as if I had just stepped back into India. When the waiter handed me the menu and asked if I'd like a drink, I eagerly inquired, "Do you have masala chai?" He politely replied no, explaining they only served "dip dip tea" (the kind with sachets). The menu also seemed a bit off—it didn't feature the dishes I was expecting. Something felt amiss, but I decided to push through and enjoy the experience without letting my disappointment show. On the bright side, the staff were friendly and welcoming.

A couple of days later, I decided to try Bombay Bay. The experience was strikingly similar. When the waiter brought the menu and asked if I wanted a drink, I once again asked for masala chai. Predictably, the response was, "We have dip dip tea." Browsing the menu, I noticed it was almost identical to the one at the other restaurant, but then something else caught my eye—there was no paneer (cottage cheese). Unable to resist, I asked, "no paneer on the menu?" The waiter, looking completely baffled, replied, "What? What pan...?

I ordered something else, and it was okay, nothing special. While paying, I casually asked the waiter, "Where are the people working here from? Which part of India?" He replied, "We're not from India; we're from Bangladesh."

Ah, that makes sense.

I ended up trying all the "Indian" restaurants in Portsmouth, but none of them were actually Indian. I'm not saying the food was bad—they made decent dishes—but it just didn't taste like what I was used to back home. I went to Gandhi Restaurant because it said "Gandhi" and not the "Sheikh Mujibur Rahman Restaurant" (no disrespect meant). I picked Bombay Bay because it said "Bombay" and not "Dhaka."

Afterall names do matter!

Aurangzeb is not just a name; it represents a symbol of historical injustices and hindu persecution. In Europe, the name Adolf Hitler is conspicuously absent from personal identities—why? The historical weight and atrocities associated with the name render it unthinkable for use. In contrast, in India, names like Aurangzeb and Timur are still invoked in political and cultural discourses, often as symbols to shape narratives. Interestingly, politicians in India frequently use their surnames to signal caste, community, or lineage, leveraging historical associations to consolidate their appeal and influence.

Separatism & Islamism

Even if we set aside the narratives of pre-independence India—marked by colonization, invasions, persecution, and humiliation—

the political discourse on modern Indian history post-independence largely remained stagnant until 2014. The short but intense history shared by India and Pakistan is filled with wars, proxy conflicts, and deep-seated animosity. Despite this turbulent past, Indians hold diverse perspectives on these events. What's more troubling is that separatist ideologies, rather than being countered decisively, were often overlooked or even subtly encouraged over the decades.

Consider the case of terrorism. When the Indian Army neutralizes a known terrorist or mujahideen, it is not uncommon to see crowds gathering to mourn him and pay respects. Politicians, activists, journalists, and social media influencers often subtly (or sometimes overtly) lend support to these movements. Burhan Wani serves as a prime example. While the army's actions were necessary, many of his supporters faced little to no consequences. Unlike Germany's systematic denazification efforts after WWII, there has been little attempt to dismantle the underlying ideology driving these actions in India. Instead, such individuals are often dismissed as "*bhatke hue*" (lost or misguided youth), allowing the root causes to persist unaddressed.

Article 370—a so-called temporary provision—granted separatist leaders the ability to maintain two flags and two constitutions within one country, effectively impeding Kashmir's integration into India. Article 35A compounded this by allowing the state to define "permanent residents" and granting them exclusive privileges, such as property ownership. The irony was stark: as an Indian, I could buy a property anywhere in the country—except in Kashmir. Even more absurd, I could buy a property in the UK or Europe but not in a part of my own country. Adding to the injustice, Kashmiri women who married outside the state lost their property rights altogether, further deepening the discrimination.

I often refer to it as separatism, but at its core, it's rooted in a medieval Islamic ideology that emphasizes control over wealth, women, and land (*zan, zar, zameen*). Slogans like "*Raliv, Galiv ya*

Chaliv" (convert, die, or flee) starkly illustrate this mindset. Provisions like Article 35A were designed to maintain demographic dominance by any means necessary.

What's intriguing is that those who vehemently defended Article 370 and even threatened violence if the Modi government attempted to revoke it were the same voices advocating for the settlement of Rohingya Muslims in India. These individuals also opposed the Citizenship Amendment Act, which was designed to support persecuted Hindus from neighboring countries. However, when Article 370 was finally abrogated, the anticipated bloodbath never materialized—only a cacophony of protests and outrage.

This isn't just about Kashmir or Hindus—it's part of a broader, global pattern. Consider Afghanistan or Arabia—are there any native Hindus left there? What became of the Zoroastrians in Iran? Why is Israel perpetually under fire? It's the same ideology at play across different regions. I once met a Pakistani couple in England who, despite holding British citizenship and having no direct connection to the region, passionately protested against Israel while supporting Palestine. Not a single word of criticism was directed at Hamas. The underlying reason? Ideology.

Even when attempts are made to shed light on the underlying ideology, they are often ridiculed rather than acknowledged. Films like "The Kashmir Files" and "The Kerala Story" are routinely dismissed as propaganda by critics of Hindutva narratives. Yet, these are not the only films tackling ideological conflicts. Similar productions in the West, such as "ISIS Bride" (2017) and the documentary "The Return: Life after ISIS" (2021), address comparable themes but rarely face the same level of skepticism or dismissal as propaganda.

Another movie that faced the label of propaganda was "Ajmer 92," which is based on real events. Interestingly, it drew parallels for me with the British TV series "Three Girls" on BBC One, which portrays the real-life story of grooming gangs in Rochdale. This led me to look at similar cases in Rotherham and Telford, where white girls were systematically abused by men of Pakistani origin. To maintain political correctness—or perhaps out of fear of being labeled Islamophobic or racist—the media and authorities often referred to the perpetrators as "South Asian men." Initially, complaints from the victims were dismissed, with some authorities even placing blame on the girls themselves. This is still an ongoing issue in the UK. What's unsettling is how closely these events mirror what happened to Hindu girls in Ajmer during the 90s—and what continues to occur in India even today. How can two places, thousands of miles apart and with vastly different cultures, exhibit such strikingly similar patterns of crime? The answer lies in the shared ideology that drives these acts.

As I write this, the UK is grappling with a legal battle involving Michaela Community School, which banned prayer sessions, prompting a Muslim student to sue the headmistress. This situation bears a striking resemblance to the hijab controversy in Karnataka in 2022. Indians should recognize that the issues like these are not isolated incidents—similar cultural clashes are unfolding globally, reflecting broader ideological and societal tensions.

Uniform Civil Code

Sharia is often a contentious issue across the UK and Europe, sparking debates about integration, multiculturalism, and the balance between religious freedom and national values. In cities like London, Birmingham, and Manchester, where large Muslim populations reside, unofficial Sharia councils operate to mediate family and civil disputes within the Muslim community. These councils primarily deal with marriage, divorce, and inheritance, but their existence raises concerns about parallel legal systems undermining national laws, especially regarding women's rights. Protests and demonstrations against Sharia councils have taken place in major cities driven by concerns over their potential to undermine British law and perpetuate gender inequality. Right-wing groups, women's rights activists, and local communities have voiced opposition, citing discriminatory practices in areas like divorce and inheritance. These protests highlight the broader tension between preserving national identity and accommodating religious practices.

In countries like France and Germany, the pushback against Sharia stems from broader efforts to uphold secularism and safeguard cultural identity. France, in particular, has enacted stringent measures to limit religious influence in public spaces, such as banning headscarves in schools and restricting halal options in state institutions. The debate over Sharia often intersects with broader issues of immigration and national security, reflecting deep societal anxieties. Right-wing parties across Europe frequently cite the existence of Sharia councils as evidence of failed integration, advocating for tighter immigration controls and policies that emphasize national identity over multiculturalism.

These discussions closely mirror the Uniform Civil Code (UCC) debates in India, where integrating personal laws into a single national framework fuels intense conversations about identity, tradition, and equality. Just as Sharia councils in the UK and Europe raise concerns about parallel legal systems undermining national cohesion, India faces the challenge of balancing deeply rooted religious customs with the demand for a unified legal structure. The UCC debate often sees proponents of gender equality and national integration clashing with defenders of religious autonomy and cultural heritage. Both scenarios encapsulate the ongoing struggle of modern nations to harmonize diversity with the ideals of equality and secular governance.

Quite interestingly, the laws, norms, and practices regarding Islam in India often feel stricter than those found in the Middle East. A close friend of mine, with roots in Egypt and Jordan, once expressed his outright rejection of practices like "Halala," "Triple Talaq," and "Four Marriages." This was surprising, given that both

Jordan (97%) and Egypt (90%) are Muslim-majority, predominantly Sunni countries. While, tennis star Sania Mirza faced widespread backlash and humiliation for wearing skirts during matches in India. Women squash players in Jordan and Egypt don't encounter such criticism, even though squash skirts are often shorter than tennis skirts. Tennis skirts generally fall around mid-thigh or just above the knee, offering sufficient coverage for the sport's dynamic movements. Squash skirts, however, are shorter to allow for the quick turns, lunges, and speed required in the game. This highlights a curious paradox: while India grapples with cultural acceptability over women's sports attire, many Middle Eastern nations appear far more relaxed about it.

The idea that Hindu nationalism is causing tension in India is misleading. Similar ideological conflicts are playing out globally, even in places where Hindus and Hindutva have no presence. In the UK, for instance, Hindus make up less than 2% of the population and are far too small a demographic to influence cultural balance or spark significant conflict. In Europe even less!

Every nation seeks to preserve and protect its cultural essence. When individuals or communities attempt to impose their own values and traditions over local ones, it often fosters an "us vs. them" dynamic, leading to friction. Across the globe, a recurring pattern emerges where one side of this conflict frequently involves Islamic ideology—whether it's clashes with Buddhists in the East, Hindus in India, Jews in the Middle East, or Christians in the West. And when external groups are not involved, the friction often manifests internally, as seen in the Sunni vs. Shia divide.

Citizenship & Citizenship Amendment

Awarding or denying citizenship is a fundamental prerogative of any sovereign state, reflecting its right to preserve cultural identity, maintain economic stability, and safeguard national security. During the 2024 US election campaign, Vivek Ramaswamy made a provocative suggestion: that all Americans should take the same test immigrants have to pass to gain citizenship. While this idea is open to debate, it underscores an important reality—acquiring citizenship in the US or any developed country involves a stringent and structured process. Countries like Germany, the UK, and the Netherlands enforce similarly rigorous rules, ensuring applicants meet cultural, linguistic, and economic integration standards before being granted citizenship.

While the specific regulations vary, these countries follow a similar framework: applicants must pay taxes for five to eight years, undergo cultural integration processes, and demonstrate proficiency in the official/national language. In Germany, for instance, conversational-level German is mandatory. Similarly, the Netherlands requires applicants to learn Dutch, while in England, a good command of English is essential. Citizenship isn't granted solely based on residency; applicants must prove their ability to integrate into the country's culture and align with its ethos.

Germany's process for acquiring citizenship is notably stringent. Applicants must reside in the country for at least eight years (or six in specific cases, such as for refugees or those completing integration courses) and consistently pay taxes. They are required to demonstrate B1-level German proficiency, pass a citizenship test covering German laws, culture, and history, and prove financial independence. Similarly, the Netherlands mandates five years of uninterrupted residence and tax contributions, along with passing the 'inburgering' (integration) exam, which evaluates Dutch language skills and cultural knowledge. In the UK, the process typically requires six years of residence (or three if married to a UK citizen), passing the 'Life in the UK' test, and demonstrating sufficient English proficiency. Applicants must also meet stringent financial criteria and maintain a clean legal record throughout their stay.

The same applies to most European countries: meeting the basic eligibility criteria doesn't guarantee approval—it only allows you to apply. The state retains discretionary power to reject applications without necessarily disclosing reasons. While reapplication is an option, approval remains uncertain. However, exceptions do exist. For example, significant financial investments—such as a million pounds in the UK—can fast-track the process, bypassing many standard requirements and significantly increasing the likelihood of approval.

Countries treat immigrants differently based on their skills and the demand for those skills. If you work in a field listed as having a "skill shortage" or hold specialized visas like the Highly Skilled Migrant (HSM) visa in the Netherlands or a Blue Card in Germany, you are likely to receive favorable treatment. In many cases, the benefits extended to skilled migrants even surpass those available to native citizens. For example, in the Netherlands, individuals relocating from more than 150 kms outside the Dutch border on a Highly Skilled Migrant visa are eligible (there is a list of criterias) for the 30% ruling. This policy allows them to pay taxes on only 70% of their income for the first five years—a financial advantage not available to the native population.

These policies are designed to advance the interests of the host nation. High-net-worth individuals contribute significantly to tax revenue, while skilled migrants help address labor shortages and ensure the economy functions smoothly. By attracting talent and investment, these measures strike a balance between benefiting the state and providing opportunities for immigrants.

So, why does the Citizenship Amendment Act (CAA) in India spark so much controversy? As an independent nation, India has the prerogative to determine its citizenship policies based on cultural integration and national interests, just like any other sovereign country. The CAA aims to fast-track citizenship for persecuted minorities—Hindus, Sikhs, Buddhists, Jains, Parsis, and Christians—from Pakistan, Afghanistan, and Bangladesh. This is not a nominal act; it specifically addresses the plight of these communities who face systematic persecution.

This raises a critical question: is India meant to serve as a *dharamshala*, open to anyone and everyone indefinitely, or should it adopt a structured immigration and citizenship policy akin to those of developed nations? The 2019 amendment to the CAA provides a clear definition of who qualifies as a minority in the context of religious persecution. Without such clarity, it would be impossible to frame and implement a transparent policy. This also prompts further deliberation—should the definition of a minority extend to linguistic groups, or should it be confined strictly to those facing religious persecution?

The Citizenship Amendment Act (CAA) in India isn't a unique policy in its approach to addressing historical and religious persecution. Many countries have implemented similar laws to address historical injustices or protect displaced communities. Israel has implemented a similar measure through its 'Law of Return,' enacted in 1950. This law was a direct response to the atrocities of Nazi Germany and the Holocaust, which exposed the vulnerabilities of Jewish communities worldwide. The 'Law of Return' grants Jews from any part of the world the right to immigrate to Israel and obtain citizenship. It serves as Israel's commitment to providing a sanctuary for Jews facing persecution or those seeking to reconnect with their heritage. Over the decades, thousands of Jews from Europe, Africa, and the Middle East have migrated to Israel under this law, enriching the nation's cultural and social fabric. The policy is a cornerstone of Israel's identity and symbolizes its resolve to safeguard its people against historical injustices.

Even Germany provides a pathway for ethnic Germans from Eastern Europe and the former Soviet Union to return and gain citizenship with the help of "Aussiedler Act". Greece offers repatriation laws for individuals of Greek descent, while Poland's "Karta Polaka" extends privileges to individuals of Polish origin living abroad. Ireland provides citizenship opportunities through its Foreign Births Register, reconnecting descendants of Irish emigrants. Similarly, Hungary allows simplified naturalization for ethnic Hungarians in neighboring countries, and Armenia provides fast-track citizenship for members of the Armenian diaspora. These laws reflect the efforts of nations to address historical displacement and cultural reconnection.

History is full of examples of people being persecuted for all kinds of reasons – religion being one of the most common and horrific ones. For people of Indic faith, especially those living in India's Islamic neighbors like Pakistan, Bangladesh, and Afghanistan, India stands as the only safe haven in the face of persecution. It's the one place they can turn to, knowing they'll be welcomed and accepted. The fear of persecution for Hindus in these countries isn't some exaggerated or baseless concern – it's very real. Over the years, many Hindus have already fled to India, seeking refuge and safety. Many of them remain stateless, caught in legal limbo.

In fact, the Citizenship Amendment Act (CAA) shouldn't be limited to addressing the persecution of Indians and Hindus in neighboring countries; its scope could be broadened to account for other pressing historical injustices. After moving to the UK, I found one such historical injustice done to some Indians which is rarely discussed today in textbooks or public discourse.

When I first arrived in the UK in 2022, I eagerly immersed myself in every Indian cultural event I could find. A standout experience was a Diwali Dinner and Dance. The moment I walked into the venue, I was greeted by the lively sounds of Bollywood music, the cheerful chatter in Hindi and Gujarati, and the rich aroma of North Indian cuisine. It felt like stepping back into a vibrant slice of home. That evening, I formed friendships that have not only endured but have also deepened my understanding of the diaspora's unique experiences and the historical connections that bind them to both India and their adopted homeland.

On the surface, the UK appears to have a significant Indian population, but the reality is more nuanced. Much of the British-Indian community traces its roots to India, yet many have never lived there, apart from the occasional holiday. A considerable number of them arrived in the UK during the 1970s and 1980s—not directly from India, but from African countries like Kenya, Uganda, and Tanzania. Their identities reflect a blend of cultural influences, making them British in nationality but deeply connected to their Indian heritage.

Some of the people I met shared stories of their families being forced to leave Uganda during a regime change. In 1969, a military coup in Uganda led to a directive giving South Asians—primarily Indians—less than three months to leave the country. Families were compelled to abandon their homes, businesses, and possessions, permitted to carry only 55 pounds in cash as they fled.

The irony? Despite their Indian origins, many did not hold Indian passports. Their families had lived in Africa long before India's independence, retaining British India passports. This left them stateless, with no country willing to take them in. India argued that, as holders of British-Indian passports, it was Britain's responsibility to accept them. India even issued temporary visas to about 5,000 refugees but only under the condition that Britain would eventually grant them citizenship.

Britain reluctantly agreed but with significant hesitation. Concerns about the increasing South Asian population and its potential impact on Britain's demographics led the government to impose a cap—allowing only 1,500 British-Indians to settle annually. As the crisis in East Africa worsened, these restrictions were gradually eased. However, their reception was cold; many Brits were uneasy about the influx of refugees, and there was little effort to make them feel welcome.

It makes you wonder—if Britain hadn't intervened, what would have happened to those people? Where else could they have sought refuge? Even when these individuals found shelter in Britain, it was far from what could be called a home. Britain in the seventies and eighties was not the racially tolerant society we see today. These refugees often endured life as second-class citizens, facing widespread hostility from the locals who left no stone unturned to push them to the margins. Racial slurs were commonplace, and harassment by local gangs was a constant reality. All of this happened because India, their ancestral home, failed to protect their interests and denied them a rightful place to call home. It remains a tragic failure of responsibility.

The Citizenship Amendment Act (CAA), passed in 2019, seeks to address the plight of persecuted minorities by fast-tracking citizenship for Hindus, Sikhs, Buddhists, Jains, Parsis, and Christians from Pakistan, Bangladesh, and Afghanistan. The law provides these communities with a pathway to formal recognition as Indian citizens. These people have been living in their own homes for decades as refugees. For many, this isn't about acquiring something new—it's about reclaiming a sense of belonging they feel was historically theirs. By offering a refuge from religious persecution, the CAA ensures that these individuals can find a safe and secure home in India, free from the threat of deportation or further marginalization. Where should the people of Indic faiths go if not India?

Nationalism

The Citizenship Amendment Act (CAA) not only raises questions about who qualifies for Indian citizenship but also delves into deeper themes of identity, belonging, and national sovereignty. This naturally connects to broader discussions of nationalism, particularly in the context of India's emphasis on "*Aatmanirbhar Bharat*" (Self-Reliant India). The ruling party frames "*Aatmanirbhar Bharat*" as a necessary assertion of national pride and economic independence, while opposition elites often critique it as jingoism or hypernationalism.

Similar ideologies can be observed in the UK through Brexit and in the US with "Make America Great Again" (MAGA). Both movements center around themes of national pride, sovereignty, and cultural identity—key pillars of nationalist ideology. Despite their origins in vastly different continents with unique historical and cultural contexts, these movements converge on shared objectives: prioritizing national interests, promoting selective globalization, and asserting cultural and economic sovereignty.

They also reflect shared fears and anxieties, including changing demographics, the perceived erosion of cultural and traditional relevance, and concerns about immigration. For example, MAGA emphasizes prioritizing American interests in global trade, diplomacy, and defense, often at the expense of multilateral agreements. Policies such as renegotiating trade deals (e.g., NAFTA to USMCA) and withdrawing from international accords (e.g., the Paris Climate Agreement) exemplify this nationalist stance. These actions are framed as efforts to restore control, protect national interests, and bolster strength, resonating deeply with sections of the population who feel marginalized by globalization.

The Brexit campaign's key slogan, "Take Back Control," symbolized the UK's desire to reclaim legislative and policy-making authority from the European Union (EU). Nationalists argued that EU membership eroded British sovereignty, imposing laws and regulations often perceived as lacking adequate representation or consent. Brexit supporters frequently highlighted a distinct British identity, contrasting it with the broader European identity promoted by the EU. Nostalgia for a "great" and independent Britain, often linked to its imperial past, resonated deeply with nationalist sentiments. This rhetoric appealed to those who believed globalization and EU policies diluted Britain's unique cultural and national identity.

Immigration, particularly from Eastern Europe under the EU's free movement policy, emerged as a significant driver of the Leave vote. Campaigns emphasized fears that immigration was overburdening public services, threatening local jobs, and disrupting cultural homogeneity. These anxieties were magnified by nationalist narratives framing the EU as a barrier to the UK's control over its borders and economic policies. This confluence of concerns strengthened the appeal of Brexit as a path to reclaiming national pride and sovereignty.

India's diversity sets it apart from the West in many ways. Hosting over a billion people with varied traditions, customs, languages, and cultures under one flag is no small feat. This challenge is compounded by unfriendly neighbors who have openly expressed intentions to destabilize the country through strategies like "bleeding India by a thousand cuts." Over the years, India has faced its fair share of secessionist movements, including those in Kashmir, Khalistan, and the Northeast regions such as Nagaland and Manipur.

Similar movements exist in the West, though they are relatively rare. For instance, Quebec's independence movement revolves around preserving the French language and culture. However, it is markedly different from the Khalistani movement. Quebec's movement enjoys strong support from people living within the province, making it influential in both provincial and federal elections. There are established political parties, such as the Parti Québécois, that openly advocate for Quebec's independence. Quebec's independence movement has profoundly influenced Canadian politics. The 1980 and 1995 referendums on Quebec's independence, especially the latter with a narrow defeat of 49.42% voting for separation, underscored the region's strong nationalist sentiments. These referendums shaped federal policies, leading to the introduction of the Clarity Act in 2000, which established clear guidelines for any future referendums. The rise of the Bloc Québécois, a federal party advocating for Quebec's sovereignty, has significantly impacted Canadian general elections, often preventing majority governments and ensuring Quebec's interests remain central to national politics.

In contrast, the Khalistani movement lacks significant support among Sikhs living in Punjab, India. For example, in the 1985 Punjab elections following Operation Blue Star and Indira Gandhi's assassination, the focus shifted to justice and peace rather than separatism, leading to a strong performance by the Shiromani Akali Dal. By the 1997 elections, Punjab voters had largely rejected pro-Khalistan rhetoric, emphasizing development and stability. In recent years, diaspora-driven pro-Khalistan activism has found limited traction within Punjab, as seen in the 2022 elections, where no major political party endorsed separatist demands. Instead, much of its backing comes from the Sikh diaspora in countries like the UK and Canada. Additionally, no major Indian political parties, including the BJP, INC, or AAP (currently in power in Punjab), endorse the idea of Khalistan. In fact, any party that explicitly supports Khalistan tends to lose public trust and elections in Punjab because of this stance. Unlike Quebec's organic, locally driven movement, the Khalistani movement often appears as a managed event, utilized by various groups for their own purposes rather than representing a genuine grassroots demand.

India will always require a consistent reinforcement of its identity as a unified nation, symbolized by one flag and one anthem. This unity is not just symbolic but essential for maintaining cohesion among its diverse population, ensuring that the idea of 'one nation' transcends regional, linguistic, and cultural differences.

It is often said that in India, every hundred kilometers the food changes, every two hundred kilometers the clothing, and every five hundred kilometers the language. The culinary traditions, shaped by local geography and culture, vary drastically, from the dairy-rich dishes of Punjab to the seafood-centric cuisines of Kerala. Clothing styles are equally varied, influenced by climate and cultural heritage—saree drapes, for instance, differ widely between Maharashtra and Tamil Nadu. Linguistically, India is a tapestry of 22 scheduled languages and thousands of dialects, with notable shifts in accents and expressions across regions.

How can such a diverse nation, while also facing external threats, remain united? The answer lies in the power of shared national symbols. These symbols, whether the national anthem, bird, or language, act as threads that weave together the fabric of a nation where commonalities might otherwise be scarce. They remind citizens of their shared identity and history, providing a foundation of solidarity even amidst profound differences.

However, the opposition to these symbols, often cloaked in seemingly logical reasoning, can stem from deeper, hidden agendas. These ulterior motives, whether political, ideological, or divisive in nature, threaten to undermine the unity that these symbols strive to protect. Recognizing and addressing such challenges is critical to safeguarding the nation's integrity.

In a country as varied as India, national symbols serve as more than mere emblems; they are the anchors of identity, ensuring that the nation remains cohesive and resilient against all odds. By embracing these shared symbols, India can continue to stand united, celebrating its diversity while reinforcing its collective strength.

The Crux: Ideology in Modi's India

A nation is much more than a piece of land marked by borders. It's defined by its people—their souls, cultures, traditions, rituals, and emotions. True success comes when these intangible elements are nurtured and safeguarded against internal and external threats. It's the state's responsibility to find the right balance, whether through immigration policies or decisions about citizenship.

It's fascinating to see how the ideological fervor that has kept India on edge over the past decade isn't unique, either in time or context. Often, history provides parallels, but in this case, we don't even need to look back—similar ideological battles are unfolding worldwide today. What might seem like uniquely Indian issues, are, in reality, challenges faced by many nations. Over the last decade, countries with vastly different cultures, economies, traditions, and religions have wrestled with comparable conflicts. Despite these differences, the ideological debates remain strikingly similar.

Such struggles have been fought vigorously in the past, are being fought now, and will continue into the future. Nations without debate or ideology—like those under dictatorships—often lack spirit and dynamism. The rise of ideological discussions in India is, in fact, a testament to the vibrancy of its democracy. While disagreements are natural, every individual must have the freedom to express their views—without fear—provided they don't infringe on others' freedoms. However, freedom doesn't mean inciting separatist sentiments or manipulating people by exploiting their emotions.

The key is to continue these discussions in a civilized and constructive way. A significant challenge lies in the general apathy of many Indians toward these issues until they escalate into crises. For example, if the Citizenship Amendment Act had been addressed immediately after Bangladesh's liberation, today's situation might have been avoided. Similarly, initiatives like truth and reconciliation, de-Mughalization, and decolonization right after independence could have fundamentally reshaped the nation. If the government had been bold enough to implement a uniform civil code back then, we might now be focusing our energy on more pressing challenges. None of these issues originated in or after 2014—they have existed for decades. Governments overlooked them, and voters didn't demand action. If an elected government wasn't delivering on its manifesto, how did it win the next time? What were the voters voting for? Delays have made these issues increasingly complex. In hindsight, the progress achieved over the past ten years should have been part of India's first decade of independence.

As India strides forward, let these challenges remind us that democracy isn't about achieving unanimous agreement but about navigating diverse perspectives with integrity and respect. The future of the nation depends on its ability to embrace discourse, learn from history, and boldly shape policies that reflect the aspirations of its people. After all, a thriving democracy is one where every voice finds its place, and every challenge becomes a stepping stone to progress.

That's why it's often said that democracy is a responsibility. The question is, are we mature enough to bear the weight of that responsibility?

IDENTITY

"Janaanaam swaroopam kaalen vikritim praapnoti"
–Book II, Chapter 10, Arthashastra

"The identity of the people transforms over time as they adapt to changing circumstances."

Limited Identities

Imagine a person living in a sprawling mansion with a gray glass roof. This self-sufficient mansion has everything—sports complexes, offices, even cricket grounds—ensuring the person never needs to step outside. To other people like him, life inside feels entirely normal because it's the only reality they have ever known.

Growing up, he has only ever known a gray sun. Why would he question it? To him, that's simply how things are. The possibility that the sun might not actually be gray doesn't even cross his mind. If someone were to tell him otherwise, it could shatter his perception of reality, making him feel as though everything he believed was a lie. How would he even begin to process such a revelation? Chances are, he'd feel overwhelmed, doubting everything, and struggling to find a new sense of stability.

One day, driven by pure curiosity, he steps outside the mansion. For the first time, he witnesses the sun—not gray as he had always known, but vibrant orange. Bewildered, he questions whether his eyes are deceiving him. Perhaps the orange sun is merely an anomaly, a fleeting mistake. He retreats back inside, reassured that the gray sun is the real one and that what he saw outside was nothing more than an illusion.

But his curiosity doesn't fade. A few days later, he ventures outside again. The sun remains orange, steadfast in its hue. He wanders further—still orange. He climbs a tree for a better vantage point—it's still orange. No matter where he goes, the sun's color stays the same. Confusion takes root, leaving him questioning everything he once believed.

Compelled by an unrelenting need for answers, he embarks on a longer journey. With a modest pack of food and water, he heads toward a distant hill. Hours later, after navigating challenging terrain, he comes across another mansion. Exhausted and thirsty, he approaches the gate and politely requests refuge. The residents graciously welcome him inside.

The moment he steps inside, he glances upward and sees the sun—it's blue. He is stunned. When he casually mentions that the sun is gray, one of the mansion's residents chuckles and responds, "The sun has always been blue." To them, the idea of a gray sun is utterly absurd. No one believes his account. After resting for a while, he steps outside again and, as expected, the sun is orange once more.

He continues his journey toward the hill and comes across another mansion. Curious, he decides to step inside. This time, the sun appears green. He smiles knowingly, almost anticipating the change by now. However, unlike the previous mansion, the residents here are far less welcoming. They adamantly insist the sun is green and pressure him to agree. The atmosphere quickly turns hostile, compelling him to leave without delay.

Outside, the sun is, as expected, orange. Exhausted but resolute, he presses on. Another mansion comes into view, and inside, the sun appears red. Having learned from past encounters, he decides to remain silent about the colors. Later, when the topic arises casually, he discovers that everyone there is firmly convinced the sun has always been red.

Finally, he reaches the hill. After a long and arduous journey, he climbs to the top. Standing at the peak, he gazes at the sun—still orange, just as it has always been. Looking down at the mansions below, everything becomes clear. From this vantage point, he sees that each mansion has a distinctively colored glass roof. The one he just left has a red roof, the one before that green, and the one prior to that blue. His own mansion, of course, has gray. The sun was always orange—its appearance only changed because of the tinted glass through which it was viewed.

And just like that, it all makes sense.

Just as the colored glass roofs altered the appearance of the sun in the mansion story, our cultural, social, and historical contexts influence how we perceive and engage with the world around us. These unseen filters shape our beliefs, interactions, and understanding of reality.

Understanding that we all see the world through different lenses isn't a groundbreaking concept—most people get it. But putting this understanding into practice in everyday life? That's where it gets complicated. For one, recognizing the lens you're using can be surprisingly difficult. How can you imagine the true color of the sun if you've never stepped outside your own mansion? Chances are, your perspective is already shaped by a cultural lens, or perhaps a religious, a caste, a gender, a regional, or a linguistic one. The list of possible filters is endless.

These biases or lenses we adopt from time to time are the "limited identities" that shape how we perceive the world and also influence how we think the world perceives us.

So, what is my identity? It sounds like a simple question, doesn't it? Yet in India, identity is far from straightforward. Reflecting on my own life, I realize how my "limited identities" have evolved over time—shaped by where I lived, what I was doing, and the various stages of life I experienced. This constant evolution transforms what seems like a simple question into one of profound complexity.

Understanding and embracing identity is crucial—not only for building a cohesive nation but also for fostering personal growth and meaningful connections. It encourages inclusivity, empathy, and a more tolerant society. However, problems arise when we cling too tightly to a single identity, as it confines us, much like living in a box or a mansion like that person, limiting our perspective to a narrow, self-contained view of the world.

Social media and AI algorithms amplify this effect in several ways. First, they create echo chambers by prioritizing content that aligns with what we've previously liked or interacted with, exposing us repeatedly to similar viewpoints and reinforcing existing beliefs. Second, they foster filter bubbles, where opposing perspectives and diverse ideas are effectively filtered out, making it harder to see beyond our own "mansion." Third, these algorithms cater to confirmation bias, validating pre-existing beliefs and discouraging critical examination. Fourth, this reinforcement of singular perspectives contributes to societal polarization, with groups becoming more entrenched in their views, making dialogue and understanding increasingly difficult. Finally, by feeding agreeable content, social media and AI can reduce critical thinking, leaving individuals less likely to question their assumptions or broaden their perspectives. This process shrinks the box even further, creating an illusion that everyone shares our reality and reinforcing the idea that our view is the only truth.

While this is convenient for entertainment—delivering reels, music, stories, and videos tailored to your preferences without effort—it also extends to current affairs articles, videos, and commentary. The algorithms ensure you're constantly exposed to content that aligns with your views, reinforcing the illusion that everyone shares your reality. Over time, this perpetuates the belief that your perspective is the only truth, making it harder to question or see beyond it.

In India, identity-driven agitations are a common occurrence, with groups rallying around caste, religion, gender, class, profession, or region. These movements often stem from feelings of neglect or injustice, which, when left unaddressed, lead to widespread unrest and demands for change.

In the earlier story, the person was fortunate enough to step outside his mansion, equipped with the means, motivation, and curiosity to seek answers. In reality, most people are deeply immersed in their daily routines—working hard, raising families, and managing life's challenges. Taking time to reflect on biases or question their identity often falls low on the list of priorities. It's understandable why someone might cling to content that resonates with their personal experiences or assumptions, even if it is incomplete or fundamentally flawed.

Over the years, living and working across various states in India and spending the last decade abroad in Europe and the UK, I've witnessed how my identity has continuously evolved. The perceptions of those around me played a significant role in shaping my own self-image. Experiences like personal growth, cultural assimilation, adapting to new roles, and navigating diverse environments constantly challenged my worldview and expanded my perspective. It's as if I finally stepped outside and saw the sun for what it truly was—unfiltered by the tinted glass that once defined my reality.

NRI - a Non Resident Indian

Bremerhaven is a port city in northern Germany where I had moved to pursue my Master's in Embedded Systems Design. It's a quaint, modest city where, like in many small towns across Germany, English isn't commonly spoken. Fortunately, the university offered a "student buddy" program, pairing international students with local counterparts. My buddy proved invaluable, guiding me through the essentials of life—from which app to use for train schedules to navigating the intricacies of German administrative tasks.

One evening, my buddy and I decided to grab drinks at a local pub. Over time, red wine became my drink of choice for these outings. After 25 years as a teetotaler, I hadn't developed a taste for beer—it always seemed bitter and unpleasant to me. Some types even gave me headaches (not the hangover kind, just immediate ones). Red wine, on the other hand, did not do any such thing and was quite easy to order. The phrase "*Rot Wein*" was easy to spot on any German menu, and with a quick, "*Einen Rotwein für mich, bitte*," I was all set. With drinks in hand, we found a spot at the far end of the L-shaped bar. The pub was packed with Germans, and I'm fairly certain I was the only brown person there, standing out like a beacon.

At one point, I noticed a woman sitting diagonally across from me, her gaze fixed intently in my direction. It felt as though I were some kind of curiosity on display. I offered her a polite smile and turned away, but the sensation of her eyes lingering on me didn't fade.

After a while, she walked over and asked, "How come you're drinking wine?"

I blinked, momentarily taken aback. I understood her words, but the context left me puzzled. Sensing my confusion, she elaborated, "Isn't it forbidden in your religion? In Islam?"

Oh! I'm not a Muslim," I replied, caught off guard by the unexpected question. It was the first time I'd encountered such an assumption in a conversation.

She was polite, and we ended up chatting for a while. She expressed genuine curiosity about India and its diversity. She explained her assumption: in her experience, most non-Germans in the town were either of Turkish or Pakistani origin and were predominantly Muslim. To her, I seemed to fit that profile for a couple of reasons. First, my skin tone was closer to that of Turkish or Pakistani people compared to the South Indian students, who made up the majority of Indian students in Germany. Second, my accent didn't align with the typical South Indian students either. Additionally, the similarity between spoken Hindi and Urdu likely contributed to her confusion.

Over the next few years in Germany, I came to realize that her assumption wasn't unique. As I interacted more with locals, I started to see myself as an "Indian who isn't a Muslim," a brand new identity for me. A glass of wine became more than just a drink—it turned into an unspoken signal that I wasn't from Pakistan and wasn't a muslim. They say red wine has antioxidants and might reduce heart disease; while I can't vouch for that, I can say with certainty that a simple glass of wine can shape perceptions and even influence a part of your identity.

You might be surprised by how little Europeans know about India—and even less about Hinduism, let alone Sanatan Dharma. Awareness is slightly better in the UK, but there's still a significant gap. Hindus remain somewhat of a mystery in Europe and the UK, and unfortunately, much of what is known isn't particularly positive. I'm still asked whether elephants and snakes roam freely in the streets or if people ride on the roofs of trains. Astonishingly, India doesn't even rank as a top travel destination for most Europeans; even Bhutan seems to surpass it in appeal.

Questions like "Do Indians know how to use a fork and a knife?" or "Can Indians drive?" or "How do you speak English so well? Can Indians speak English?" inadvertently heightened my awareness of my Indian identity, often in ways I hadn't consciously considered. Maybe that's why NRIs often grow more patriotic the longer they live abroad—constantly being reminded of their Indian identity through contrasts with their adopted surroundings.

Roll Number 5

Even though I was born and raised in India, being 'Indian' was never an active or dominant part of my identity until I moved abroad. In India, everyone was Indian—it was a given fact, not something anyone dwelled on. Outside school, I was known as "Doctor Saab's elder son," a label that defined my identity as long as I lived with my parents. In school, I became "Roll Number 5." Studying in the same school until senior secondary (Class XII) meant seeing the same faces every year, with new additions being rare. As a result, my roll call hardly changed: "Roll Number 5—Present, Ma'am!" That became my identity.

What kind of an identity is "Roll Number 5", you might ask.

Many of us, myself included, were not particularly fond of the idea of roll numbers and roll calls. After all, we had real names, so why couldn't we just be referred to by the names? To make matters more perplexing, during the end-of-year exams, students weren't even allowed to put their names on the answer sheets—only their exam roll numbers (which differed from the class roll numbers).

Never made sense to me as long as I was in school.

Now that I have experienced more of life than I had back in school, I have come to appreciate that "Roll Number 5" was in fact the one identity entirely free from prejudice and discrimination. It was the only identity I ever had that wasn't confined by societal, circumstantial, or any other limitations. Roll Number 5 carried no caste, no religion, no color, no region, and no ethnicity—it was an identity brimming with untapped potential, ready to make its mark.

Uniforms were another aspect disliked by many. The same attire every day led some to claim it was merely a way for schools to generate money. Everyone wore the same clothes: white shirt, green sweater, green blazer, green tie, gray shorts or trousers (trousers for Class IX and above), or skirts for girls. Each morning during assembly, strict rules were enforced. If a skirt was shorter than the knee-length, a trouser didn't touch the shoe collar, nails were painted or unkempt, or boys' hair was longer than expected—students could expect swift consequences.

It did look unfair at that time without any reason, it wasn't an army school, then why all this fuss?

The purpose was to ensure that everyone appeared the same, regardless of differences in shape, size, or background. It was not only essential for teachers to view all pupils equally but also for students to perceive one another without biases. With roll numbers and uniforms, there was minimal room for discrimination based on wealth, caste, religion, ethnicity or social status. This approach was particularly significant during school years—a critical period for neurological development when values, whether good or bad, become deeply ingrained and often last a lifetime.

I understand why schools and educational institutions might choose to ban symbols, whether religious or otherwise. Such symbols contradict the principles behind roll numbers and uniforms, which aim to promote equality and minimize distinctions. At the same time, I also recognize why some groups or sections of society feel compelled to prominently display their symbols—often as a way of asserting their identity or claiming superiority with messages like, "We are better than you" or "My religion is the one true faith." This creates a paradox: some go to great lengths to stand out, yet when these differences are acknowledged or questioned, it can quickly escalate into controversy.

School uniforms and hijab became a focal point of controversy in India, particularly during the events in Karnataka in 2022. The issue arose when some students were prohibited from wearing hijabs in class, citing school uniform policies. This incident sparked nationwide debates about secularism, religious freedom, and the balance between individual expression and institutional rules. Supporters of the ban argued that allowing religious attires or symbols like hijab disrupted the uniformity intended by dress codes, while opponents saw it as an infringement on constitutional rights and personal freedoms.

The controversy over hijab is not limited to India; it has also been a contentious issue across Europe and the UK. Countries like France, known for their strict secular policies, have implemented outright bans on religious symbols, including the hijab, in public schools and government spaces. The French government defends these measures as necessary to maintain secularism and prevent religious influence in public life. However, exactly like in India critics argue that such policies disproportionately target Muslim communities, creating a sense of exclusion and alienation.

In the UK, while there isn't a blanket ban, hijab has sparked debates around integration, identity, and women's rights. Some schools and institutions have attempted to regulate its use, citing dress code policies, but these moves often face backlash for infringing on religious freedom.

In Germany the state of Baden-Württemberg where I lived for a few years, restricts teachers from wearing religious symbols, including hijabs, in public schools. The Netherlands introduced a partial ban on face coverings, including the niqab, in schools, hospitals, and public transportation. Some Belgian schools prohibit hijabs under their dress code policies. In 2020, the Constitutional Court upheld such bans, citing the need to ensure neutrality in education.

Schools are more than places for academic learning—they are environments where children develop social skills and learn to coexist. In multicultural, multi-faith societies, it is crucial that children are taught to view one another without bias or prejudice. Roll numbers and uniforms play a role in fostering this equality by minimizing visible distinctions, including those conveyed through symbols of superiority.

General (GEN)

I was soon going to realize that life truly begins after school. While school might have tried its best to place all students on an equal footing—same uniforms, same rules, same perspective—the real world was far less uniform.

Roll Number 19 was another spirited identity, my closest friend since Class VI, both in school and beyond. His father, like mine, was a doctor, and we lived in the same hospital campus. As kids, we rode the same school bus; as we grew older, we cycled to school together. We shared our lunches, played table tennis after school, represented our school in various sports, and even brought home some trophies during our six years of friendship.

We prepared for the IIT JEE (Indian Institute of Technology Joint Entrance Exam) together, and I still remember the day we went to a cyber cafe to check our results side by side.

Days later, I came to realize that we weren't the same after all. Despite scoring 16 marks less than me, he secured admission to one of the best IITs. I wasn't the only one who had outscored him—there were others I knew in a similar position—yet none of us made it to any of the IITs but him, and that to IIT Delhi.

Clearing the IIT JEE Mains or securing an AIIMS (All India Institute of Medical Sciences) seat was considered the pinnacle of achievement in my city. Students often began preparing as early as Class IX, with many enrolling in coaching institutes. Kota, renowned for its intense coaching culture, was a name everyone associated with such aspirations. Opportunities to prove oneself in my school or my city were limited. You could win consecutive sports tournaments, dominate school debates, or perhaps outwit a teacher in an argument to earn recognition. Yet, nothing compared to securing a seat at one of the IITs or AIIMS. That accomplishment crowned you as "The Alpha," no questions asked. Of course, cracking the UPSC (civil services) exam also conferred a similar level of unmatched prestige.

Once the dust settled, I came to terms with the fact that Roll Number 19 and Roll Number 5 were never truly the same. The school's efforts to equalize us, through uniforms and roll numbers, couldn't erase the deeper disparities that shaped our lives. Roll Number 19 was set to graduate from one of India's elite technical institutions, the Indian Institute of Technology. I, on the other hand, found myself lost among the 15 million engineers the country produces annually. Since childhood, I had believed that he and I were sailing in the same boat, fighting the same demons together. But not this time. This time, I was sinking alone. It felt as though the Titanic had sunk, and I was left floundering in the vast sea, surrounded by others equally directionless, struggling to find a way forward.

For the first time in my life, my identity transformed, with a brand-new suffix added: The General (GEN) category.

Caste-based reservations were introduced in India as a mechanism to address historical injustices and provide social and economic opportunities to marginalized communities. Rooted in the principles of affirmative action, these policies aim to level the playing field for Scheduled Castes (SC), Scheduled Tribes (ST), and Other Backward Classes (OBC).

At seventeen, I struggled to comprehend how, despite living on the same campus, attending the same school, studying from the same books, and facing the same challenges—including braving the same bullies—we could still be so fundamentally different. How could he be at a disadvantage while I was perceived to hold an imaginary advantage?

The university I joined later only deepened this struggle, constantly reinforcing the "general" identity over the next four years. It felt inescapable—half the class openly carried their 'reservation' status, while every form, from exam fees to postgraduate entrance applications, required me to mark "GN", repeatedly reminding me of the label I couldn't shed.

This wasn't unique to me; many twenty-somethings in India have grappled with the complexities of caste identity. The nation has even witnessed extreme acts like youth self-immolating in protest against caste-based policies. The Mandal politics of the 1990s further cemented caste as a pivotal factor in Indian socio-political life. In my home state of Uttar Pradesh, caste has long been a cornerstone of politics. I grew up observing the clear demarcation of vote banks among political parties: the Bahujan Samaj Party (BSP) heavily reliant on Muslim and Dalit votes, while the Samajwadi Party (SP) leaned on its "MY" alliance, strategically leveraging Muslim and Yadav support. Similarly, in Bihar, the Rashtriya Janata Dal (RJD) has wielded the "MY" alliance to secure electoral victories. However, this reliance on caste-based alliances has also limited these parties' influence beyond regions with significant Yadav populations, confining their success to specific states.

Mentioning anything good or bad about reservation is like opening a can of worms. Those who strongly identify with a caste-based "limited identity" often react intensely. If you bring it up on social media, brace yourself for a storm. To be fair, blaming politicians and political parties today for exploiting such sentiments isn't entirely justified. They can only do so because deep-seated prejudices and biases exist within the society. If these politicians didn't capitalize on it, someone else inevitably would.

After college, I was fortunate to secure a job with a software company. Within two years, I relocated to Pune for a new role, and this move marked the beginning of a shift in my perspective. Distance, as they say, lends clarity, and living away from my home state gradually allowed me to shed the weight of my caste-based identity when I encountered a new label, a new limited identity in Maharashtra. I was no longer just a (General Category); instead, I became a "*UPwala*" or "*Dilliwala*." When I later moved to Bangalore, Karnataka, these labels morphed further, branding me as "a North Indian." This new identity became a focal point in my life for the next few years.

While my mind was preoccupied with this new identity, my caste identity gradually faded into the background—to the point where I could reconnect with Roll Number 19 as a friend once more. It was during these renewed conversations that I realized I wasn't the only one whose identity had evolved the day our JEE results came out. He, too, had acquired a new label: "reserved." Up until that day, he too had viewed us as equals, just as I had. But just as my time at the university didn't allow me to move on from my "general" identity, his university experience similarly anchored him to his "Reserved" label.

While I worked hard to develop resilience and push through an unfair system, he struggled with insecurities and an overwhelming sense of inferiority. He couldn't shake the fact that he had scored sixteen marks less than his best friend and still made it to an IIT while his best friend couldn't. This disparity planted seeds of self-doubt, which only grew when he found himself surrounded by students consistently outperforming him. The same unfair system that made me put extra effort and spend extra time in years to achieve my long term goals and dreams took an even greater toll on him—not just in terms of time and effort, but also in the form of his most precious asset: peace of mind. Sometimes I wonder if I had not moved away to a different state and a different identity, I would have never seen the fact that the system hurt him more.

North Indian & Hindi

Interestingly, after spending some time in Maharashtra, the prominence of caste issues seemed to fade into the background for me. This wasn't because caste concerns were nonexistent in Maharashtra or Karnataka, but rather because my North Indian identity was constantly under scrutiny and amplified. On numerous occasions, locals went out of their way to remind me that I didn't belong and was perceived as an outsider.

Bangalore, often referred to as the Silicon Valley of India, is a melting pot of software professionals from across the country. The city boasts a rich culinary tapestry, offering everything from Dosa, Uttapam, and Medu Vada for breakfast to Chole Bhature and Stuffed Paratha for lunch, alongside an array of global fast food chains like Domino's, Pizza Hut, and McDonald's for dinner. With its blend of cultural diversity, modern infrastructure, and global connectivity, Bangalore truly lives up to its reputation as a vibrant, expat-friendly metropolis.

However, strong regional identities and deeply ingrained linguistic prejudices persisted.

I started attending German classes with the intention of making my weekends more productive. However, my deeper motive was to explore opportunities at German engineering institutes. I aspired to secure admission to a university offering courses in embedded systems.

In hindsight, it turned out to be one of the best decisions of my life. I often wonder if I should have pursued this path for my bachelor's degree rather than waiting until my master's. Is it worth dedicating 12 to 14 hours a day, navigating intense competition, just to secure admission to a decent engineering college in India? Or does it make more sense to take an alternative route—one that avoids reservation constraints on the already limited number of available seats? Writing the GRE (Graduate Record Examinations) and IELTS (International English Language Testing System) to gain entry into a reputable German university feels significantly easier compared to excelling in GATE (Graduate Aptitude Test in Engineering) or CAT (Common Admission Test) to secure a spot in a prestigious Indian engineering institute or business school. Furthermore, state-funded German universities often provide scholarships for specific courses, making the prospect even more appealing. Feel free to connect with me on LinkedIn or via my personal blog "www.infiniteseaofopportunities.com". if you have questions about higher studies in Germany or Embedded Systems Design in general.

Every Saturday, I would take an hour-long bus ride from BTM Layout to the Goethe Institut/Max Muller Bhavan in Indira Nagar to attend German classes. After a few sessions, I discovered that one of my classmates happened to live in the same building as me. He was a Telugu speaking software professional learning German over the weekends. While his mother tongue was Telugu, he was fluent in Hindi, spoke some Kannada, and knew English, although his Hindi was stronger than his English. We quickly became friends and started spending more time together. He often helped me communicate with our building's caretaker, who spoke only Kannada and neither English nor Hindi.

After every class, my Telugu friend and I would stop at the chai shop just outside the Bhavan. One day, as we were chatting in Hindi as usual, another person from the institute joined us. We didn't know him well, but we had exchanged a brief introduction in the past. He had moved from Chennai, Tamil Nadu, where he had completed A1, A2, B1, and B2 levels in German. He was a teaching assistant at the institute while pursuing his C1 certification, after which he planned to move to Berlin to work with the embassy as an official German-English translator.

He remained silent while my Telugu friend and I chatted away in Hindi. After about five or six minutes, we noticed his quiet demeanor. Realizing this, I asked him if he understood Hindi and whether we should switch to English. He simply said, "No."

My Telugu friend casually remarked, "That's bad." The Tamil guy immediately erupted, "Why? Why is it bad? Why should I learn Hindi?" He paused briefly to catch his breath, and my friend attempted to explain that he only meant it would have been easier to communicate in Hindi rather than switching to English. However, the explanation failed to calm him. Those two words, "That's bad," seemed to hit a raw nerve, leaving the Tamil guy visibly upset. He continued murmuring, "Why does everyone need to learn Hindi? Why? Why are North Indians trying to shove Hindi down our throats?"

Both of us were taken aback by the intensity of his reaction. Nevertheless, we paid for our *chai* and left, hoping to move past the awkwardness of the situation.

Fast forward to 2021. Frankfurt Airport was my regular transit point for trips to Delhi. While sipping coffee at a café inside the airport, having arrived several hours before my flight, I noticed a familiar face in the crowd. It took a moment, but as I looked closer, I instantly recognized him. I waved and said, "Hi." His eyes lit up almost instantly. “Hello, long time!” he replied warmly. He was the teaching assistant from 2013. He was on his way home for annual leave, accompanied by his wife and their son. We quickly exchanged pleasantries, both surprised to see each other in such an unexpected setting.

We sat in a coffee shop and chatted about Indian affairs for the next two hours. Our conversation ranged from the pandemic and Covid-19 to the vaccination drive, discussing how India had managed the crisis compared to Germany. We even touched on topics like the Demonetization of 2016. His son occasionally interrupted with his endearing questions. I noticed he spoke fluent German, addressing his father in German but switching to English with his mother. My friend later remarked, “It is extremely important for him to excel in German if he wants to live in Germany; otherwise, it will be quite difficult for him to integrate with Germans.” I nodded in agreement, and, amusingly, so did his son.

I was taken aback by his conviction. My last memory of him was his intense reaction to someone asking if he spoke Hindi. What changed over the past nine years? He had made his son prioritize learning German over Tamil. Why? What had happened to his Tamil pride? He wanted his son to be fluent in German because approximately 84 million people speak it in Germany, making it easier to integrate. Yet, he had never considered learning Hindi himself, even though over 500 million people speak it in India.

Some people have a natural aptitude for learning multiple languages, while others may not. Choosing to learn a language—or not—is a matter of personal preference. However, turning a language into a rigid identity and clinging to it indefinitely can hinder progress. During my visit to Bengaluru last year, I was struck by the overwhelming display of Kannadiga Pride. Navigating the city has become challenging as hoardings, shop names, and signs were now almost exclusively in Kannada, with little to no English. Auto drivers were even insisting (it's a polite word) that passengers learn Kannada. This was a stark contrast to my last visit in 2013-14. Ironically, while countries like Germany and the Netherlands are embracing English as a secondary official language to enhance global communication, Bengaluru seems to be moving in the opposite direction, prioritizing regional identity over accessibility.

Dutch and German serve as both national and official languages in their respective countries, reflecting their dual role in cultural identity and governance. There is a significant difference between a national language and an official language. A national language symbolizes a country's cultural identity and heritage, whereas an official language is designated for use in government, legal, and administrative functions. India has twenty-two official languages but does not have a designated national language. This distinction highlights the country's effort to embrace its linguistic diversity while avoiding the elevation of one language over others as a symbol of national identity. All this resistance to pick a national language is out of political motivation and ignorance. Given the ongoing debates and the divisive nature of language politics in India, I believe Sanskrit could serve as a more neutral and unifying choice for a national language than Hindi. Sanskrit, being the root of many Indian languages, represents the country's shared cultural and historical heritage. It carries a pan-Indian identity that transcends regional and linguistic divisions, offering a symbolic link to India's ancient past while fostering a sense of unity.

The Crux: Modi's India and the limited identities

Over time, I've come to recognize various layers of identity that shape the lives of people in India: Individual or family Identity, Caste Identity, Regional or Linguistic Identity, Religious Identity, National Identity, and finally, Global Identity (where we view ourselves as part of humanity). Of course there are other identities like gender that overlap all of them. Each step outward broadens our understanding and fosters greater inclusivity, with the national and global identities encouraging the most expensive worldviews. If I were to draw an image, it would look something like this:

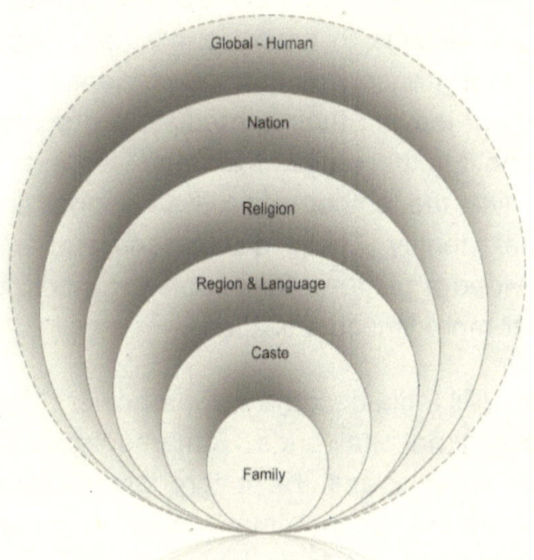

The smaller the circle, the more restricted the identity becomes, which often leads to biases and a narrower perspective. Smaller identities, like caste or regional affiliations, tend to focus inward and limit inclusivity, making it harder to appreciate diversity.

It took me years of moving to different places and taking on various roles to finally start identifying as Indian. Once I embraced this broader identity, I was able to view other, more limited identities with greater maturity.

But it shouldn't take everyone a decade of grappling with narrow identities to realize their inherent biases and how those biases can influence opinions. If I had read something like this at eighteen, I might have felt differently about many things—less hurt, less betrayed and less disappointed. That's one of the reasons I wrote this book: to help young adults or anyone struggling with an identity crisis. Life doesn't end if you don't make it to IITs. There are plenty of other ways to become a good engineer. Of course, easier said than done. I hope it provides the kind of clarity and comfort that I now feel after understanding the limitations and pitfalls of restricted identities.

Over the last ten years in Modi's India, the political environment has encouraged citizens to embrace a strong sense of national identity—one that transcends narrower identities like caste or region, all without leaving their immediate surroundings. Debates around standing for the national anthem, for example, highlight how symbols like the anthem and the national flag reinforce a shared national identity. These discussions and arguments have ultimately provided a platform for people to prioritize their identity as Indians over more limited affiliations.

Questions like "Will India become a superpower?" frequently arise, reflecting growing national pride. Statements such as "India is showing Pakistan its place, be it through airstrikes or surgical strikes" showcase the common man's nationalist sentiment. While it may not matter whether India becomes a superpower, what's crucial is that people now think of themselves as Indians first, rather than aligning primarily with caste or regional identities. For both nation-building and personal growth, it's essential for Indians to associate with the largest possible identity—the national identity—rather than smaller, divisive ones.

There are still political parties, groups, and communities that actively work to keep these limited identities alive. For instance, some political parties base their entire election campaigns on advocating for a caste-based census or pushing to increase the reservation cap beyond 50%. These actions reinforce caste-based identities in people's minds. Similarly, the promotion of "north versus south" controversies by some parties—whether through language debates or claims like "South Indians are more educated or civilized than North Indians"—further entrenches these divisions. There is a fine line between fighting discrimination and using social justice as a tool for personal or political gain. In today's India, there is no room for caste-based discrimination, nor is there any justification for using affirmative action as a means to secure a vote bank

In India, social justice has often been weaponized by certain political parties to serve their own interests rather than genuinely uplift underprivileged groups. For example, reservation policies, which were intended to address historical inequalities, are frequently used as electoral tools rather than mechanisms for real socio-economic improvement. The current reservation system allows governments to deflect accountability by saying, “We have provided xyz% reservation to xyz community; if they are not progressing, it’s their fault.”

If the true aim is to uplift impoverished and underprivileged communities, affirmative action must focus on equipping them with the tools and opportunities to compete effectively with others, rather than perpetuating dependency or limiting their potential.

I was quite pleased to see Mr. Mohan Yadav, a politician from the Bharatiya Janata Party (BJP), take the oath as the Chief Minister of Madhya Pradesh, directly challenging the SP and RJD’s traditional hold over the Yadav community and addressing the underlying caste bias. This shift means that Yadavs in Uttar Pradesh and Bihar can no longer rely solely on caste to guide their votes for SP or RJD; they are being encouraged to think beyond those narrow identities.

In Modi's India, political parties like SP, BSP, RJD, Shiv Sena, and other regional parties have been struggling to maintain their relevance. Their decline could be seen as a positive shift for the country, as it paves the way for citizens to move beyond narrow identity-based politics. When such parties fade away, it becomes easier for people to unite under a shared national identity and work collectively towards common goals.

INSTITUTIONS

"Sanskriti aur shiksha sansthaanon ka sammelan rashtra ki unnati mein sahayak hai"
–Book II, Chapter 16, Arthashastra

"The collaboration of cultural and educational institutions aids the progress of the nation."

Social Norms

Every now and then, we hear that public institutions like the judiciary, election commission, and policy-making bodies are under attack. However, the reality is that these institutions have faced challenges and exploitation for as long as they have existed. History offers countless examples of these institutions being undermined, incapacitated, or manipulated for personal or political gains sometimes even within the bounds of democracy. The imposition of emergency was perhaps the pinnacle of such attacks but only the tip of the iceberg.

The root cause of their struggles lies in the weakening of the social institutions that laid their foundations. Social institutions such as family, education, marriage, media, peer groups, community organizations, religion, and cultural institutions play a crucial role in shaping the progress and character of a nation, including its public institutions. These institutions establish norms and rules that guide social conduct, relationships, behaviors, and mindsets, creating the resilience necessary for societal stability.

While infrastructure, industry, and innovation often dominate discussions on development, social institutions and norms are frequently overlooked or dismissed in debates.

Living in Europe and the UK for an extended period helped me appreciate the nuances of their social norms and institutional frameworks, which often contrast sharply with those in India. These insights would not have been possible through brief visits or tourism. Daily interactions with locals revealed gaps in my understanding of Western ways of life and even greater gaps in the West's understanding of Indian traditions and societal structures. The Indian way of life, deeply rooted in centuries of diverse traditions and community-centric values, contrasts with the individualism that defines many Western societies. Differences in education systems, lifestyles, and mindsets are profoundly shaped by the institutions that support each culture.

These contrasts extend beyond education and lifestyle to include work culture, governance, healthcare systems, and community engagement. Family dynamics, gender roles, and societal constructs like individualism, feminism, and classism reveal nuanced differences between India and Western societies. Concepts such as diversity, equality, and activism, especially in environmental movements, also take on distinct forms in Western contexts compared to India.

The crisis emerges when we start adopting fragments of the Western system without fully understanding or adapting the broader context and foundational principles that support it. A piece from one puzzle, crafted for a specific framework, does not seamlessly fit into another, even if it appears appealing or sophisticated.

Mission Buniyaad

During my time at the University of Bremerhaven, I joined a voluntary non-profit club called Rotaract, the youth and student division of the Rotary Club. While the Rotary Club sponsored various activities, Rotaract members were responsible for executing them. Joining clubs like these was a strategic way to build both social and professional networks. Networking holds significant importance in Germany, where students frequently engage in such activities to enhance their career prospects.

One of the first tasks I took part in was painting the fence of a Gymnasium. At first, I thought a Gymnasium referred to a gym or fitness center, but I quickly learned it was actually a type of school. One of the girls in our group, who was an alumna of that particular Gymnasium, explained its significance. Curious, I asked her about her time studying there. She clarified, saying, "This isn't just a school; it's a Gymnasium." Naturally, my next question was, "What's the difference?" While she tried to explain, I only grasped that it was distinctly different from Hauptschule and Realschule. Her explanation opened my eyes to an educational system that was vastly different from what I knew in India, piquing my curiosity to dig deeper into these differences.

I was curious, but I decided to leave the conversation and kept myself busy with the other things—a bit of fence painting, taking photos, exploring the area, and, of course, enjoying lunch. Lunch was chicken soup with a loaf of bread. I thought it was just an appetizer at first, but to my surprise, it turned out to be the main meal. It was my first lesson in how cultural perceptions of meals differ. Later, at another seminar, I discovered that fried chicken and potatoes could also qualify as a full meal rather than just starters. These little moments kept adding to my growing understanding of how things that seem ordinary could vary so much across cultures.

As I spent more time in Germany, the differences in outcomes for students from Gymnasium and Hauptschule became increasingly clear. Most of the professionals I met at workplaces or seminars had studied at a Gymnasium. On the other hand, individuals working in trade or service jobs—like gym receptionists, Aldi cashiers, plumbers, electricians, and food kiosk workers—typically had a Hauptschule education. Interestingly, almost every Turkish person I interacted with who shared their educational background had attended Hauptschule. The contrast was striking: individuals from Hauptschule often worked in physically demanding roles, where their fitness and strength were evident, while those from Gymnasium typically pursued higher-paying professional careers, characterized by "six-figure" salaries and academic prestige.

In Germany, students are divided into three educational tracks after the fourth grade (around age 8-9): Hauptschule, Realschule, and Gymnasium. This division is primarily based on academic performance and, to a significant extent, the socio-economic background of their families.

- Gymnasium: Designed for academically strong students, often from well-off families, Gymnasium students are prepared for university education by default.
- Hauptschule: This track focuses on vocational training, preparing students for apprenticeships in trades such as electricians, plumbers, and receptionists. University education is not an option for these students.
- Realschule: Positioned between the two, Realschule offers pathways to both vocational education and, with additional certifications, university admission. For instance, a technician at my workplace had successfully transitioned from Realschule to higher education.

This tiered system significantly contributes to Germany's strength in research and development. By funneling the top third of students—those in Gymnasium—into higher education, Germany ensures its universities are populated with highly capable and academically driven individuals. However, when domestic enrollment falls short, international students like myself step in to fill the gaps. This is likely why my master's course in Embedded Systems Design was offered in English rather than German, accommodating the diverse international student body.

Despite its successes, this system has notable drawbacks. A child's placement is heavily influenced by their socio-economic background. Children from affluent, educated families are significantly more likely to excel in the fourth grade and secure a spot in Gymnasium, while those from underprivileged families often find themselves tracked into Hauptschule. This early categorization can have lasting psychological effects, fostering feelings of inferiority and low self-worth, particularly among Hauptschule students. These challenges have sparked protests, leading some states to modify the rigid three-tier system into a two-tier model. However, the foundational structure of the framework remains mostly unchanged.

The Delhi government's Mission Buniyaad, launched in 2018, reflects a similar intent to Germany's tiered education system: acknowledging that students have diverse learning needs and require tailored support. Like Germany's Hauptschule, Realschule, and Gymnasium, Mission Buniyaad categorizes students into three groups based on their academic proficiency:

- Ujjawal: Students performing at or above grade level, receiving enrichment activities to enhance their learning.
- Udyam: Students with foundational skills but needing additional support to reach grade-level expectations. They receive targeted interventions and remedial teaching.
- Utkarsh: Students with significant gaps in foundational skills, requiring intensive, individualized support.

The categorization under Mission Buniyaad, however, only applies until Class VIII. Beyond this point, all students follow the same curriculum, and the tailored study material for these groups is limited to just three months.

While Germany's model supports long-term excellence among Gymnasium students, Mission Buniyaad falls short due to its lack of a continuation strategy, making it appear more like a gimmick rather than a well-rounded, enduring solution. This experimental and superficial approach not only risks creating unnecessary stigma for students in lower-performing groups but also fails to deliver the sustained benefits observed in Germany's system.

Labeling students early in both systems can result in significant psychological challenges, such as diminished self-esteem and feelings of inadequacy. Germany's structured vocational training mitigates these issues to some extent by providing Hauptschule students with clear pathways into skilled trades and successful careers. In contrast, Mission Buniyaad lacks such a comprehensive follow-through, leaving many students without a defined long-term strategy for academic or professional growth.

This isn't the only example of a policy created for appearances rather than meaningful impact. Similar initiatives can be seen across various sectors, emphasizing the urgent need for thoughtful and inclusive policymaking that focuses on sustainable, long-term outcomes rather than short-term optics.

Compulsory Education

On June 15, 2019, I was flying back to EuroAirport Basel after a week-long trip and reunion with a university friend. This time, we had chosen Budapest, Hungary, as our meeting spot. Navigating EuroAirport Basel turned out to be more complicated than I had anticipated. The airport, located at the intersection of France, Germany, and Switzerland, was quite unique. I needed to exit on the German side to catch a train to Villingen-Schwenningen, where I lived and worked. However, I mistakenly exited on the Swiss side first and had to re-enter the airport, go up a level, cross the internal border (yes, there was a border inside the airport), and finally come down on the German side to exit correctly. Fortunately, I had a flexible train ticket, so missing the first train wasn't an issue as the next one was a couple of hours later.

Just outside the gate, I spotted a food van and decided to grab a sandwich while waiting in the queue. Suddenly, there was a commotion near the airport gate—screaming, sobbing, and an overall sense of chaos. Unfortunately, everything was happening in German, so I couldn't fully understand the situation. A large number of police officers and officials had gathered around a family with three children, and the mother was yelling at the cops.

Curiosity got the better of me—I had to know what was going on. This kind of commotion was so unlike Germany, where people are usually reserved and quiet. While I was still waiting in line, I noticed two friendly-looking girls just ahead of me. I decided to ask, "Hi, do you know what's happening over there? My German isn't great, so I'm struggling to understand." One of them smiled and explained, "Those three kids apparently skipped school to go on holiday before the official holidays started. Now the cops and child care services are here to penalize the parents."

This sounded absolutely absurd to me. The disbelief was likely written all over my face, prompting the girl to continue, "It's normal here. The cops and child services were probably here since morning, and this is most likely not the first case they've handled today. It's always like this right before the holidays."

Their sandwiches were ready, and with a quick "*ciao*," they left. There's a common stereotype that Germans are rude, but in my experience, they are quite polite and helpful. The language itself might sound harsh to non-native speakers, but the people are generally warm and considerate. For instance, my colleagues at work would always switch to English as soon as they saw me, just to make me feel comfortable.

I even developed a little trick for navigating meetings when my German wasn't strong enough: I'd make sure to be the first person to join the meeting room—whether in-person or virtual—and start a casual conversation in English with the next person who arrived. The colleagues were so polite that they refrained from switching to German, and the entire meeting would often proceed in English. This strategy worked for a couple of years until one day, a technician joined who didn't speak any English. Suddenly, someone asked, "If everyone is comfortable, can we switch to *Deutsche*?" It was a humbling moment, but it also made me appreciate how accommodating my colleagues had been.

Returning to the food van outside EuroAirport Basel, I waited there a little longer until my train arrived, precisely on time as expected. The following Monday at work, I couldn't wait to share what I had witnessed at the airport. Lunchtime was usually when I gained the most insight into German culture, as my colleagues often shared their perspectives. Mondays were our burger days (Thursdays were reserved for Indian food), and my colleague always gave me a lift to the restaurant. As soon as I got into the car, I couldn't hold back and started, "You won't believe what I saw at the airport..." I explained the scene in detail, and he responded with almost the exact same explanation the girls at the food van had given me: "It's normal here. The cops and child services were probably there since morning, and this was likely not their first case of the day. It's always like this just before the holidays."

I asked, "Why specifically before the school holidays? What's so special about that time?" The reply came quickly: "The tickets are cheaper. Prices skyrocket as soon as the holidays begin because everyone with kids or those associated with schools and universities start traveling." That explanation made perfect sense, and it turned out to be a valuable tip for me. From then on, I avoided traveling during school holidays, managing to save anywhere between two to four hundred euros on tickets and accommodation.

As we arrived and stepped out of the car, he asked me, "Is education compulsory in India?" I was stumped—I had no idea! While walking towards the restaurant, I quickly googled "compulsory education India," hoping to at least provide a straightforward yes-or-no answer. I was eager to affirmatively respond. For NRIs like me, such questions often feel like a matter of pride because many people in Europe and the UK know very little about India. Worse, much of what they think they know isn't flattering: "People still live with snakes, travel on elephants or on the roofs of buses and trains, and don't know how to use forks and knives." These stereotypes persist because most affluent Europeans have never visited India. Their perceptions are shaped by social media and news reports, which often paint a skewed picture.

Indeed, I found "The Right of Children to Free and Compulsory Education Act, 2009," which provided just enough information for me to respond confidently. I told him, "Yes, we do have a law for free and compulsory education." That seemed to satisfy his curiosity, and we shifted our focus to choosing burgers and chatting about other topics. However, when I got home later that day, I felt compelled to learn more. I looked up the act and read through the PDF version. To my disappointment, it turned out to be vastly different from the German system and, in some ways, quite flawed.

Two lines from Section 10 of the act highlight the core issue: "It is not the intention of this provision to compel parents/guardians and children/wards, who do not wish to avail of free and compulsory education, to necessarily admit their children/wards in a neighbourhood school." The term "compulsory" in the act's title does not actually apply to parents. This raises critical questions: Why wouldn't a parent want to send their child to school if the government is offering free education? What are these children doing instead of attending school? Would a mandate requiring parents to send their children to school help address issues like child labor?

While India has several laws prohibiting child labor on paper, the reality is quite different. It's not uncommon to see a "*chotu*" serving tea at a roadside dhaba, reflecting the significant gap between policy and practice. Moreover, the act has turned into a mockery of effective education policy. The consequences of its shortcomings are visible today, but they remain unaddressed by policymakers.

The act explicitly states that no student shall be detained or expelled until Class VIII. This leads to a fundamental question: Will a child make an effort to study if they know they cannot fail? Personally, I wouldn't have been motivated to study at all without the fear of exams. Would you? On paper, these children might be labeled as literate, but in practice, they barely learn. Instead of addressing these shortcomings, authorities merely deferred the problem to the next level, creating a cascading effect.

For example, Class X Board Exams, which were considered a significant academic milestone until 2009, were rendered insignificant and optional, accompanied by the introduction of a grading system. To further defer the problem, the difficulty levels of both Class X and Class XII exams were lowered. This is evident from the sharp increase in students scoring above 90-95%, with an unprecedented number achieving perfect scores in many subjects. Additionally, widespread leniency towards cheating during exams further worsened the situation. This was starkly revealed when the Class X exam was reinstated as mandatory and conducted under stricter, fair conditions—resulting in a significant drop in pass percentages. Remarkably, one former Chief Minister of Uttar Pradesh even publicly stated that some level of cheating is acceptable - he confidently misled people by comparing this to open-book tests conducted in many European universities. However, open-book tests come with their own challenges and nuances, which I will elaborate on later in the book.

These developments underscore systemic flaws and the unintended consequences of poorly implemented policies, highlighting the urgent need for thoughtful and effective educational reforms.

As an NRI, I can't tell the reality of the compulsory education act in India to anyone in Europe. Can I? It would further deteriorate the already deteriorated image of India.

When I moved to the UK, I noticed that the law here differs from Germany's and somewhat mirrors India's. Sending children to school is not mandatory; parents have the option to educate them through alternative methods, including homeschooling. For instance, one of my colleagues, who holds fairly orthodox religious views, chooses not to send his children to school. His reasoning is to protect them from the perceived negative influences of schools and their peers. Instead, he homeschools them with the help of a private tutor and supplements their education by sending them to a Madarsa.

However, there is a significant difference between how homeschooling and *Madrasas* are handled in the UK compared to India. In the UK, both are strictly regulated under a well-defined code of conduct that ensures children receive a structured and standardized education. Parents who choose homeschooling must register their children with local authorities and provide evidence of adequate progress through periodic assessments. Similarly, *Madrasas* are overseen to ensure they meet educational standards and adhere to child welfare regulations.

In contrast, India lacks a cohesive framework to regulate homeschooling and *Madrasas*. While some state governments, such as Uttar Pradesh under Yogi Adityanath's chief ministership, have attempted to introduce guidelines for *Madrasas*, these efforts have faced resistance and are perceived as targeting minority communities. This absence of standardized regulations has led to inconsistencies in educational quality and limited accountability. Without proper oversight, homeschooling and *Madrasas* in India operate in a fragmented and largely unmonitored system, emphasizing the urgent need for a structured and standardized approach to alternative education methods to ensure equitable and effective learning outcomes.

Mission Buniyaad and the Compulsory Education Act are paradoxical in their outcomes: one denies deserving students the opportunity to qualify for universities, while the other allows even under qualified students to become eligible for university admission.

Education Crisis

It's not that everything was perfect before the Compulsory Education law or Mission Buniyad—far from it. My disappointment lies in the fact that the state of education, already dismal, has worsened rather than improved.

I recall an incident from my B.Tech days. During one of our internal exams, a student in the seat behind me stood up and claimed that a particular question was incorrect. I was confused since I had just started answering that very question. Soon enough, the “topper” group—the teacher's favorites who always attended classes, submitted assignments on time, and followed instructions diligently—supported his claim.

The invigilator, unsure of the situation, decided to consult the professor who had set the question paper. Until then, she instructed us to proceed with the other questions. When the professor arrived, the student reiterated his claim, and the topper group echoed his concerns. However, the professor stood firm, stating, “The question is correct as per my understanding. Complete the exam, and we’ll discuss this further during the answer sheet review.” The students reluctantly complied.

When the results were announced, chaos erupted. The contentious question had been discussed in class weeks earlier, but in the question paper, a single value was changed—from “9” to “7.” The students who had memorized the problem with “9” insisted the question was invalid. The discrepancy rendered their rote-memorized answers unusable.

Fast forward to 2015, during my master’s program at Hochschule Bremerhaven. I had chosen Robotics as an elective, which required me to attend classes at the University of Bremen due to low enrollment at Bremerhaven. This course was open to both bachelor’s and master’s students. It was challenging, with more mathematics than I had anticipated.

When the semester ended, the professor distributed past exam papers and explained the test format: it would be an open-book exam. Students could bring notes, textbooks, calculators—whatever fit on their desks. However, sharing materials during the exam was strictly prohibited. Having never taken an open-book exam before, I was curious and apprehensive.

On exam day, students arrived armed with notes and reference materials. As the invigilators handed out the question papers, my heart sank. The questions looked entirely unfamiliar. After several readings, I realized these were completely new problems, designed to test the application of concepts we had learned. This was no 9 to 7 change—it was a genuinely novel challenge.

What struck me most was the classroom's atmosphere. No one protested. Students, particularly the Europeans and even the South Asians, appeared calm and focused. Nobody panicked and no protests!

This was a stark contrast to my undergraduate experience, where students often retaliated. Why? What's the difference?

The difference lay in the students' motivations– those in the master's program, including South Asian students, had chosen to study the course out of genuine interest, while many students back home were compelled into engineering programs for reasons unrelated to personal passion or curiosity.

Years later, as I browse through LinkedIn, it's evident that many of my undergraduate peers are no longer working as engineers. Some pursued MBAs immediately after completing their B.Tech, while others joined ITES (information technology enabled services) companies as a stepping stone to business schools. Many transitioned into careers in banking, civil services, family businesses, or entirely unrelated fields. A significant number of the females in the class were waiting to get married soon after graduation, with some even getting married before earning their degrees. The situation is even more challenging for electronics engineers, many of whom eventually moved into software roles, assuming they stayed in the engineering domain at all.

Reports claiming that 90–95% of Indian engineering graduates cannot write functional code often lack nuance. These statistics lump together all graduates, regardless of their career paths. If the surveys focused solely on graduates who remained in core engineering roles five years after graduation, the numbers would tell a very different story—albeit the number of such engineers would be extremely small to start with.

Whenever the crisis in engineering and employment is discussed, the conversation often concludes with calls to overhaul the education system. Yet, the same system produces brilliant engineers as well. All these engineers shine somewhere, India or abroad. Not to forget the missing university-industry collaboration in India. I don't think I need to provide a detailed list of Indian origin engineers who made it big in the west with the exact same education. The deeper issue lies in the motivations for pursuing engineering. In small-town India, students scoring 75% or more in high school are funneled into math or biology streams, leading to medicine or engineering. For many, engineering is not a passion but a means to an end—a degree for social prestige or better job prospects.

Interestingly, most Western countries I encountered have some way to regulate the number of students applying for university. European countries, for instance, implement educational frameworks akin to Germany's three-tier system, which tracks students early and limits university eligibility for some. These frameworks emphasize vocational training and apprenticeships, effectively guiding many students toward careers that do not necessitate a university degree.

Switzerland employs a dual education system akin to Germany's, dividing students into distinct tracks based on aptitude and career aspirations. The *Gymnasium* (Academic Track) prepares students for university, the *Sekundarschule* (Middle Track) leads to technical schools or vocational training, and the *Realschule* or *Oberschule* (Lower Track) focuses on apprenticeships and trades. Similarly, Austria's system includes the *Allgemeinbildende Höhere Schule* (AHS) for university-bound students, the *Mittelschule* for vocational training or secondary technical colleges, and the *Polytechnische* Schule for apprenticeships or technical professions. The Netherlands features a comparable structure: VWO (*Voorbereidend Wetenschappelijk Onderwijs*) for university preparation, HAVO (*Hoger Algemeen Voortgezet Onderwijs*) for applied higher education, and VMBO (*Voorbereidend Middelbaar Beroepsonderwijs*) for vocational training. Similar frameworks exist in other European countries, such as France and Italy, ensuring a clear pathway tailored to both academic and vocational pursuits.

These frameworks establish a robust vocational track that alleviates pressure on universities while contributing to economic stability by addressing demands in trade and technical job markets. By directly linking vocational pathways to employment opportunities, these systems significantly contribute to the notably low unemployment rates in many European countries. Countries like the UK and the US lack rigid filtering frameworks, but the exorbitant cost of university education often acts as a deterrent, prompting many students to pursue vocational courses instead. This allows them to enter the job market earlier and avoid the financial burden associated with higher education.

In contrast, India's education system lacks the rigid frameworks seen in Germany's three-tier system or the selective processes utilized in the UK, which limit access to universities and ensure alignment with specific career pathways.

The Right to Education (RTE) Act and Continuous and Comprehensive Evaluation (CCE) policies have made it increasingly difficult for students to fail during their schooling years. This "no detention" policy ensures that students progress through grades, often regardless of performance, until at least Class 8. While this inclusivity expands access to education, it can lead to high enrolment in universities without aligning with job market needs. Many graduates may find themselves underemployed or unemployed due to a skills gap between education and industry demands. This contributes to high youth unemployment rates, as degrees often outnumber job opportunities. Further compounding the issue is India's reservation system, which allows at least fifty percent of the students belonging to the reserved categories to reach university at a lowered benchmark.

Quantity & Quality

The high influx of students into universities, driven by inclusive policies and the allure of higher education, has intensified competition to unhealthy levels. The pressure to succeed academically, often reduced to a numbers game, has led to a surge in mental health issues among students. The race for marks, degrees, and prestigious institutions leaves little room for creativity, curiosity, or critical thinking.

It is now more about the quantity rather than the quality -more students and more engineers rather than better quality engineers and better quality codes.

This conflict between quantity and quality is not limited to education but extends to other sectors as well. The entertainment industry mirrors this shift. Bollywood, once revered for its powerful storytelling and compelling performances, now often revolves around box office numbers and star power. The success of a film is frequently gauged by its opening weekend revenue rather than its artistic value or narrative depth. Strong PR takes over quality content and organic marketing. This might explain why many companies specializing in special effects and VFX relocated abroad - the limited domestic demand for these services in India, reflecting the nature of the Indian entertainment industry and its prioritization of traditional formats over high-budget, effects-driven, good quality productions. Social media amplifies this transformation, enhancing the reach and influence of actors based on follower count and engagement rates. A viral post or trending hashtag can significantly boost an actor's brand, sometimes more than the quality of their performances.

Social media, as the great equalizer, has further entrenched this culture of quantity over quality. Algorithms reward content that garners views, likes, and shares, regardless of substance. In today's India, this dynamic also shapes public opinion and discourse, where the loudest voices, not necessarily the most informed, dominate the narratives. The proliferation of influencers, content creators, and online personalities exemplify how digital platforms value attention over authenticity. Whether in politics, business, or entertainment, success is increasingly defined by metrics that prioritize reach over resonance. In education, this manifests as a race for marks rather than knowledge; in sports, as brand-building over mastery; and in entertainment, as blockbuster hits over cinematic brilliance.

This obsession with numbers fosters a superficial culture where the pursuit of instant gratification often eclipses long-term growth and meaningful achievement. Consider the case of rising cringe content on social media, where creators amass significant wealth and fame through sensationalism. Such success stories trigger a domino effect, inspiring younger generations to follow a similar path, often sidelining traditional skill development.

Yet, this cultural shift also reflects the ambitions of a young, aspirational India. In a rapidly transforming economy, visibility can be a pathway to opportunity, and social media provides a platform for millions to showcase their talent. However, the challenge lies in striking a balance—ensuring that the pursuit of popularity does not come at the expense of quality and substance.

Cricket, India's most cherished sport, exemplifies this obsession with quantity over quality. Traditionally, cricket celebrated skill, strategy, and on-field excellence. However, the focus has increasingly shifted towards cultivating stardom. Cricketers are judged not just by their performance but by their social media presence, endorsement deals, and personal brand. A cricketer with a massive social media following may command more attention and financial rewards than a technically proficient player who lacks visibility. This commercialized approach prioritizes fame over genuine talent and consistency, reinforcing the notion that popularity often outweighs merit. In this setup, the batsman who scores a boundary with a thick inside edge is as celebrated as one who plays a textbook cover drive. The reluctance of selectors or captains to highlight technical flaws reflects this shift. Australia's six ODI World Cup titles starkly contrast with India's two triumphs, underscoring the cost of prioritizing stardom over sustained excellence.

Cricket

When I moved to Portsmouth, England, from the Netherlands, I began searching for a gym near my residence. Several options were available, but I chose the one closest to me. It wasn't fancy, but it seemed adequate for my needs. After inquiring about the prices and facilities, I was preparing to leave when a guy, seated slightly inside the reception area, asked me an unexpected question: "Do you play cricket?" Apparently, their cricket team was short of players.

His question both surprised and delighted me, and I immediately said yes. While planning my move to England, I had eagerly anticipated exploring Indian food but was equally thrilled at the prospect of playing cricket again. He led me to the cricket ground, just a short five- or six-minutes walk from the gym. Along the way, he mentioned that Rahul Dravid, my favorite cricketer, had scored his maiden century on that very ground during the British County Championship in 2000 while playing for Kent against Hampshire. This anecdote only heightened my enthusiasm.

He explained that the cricket season would start at the end of April and promised to introduce me to the team and the captain. We exchanged contact details, and as we parted, I asked, "Do you ask every new person at the gym the same question?" He laughed, replying, "Of course not. But as soon as you mentioned you were from India, I was certain you played cricket." We shared a laugh and went our separate ways.

By April, I received a message notifying me that training would begin that Thursday at 5:00 PM. Arriving on time, I used the entry code sent to me and walked to the nets at the far end of the ground. The same man was there and introduced me to the rest of the team. Interestingly, while he wasn't the best player, he managed the team and handled its affairs. What struck me most was the team's composition. Besides him, only two other players were British. The rest were international —primarily from India, with a few from Pakistan, Bangladesh, and one from Africa. Some were working professionals like me, others weren't. I had anticipated more English players, considering I was in England. We trained for a couple of hours and dispersed. I later joined the club and played for them throughout the season.

At work, I noticed a similar trend– while cricket was widely recognized, it wasn't particularly popular among young professionals in my department. Unlike in Germany or the Netherlands, where cricket is virtually unknown, it was a familiar sport in England, yet few actively played it. Intrigued by this disparity, I sought insights from a colleague nearing retirement. He explained that cricket, while once integral to English culture, has lost its prominence. Soccer now commands the nation's attention, followed by rugby, relegating cricket to a distant third. This shift reflects a cultural preference for faster-paced, more commercially dominant sports that better capture the public's interest.

This revelation intrigued me further when a colleague from Australia noted a similar hierarchy there. Australian football dominates, followed by rugby league, with cricket ranking third. The contrast became even more striking when compared to India, where cricket is more than just a sport; it's a national obsession. No other sport in India comes even remotely close to cricket's fan following. Yet, despite this overwhelming popularity, Australia boasts six World Cup titles compared to India's two. This paradox raises a significant question– How can a nation of over a billion people, where cricket is almost a religion, consistently lag behind nations with comparatively less enthusiasm for the game?

India's cricket board, the BCCI, is the wealthiest in the world, and cricket infrastructure in India far exceeds that of any other sport in the country. The common justifications for underperformance, such as inadequate facilities or insufficient financial backing, simply do not apply here.

South Asian cricket, not just in India, exemplifies how quantity often overshadows quality. The sport frequently transforms into a spectacle, prioritizing glamor, commercial interests, and fanfare over the core fundamentals of the game. A vivid illustration of this was the 2023 ICC Men's Cricket World Cup. The highly anticipated India vs. Pakistan match at the Narendra Modi Stadium drew an audience of over 100,000 spectators, creating an electrifying and charged atmosphere. Following India's victory, however, some Pakistani fans and team management voiced grievances, attributing the result to the overwhelmingly one-sided support. Complaints ranged from the DJ's failure to play "*Dil Dil Pakistan*" to the stadium's dominant sea of blue, reflecting the fervent nationalistic undertones that often overshadow the spirit of the game.

During the final at the same stadium, Australia triumphed decisively, silencing the overwhelmingly pro-India crowd. Pat Cummins, Australia's captain, aptly remarked, "It's a great feeling to silence 100,000 spectators." Why couldn't India leverage its home advantage and fervent fanbase in such a pivotal match? The underlying issue lies in how cricket has evolved in countries like India and Pakistan. Despite the sport's massive popularity and resources, its focus has shifted away from core skill development and strategic depth. The lackluster performance in the final reflected systemic shortcomings—a reliance on individual brilliance rather than a cohesive team effort, compounded by an underinvestment in nurturing diverse skill sets, such as quality bowlers and batsmen. It's a team sport and it can not be played by one quality batsman, one quality bowler and nine social media stars. This outcome, though disappointing, was a foreseeable consequence of these persistent structural issues.

For decades, India leaned heavily on its formidable batting lineup, while systematically neglecting the development of a balanced and robust pool of quality bowlers. This over-reliance on batting prowess led to a lopsided strategy that took years, even decades, to recognize as unsustainable in the long run. Acknowledging the need for change is often the most challenging step. The first step to solving a problem is recognizing that it exists. In the context of Indian cricket, this means critically evaluating the structural and cultural aspects that have allowed complacency to set in. Addressing the imbalance between commercial interests and player development, investing in grassroots programs that nurture diverse skill sets, and fostering a team-oriented approach are critical steps forward. So, the question remains – will India take the necessary measures to transform its cricketing ecosystem, or will it continue to rely on fleeting moments of individual brilliance in an increasingly competitive global arena?

Knockout

India’s cricket journey is marked by consistent dominance in the group stages, only to falter repeatedly in the knockout rounds. Since 2011, this pattern has become all too familiar. It’s not merely a stroke of bad luck; the frequency with which it occurs suggests deeper systemic issues, particularly when such struggles are notably absent in teams like Australia. When the stakes are highest, Team India seems unable to deliver, as if the gears seize under pressure. Losing occasionally is natural, but when setbacks become habitual, it signals a need for introspection and change. Perhaps the allure of stardom and the distractions of lucrative endorsements contribute to this recurring shortfall.

Knockout events are not confined to cricket; they permeate every facet of life. These pivotal, make-or-break moments test our ability to perform under pressure, where success often hinges on a single opportunity. Whether it's a cricket final, a high-stakes school examination, a crucial work presentation, or even a performance in a cherished hobby, the principle remains the same. Despite meticulous preparation, everything can boil down to executing flawlessly at that critical juncture. Life, much like cricket, often challenges us to deliver our best when it matters most.

For a performer, every time he or she steps onto the stage, it feels like a mini knockout event. He or she might rehearse flawlessly in private, but a single missed note during the actual performance is what the audience remembers. Similarly, in professional settings—whether pitching to clients, sitting for job interviews, or delivering critical presentations—these are all knockout moments. No matter how many times one practices, the ultimate success hinges on the ability to deliver when it truly counts.

Consider this: I may excel in every unit test throughout the year, but if I falter in my Class X or XII board exams, all that effort can feel meaningless. The same principle applies to high-stakes entrance tests like NEET, IIT JEE, or UPSC. Those countless late-night study sessions and flawless mock test performances hold little value if I can't deliver on the exam day. These are knockout events—high-pressure moments where it's all or nothing, with success or failure being the only outcomes.

I used to struggle with exams, often overwhelmed by anxiety and nervousness that persisted until I saw the question paper. This pattern wasn't limited to academic tests; it extended to job interviews and dissertations as well. For the longest time, I believed it was normal—an inherent emotional weakness I had no control over.

When I began working in Villingen, Germany, my colleague and I were assigned to design two IP cores (Intellectual Property cores—functional units that perform specific tasks and can be sold or integrated into larger designs). We successfully completed the assignment on time, and later it was announced that our prototype would be showcased at the auto expo in Nuremberg in February 2020. While I was filled with nervous anticipation about the event(which did not happen because of covid), my colleague remained completely indifferent. As the expo drew closer, my anxiety only intensified, yet he appeared unaffected, as though the announcement had no bearing on him whatsoever.

Noticing the stress on my face, he asked, "How's everything?" Hesitantly, I shared my nervousness and admitted, "What if my IP doesn't work?" Expecting a philosophical reassurance like, "You did your best; if it doesn't work, it doesn't work," I was caught off guard by his direct question: "Why won't it work?" His question left me momentarily speechless. I didn't have an answer. Why was I doubting my work in the first place?

"Did you simulate the design?" he asked, following up. I nodded—yes, I had. And at that moment, the reason for my nervousness became clear. I had indeed simulated it, but the code and simulation setup were rushed—"quick and dirty." My sole focus had been meeting the deadline; once it worked, that was enough for me. However, the simulation lacked the depth and thoroughness it required. My colleague's approach, by contrast, was meticulous. He had developed significantly more test cases and invested additional hours to account for corner cases. This rigorous preparation gave him the confidence I realized I lacked.

I realized that I had been repeating the same pattern since childhood. The root of my nervousness, anxiety, and lack of confidence was my tendency to not invest sufficient effort and preparation. I was not alone in this habit; there are many, even the "topper" group I mentioned earlier shared a similar shortcoming. While they worked hard, their approach was flawed. Their success relied heavily on familiarity with the material, and they knew that if the exam presented unfamiliar questions, they would likely falter.

The problem with contemporary India lies in the pervasive obsession with shortcuts. The current generation craves instant results, leading to the proliferation of scams promising quick riches. From Ponzi schemes to dubious chit funds, the lure of "doubling your money in twenty days" has ensnared countless individuals. While the inclination towards shortcuts is not new in India, the situation has progressively worsened. In earlier times, it was primarily anti-social elements exploiting vulnerable masses under the guise of religion. Today, however, even the educated youth are falling victim to manipulative influencers. A striking example is a recent controversy involving a program that falsely claimed to impart MBA-equivalent skills in just a couple of weeks.

The Indian cricket team exemplifies this principle of preparation and consistency. During a World Cup match against England, Mohammad Shami demonstrated exceptional precision by pitching six consecutive deliveries to the exact same spot. This relentless accuracy frustrated Ben Stokes to the extent that he played a reckless shot and lost his wicket. Shami's performance was a testament to the rigorous effort and meticulous preparation he had undertaken well before the tournament. In contrast, during the semi-finals against New Zealand, Mohammad Siraj struggled to meet the required tactical precision. He was instructed to bowl around the wicket and consistently aim just before the wide line but failed to execute this plan effectively (as noted in post-match interviews). This stark disparity highlights the indispensable role of disciplined practice and preparation in achieving precision under pressure.

One of Pakistan's renowned seam bowlers once remarked in an interview that while a bowler cannot control how the pitch behaves after the ball is pitched, however, consistently landing the ball at a specific spot is entirely within the bowler's control. Achieving such precision requires an enormous amount of practice. Similarly, MS Dhoni, India's former captain and widely regarded as one of the finest wicketkeepers, was known for his uncanny ability to hit the stumps without even looking. This remarkable skill was not mere luck but the result of countless hours of rigorous practice. It was this dedication that made him an unwaveringly reliable presence behind the stumps.

Flying an aircraft is another example of a high-stakes knockout event, though it often goes unnoticed due to the extensive preparation involved. Commercial airline pilots are required to log approximately 15,000 hours of flight training before they are entrusted with the responsibility of carrying hundreds of passengers. This immense level of practice ensures their ability to perform flawlessly under pressure, highlighting the critical importance of rigorous preparation and the mastery of skills through repetition.

As the saying goes, there are no shortcuts to success or rather sustainable success.

Lifestyle

One of the things I really admire about life in the West is the way people genuinely value their hobbies – and how accessible it is to explore something new. There's an established culture of joining clubs for practically any interest you can think of. Whether it's a cycling group, a pottery class, or a weekend hiking club, there's always a space to connect with others who share your enthusiasm. Community centers and local gyms often serve as social hubs, making it easy to discover and join these activities. In many ways, it feels like having a hobby isn't just encouraged but almost expected – everyone seems to have something they're truly passionate about outside of their professional lives.

In India, hobbies are undoubtedly appreciated, but they often take on a more informal shape. For example, many sports I learned—like chess, table tennis, or cricket—were taught to me by my dad. During my time at home, I played with my brother, cousins, or neighbors. Activities like badminton are usually picked up with friends at local courts, and weekends often involve playing cricket in neighborhood parks. The concept of enrolling in a formal club is not as prevalent—at least, not yet. What happens when you move away for studies or work?

Things are gradually changing, particularly in urban areas, where hobby groups and meetups are becoming more common. Still, for many, hobbies take a backseat to the demands of academics or work. When free time does emerge, it is typically spent with family or friends rather than exploring an individual passion project.

When I started my blog(www.infiniteseaofopportunities.com) back in 2018, I kept it to myself for the first few months. It wasn't until later that year, once I'd developed a consistent writing habit, that I decided to share it with friends. One day, I brought it up with a friend who wasn't particularly close but someone I spent a lot of time with, especially since we both enjoyed exploring restaurants. While we were having lunch at a Vietnamese place, I mentioned my blog, and he decided to check out a couple of articles right there. As he read, I found myself eagerly anticipating his feedback. Would he find the writing engaging? Did it make sense? What aspects might he criticize? I was bracing myself for some honest, constructive feedback.

After a few minutes, he looked up and asked, "Nice. Do you make money from the blog? How do you monetize it?" I explained that while monetization was an option, I hadn't enabled ads because I was doing it purely as a hobby. He seemed genuinely baffled, unable to comprehend why I would invest so much effort into something without any financial return. This reaction wasn't unique—I received similar questions from many of my Indian friends. Since the blog centered on Indian affairs and politics, I initially hesitated to share it with my German friends. However, after some time, I thought, "Why not?" and decided to tell a few of them as well.

One evening over dinner, I asked one of my German friends, who had a keen interest in painting and a knack for critical analysis, to check out my blog. When she finished reading, I asked, “And?” She gave me some thoughtful feedback – said the ideas flowed well and the article felt organized. She didn’t like the look of the website, pointing out that the layout was cluttered and the navigation wasn’t intuitive. Her feedback helped me realize how important a clean and user-friendly design is for engaging readers. That feedback actually pushed me to revamp the site – I added a search bar and better navigation. It was refreshing. She even asked about the research process and how long it took to write each piece. She was curious about the effort and process behind the blog, not just whether it generated income. This made me reflect on how hobbies are often perceived differently across cultures. In the West, there’s a deeper appreciation for the creativity, time, and passion invested in personal projects, whereas in India, there’s a stronger focus on practicality and potential returns. Her curiosity helped me see my blog as more than just a side activity—it was a meaningful way to share ideas and hone my skills. That stood out to me. The vibe was different. Most of my Indian friends, on the other hand, were fixated on whether I could turn it into a side hustle. Some of them even said, “Why spend so much time on it if you’re not earning anything?”

Having a hobby requires one fundamental prerequisite: a decent work-life balance. Without the time to unwind and recharge, pursuing hobbies becomes nearly impossible. Structured leisure policies, like paid vacations and flexible hours in the West, make it easier for individuals to take up hobbies and commit to them consistently.

On the other hand, I’ve seen colleagues in India struggle to nurture their interests due to long work hours and demanding schedules. Work-life balance directly impacts the ability to explore personal passions by providing the mental space and energy needed to fully engage. In countries like the Netherlands or Germany, there’s a strong emphasis on maintaining a balance between professional and personal life. Paid vacations, weekends dedicated to leisure, and flexible working hours are considered essential not only for productivity but also for fostering a healthier societal approach to work and relaxation. These policies encourage individuals to explore their personal interests while cultivating a culture that values rest and balance as critical to overall well-being.

When I started working at Mentor in Germany, I experienced this firsthand. I had thirty days of annual leave, and the company shuts down entirely between Christmas and New Year—a common practice in the West. Initially, I planned to visit home for a month in December to use most of my annual leave. However, in late October, HR and my manager reminded me that I needed to use at least 22 days before the year ended. This email caught me completely off guard, as such policies are unheard of in India. It underscored a cultural emphasis in the West on ensuring employees take time off to recharge and maintain a healthy balance, something that felt starkly different from the work-first approach I had experienced in India. On top of the annual leave quota, there were 8-9 bank holidays, often accompanied by bridge holidays where employees could take a day off by working extra hours earlier.

The same approach holds at my current job. Without these bank holidays, flexi days, and my annual leave quota, I would have struggled to find the time to write this book. Hobbies require time—and sometimes, a lot of it.

India, on the other hand, often leans into a more work-centric approach, especially in urban areas. Long hours, competition, and the drive to succeed can make the work environment intense. While things are changing with younger folks wanting better work-life balance, the expectation to go the extra mile still lingers. But India's informal social scene makes up for it – after a long day, chai and chats with neighbors can be the perfect way to unwind.

Also, I am not stating that everyone in the west pursues hobbies and no one in India does that, it is out of the people I have seen and encountered.

Family

In India, family is everything. The concept of a "joint family" is still common, with multiple generations living under one roof, sharing responsibilities and decisions. Even when families live apart, staying connected is a big deal. Festivals, weddings, and family gatherings aren't just events – they're huge, loud, and full of life. In contrast, Western societies lean more towards individualism. Young adults move out earlier, looking for independence and personal growth. Family bonds are still important, but gatherings aren't as frequent or elaborate. It's not that relationships are weaker – just different. Visits, holidays, and video calls keep things going.

Individualism and feminism, while empowering, come with their own set of challenges. The grass always seems greener on the other side, but moving to Europe helped me notice some of the hidden costs. Right across the street from my office in Villingen was a bus stop I frequently used when I wasn't cycling. Behind the stop stood an old building undergoing refurbishment. I later discovered it had been a traditional old-age home. In the West, old-age homes are a necessity due to the prevalence of independent living among the elderly. What stood out about this project, though, was that part of the building was being converted into student apartments. The idea was to create a shared environment where elderly residents could interact with students, reducing their sense of isolation while fostering community. It struck me as a clever solution to a problem that, in India, is often mitigated by the family structure—especially in joint families.

Depression is notably more common in the West, partly because the safety net of family support isn't as robust. In India, the constant presence of loved ones creates a built-in emotional cushion, helping individuals weather life's challenges. Even during tough times, having family around often acts as a powerful antidote to feelings of loneliness and despair. This contrast made me appreciate the nuanced role of familial bonds in maintaining mental well-being.

I've spent my fair share of time on dating apps, and something that stood out in the West was the number of single mothers looking for partners – not married or divorced, just single mothers who were never married. It's not something you see as often in India. Raising a child is already one of the toughest jobs I can think of – doing it alone, without a partner or family to lean on, seems unimaginable. In India, having family around makes parenting easier, and a joint family makes it even smoother.

Food – now that's one thing India absolutely wins at. Hands down! It's not just the spices that make Indian food so special, it's the love, time, and effort that goes into cooking. In the West, food is all about convenience – a means to get energy and move on with the day. That's it. I was honestly shocked in Mensa when I saw chickpeas and mashed potatoes served as a meal combo. One is protein, the other is carbs – technically, it checks all the boxes. But back home, boiled potatoes, boiled veggies, and lentils wouldn't exactly pass as a proper meal. I later realized it's all about time. No one here has hours to spend cooking, everyone's hustling, and everyone's got bills to pay – so who's got time to cook? Thank god for the microwave.

Feminism and individualism seem appealing, but they work best when they're backed by strong family support. What I've noticed is that in India, many people pick and choose when to embrace these ideas – often using them as a way to dodge responsibilities rather than truly embodying them.

A 20-year-old in India might want to assert his individuality like his counterpart in the West – chasing his dream of becoming a musician or a cricketer – and feels his parents shouldn't have the right to deny him that. But at the same time, he still expects them to pay his bills without complaint. What this 20-year-old often doesn't realize is that his Western counterpart is juggling part-time jobs, working tirelessly to pay his own bills, and pursuing his passion in whatever free time he can carve out. His parents aren't sacrificing their peace and retirement to fund his aspirations. If I get a chance to do it all over again, I would still choose the Indian way – with some restrictions from parents but without any need to juggle jobs for meeting the basic needs.

Similarly, I've seen feminism misinterpreted in ways that skew its essence.

Or take the example of a middle-aged couple with grown-up children. After inheriting their parents' wealth and using it to help their son establish his business, they suddenly assert their independence, wanting to step away from supporting and caring for their aging parents. They question why their parents can't simply live in old age homes, as many elderly do in the West. This kind of selective independence raises eyebrows – it's independence when convenient and dependence when beneficial.

In Modi's India, families, culture, traditions, festivals, and marriages are under pressure. Political narratives and propaganda are actively challenging systems that have worked for generations, often purely for electoral benefits. Hindu marriages are flamboyant, Hindu Fasts are unhealthy, *Holi* leads to water wastage, and *Diwali* causes air pollution. We have a state like Delhi where the state government is hell bent on killing the festival. Although the good news is still there are some politicians and states trying to keep the essence alive. For example in Uttar Pradesh, the year 2024 saw a different *Diwali* in Ayodhya, with the state authorizing a grand *Deepotsav* where lakhs of Diyas (Oil Lamps) were lit on the banks of river Saryu; traditional dance, music, and theatrical performances were organized to showcase the rich cultural heritage of Ayodhya and a spectacular fireworks display lit up the night sky. Leaving the religious aspect of the festival aside, this will help local businesses to boost their business. Somebody made those lamps, somebody sold that oil, lakhs of people paid for their travel to reach Ayodhya, they stayed in Ayodhya.

Organized firework displays are quite common in the west as well. On the new year's eve, a common place is shortlisted and the entire city watches the fire cracker show from a distance. For example in Portsmouth, a place called Southsea Common which is nothing but a very large ground where all "common" things happen like festivals, light shows, recently England celebrated D-Day so there were air shows.

Air Pollution

Every November, like clockwork, I head home for my annual leave. This ritual has become more than just a holiday; it's a moment to reconnect with my roots and reflect on the changes I observe, both in my hometown and in myself. This time, I flew from London Heathrow to Delhi IGI, ready to grab a taxi from the multilevel car park. The flight was routine, and the airport experience felt like muscle memory. But the moment I stepped outside in Delhi, I was struck by an immediate sense of discomfort. The air felt thick and warm. It wasn't just the weather; there was an overwhelming sense that the environment itself was struggling under an invisible weight.

I walked up to the kiosk right outside the exit and asked, "Where's the entry to the multilevel car parking?" The guy at the counter casually pointed to his left. "There's a signboard over there," he said nonchalantly. I followed his finger, squinting into the distance, but the signboard was nowhere to be seen. After a moment of hesitation, I asked again. This time, he glanced at me with mild irritation and added, "Oh! It's not visible right now, but just keep walking that way. You'll see it eventually." His dismissive tone and the lack of clear directions added to my frustration, which was already amplified by the oppressive and the heavy air around me.

Thick, white haze blanketed the road, reducing visibility to just a few feet. It was 4:00 AM on November 6th, 2023. I started walking in the direction he had pointed. The pilot had announced Delhi's temperature as 19 degrees, but it felt much warmer—oppressively so. The air was dense and heavy, reminiscent of a packed hall with no ventilation. Interestingly, Portsmouth, UK, had been 19 degrees when I left, but the difference was stark: that 19 felt crisp and invigorating. This, however, was suffocating and draining.

After a few minutes, I spotted a blurry signboard in the distance, and as I walked closer, the words "Multilevel Parking" gradually came into focus. The entire process felt unnecessarily tedious, adding to my growing frustration. Oddly enough, I was already feeling exhausted—and trust me, I'm no couch potato. I stay active, play squash regularly, and cycle quite a bit. But this short walk? It felt like a workout. I found my pre-booked cab and got in.

As we drove off, I gazed out the window. The white haze seemed omnipresent, cloaking everything in its path and refusing to dissipate. It wasn't just a visual obstruction; it felt symbolic of a larger, unrelenting problem—a reminder of the systemic environmental challenges looming over the city. Visibility stayed low, and the uneasiness lingered, mirroring the overwhelming weight of the air pollution crisis that permeates daily life here. I passed the remnants of the G20—bright lights, fountains, and flashy decorations—but they felt hollow against the backdrop of the smog-choked city. The grandeur seemed out of place, a stark reminder of the disconnect between global events and the local struggles overshadowing daily life. While the decorations aimed to project progress and prosperity, the oppressive haze made it impossible to ignore the urgent and unaddressed environmental crises. Less than an hour after landing, my eyes burned, and my head throbbed—a visceral reminder of the severe health impacts of Delhi's air pollution. The immediate physical discomfort underscored the urgency of addressing the city's environmental crisis, where millions endure such conditions daily, with long-term consequences far beyond my fleeting experience.

The weight of the environment pressed down on me. The initial discomfort quickly turned into guilt as I realized how fleeting my struggle with this pollution would be. For just a month—and mostly indoors—I'd endure these conditions, while the rest of the year, I'd enjoy clean air, cycle around town, and live stress-free. But for my family, friends, and the millions of others who live here full-time, this is a daily reality. It's not just unfair; it's a stark reminder of the systemic neglect that allows such conditions to persist. How do they find the strength to cope with this unrelenting burden every single day? The contrast between my temporary experience and their permanent struggles made the environmental crisis feel even more urgent.

Since its formation in 2013, the Delhi government ruled by Aam Aadmi Party has implemented several measures to address pollution, but many have been perceived as inadequate or superficial. Air pollution? They've largely pointed fingers at external factors like stubble burning. Diwali crackers? A blanket ban is enforced annually, often touted as a major solution, yet it barely scratches the surface of Delhi's air quality issues. These measures, while well-intentioned, fail to address the systemic and multifaceted nature of the problem. But here's the catch—Diwali hadn't even happened yet, and the AQI was already through the roof. Their next excuse? Stubble burning in Punjab, Haryana, and UP. Apparently, the smoke drifts over and clogs Delhi's air.

I can't help but wonder—why isn't stubble burning an issue in the UK or Europe? Why don't fireworks on New Year's Eve cause pollution in the West? I live here, and the air is clean—clean enough to spot the Milky Way with the naked eye.

In the UK, stubble burning was banned in 1993. Farmers switched to modern techniques like crop rotation, mulching, and direct drilling. Instead of burning the residue, they plough it back into the soil to boost fertility and cut emissions. Mulching not only prevents erosion but also helps the soil retain moisture, increasing yields. The government backs this with subsidies, encouraging environmentally friendly practices like using cover crops and organic fertilizers. On top of that, strict regulations and regular monitoring keep harmful practices in check. Farmer cooperatives and community initiatives also play a role by promoting sustainable methods and sharing knowledge.

Most European countries follow suit, with bans on stubble burning and incentives for modern machinery like mulchers and seed drills. The EU's Common Agricultural Policy (CAP) provides financial support and training for sustainable farming. Crop residues often end up fueling bioenergy projects, cutting the need for burning even further.

As I mentioned earlier in the industrialization chapter, Indian agriculture desperately needs reform and mechanization. However, political games have repeatedly stymied progress. The three farm bills from 2019-20 are a prime example. While similar reforms appeared in the manifestos of every major party, when the Modi government introduced them, they became a political flashpoint. Opposition parties, fearing a loss of their rural voter base, mobilized protests that turned the debate into a battleground for political gain rather than an opportunity for meaningful dialogue. As a result, the bills were repealed, leaving the core issues of agricultural reform unresolved.

Stubble burning isn't the only villain here. Industrial emissions, vehicles, and construction dust also add to the mess. As I pointed out in the infrastructure chapter, Delhi urgently needs more public transport. The cycling network is practically non-existent. Delhi could potentially take inspiration from London's congestion charges and Ultra Low Emission Zones (ULEZ). In London, vehicles entering the city center during peak hours are charged a fee, and older, high-emission vehicles pay extra or are restricted altogether. This discourages unnecessary car use and promotes public transport, cycling, and cleaner vehicles. Of course, implementing something similar in Delhi could ruffle political feathers—after all, asking people to pay for driving might clash with the popular freebies model used to win elections. Forming a government is more important than clean air!

Knee-jerk reactions like the odd-even traffic scheme and blanket construction bans during smog season often prove counterproductive. While these measures aim to address immediate issues, they frequently disrupt daily life without offering lasting solutions. For instance, blanket construction bans halt critical projects and impact livelihoods, yet the dust pollution returns as soon as the ban is lifted due to a lack of enforcement of dust control measures. Globally, construction continues even in urban hubs, but it adheres to stricter environmental guidelines, such as mandating green cover or requiring dust suppression systems. The government's inability to enforce such regulations in Delhi highlights the need for a shift from reactive short-term measures to systemic, sustainable solutions that address the root causes of pollution.

That said, there have been a couple of bright spots recently. The Eastern and Western Peripheral highways now let thousands of vehicles bypass Delhi, reducing congestion and cutting down vehicular emissions within the city. According to recent studies, these highways have contributed to a noticeable reduction in traffic density during peak hours. Additionally, the Modi government's big push for solar energy and electric vehicles has started to bear fruit. India is now among the top countries in renewable energy capacity, and EV adoption has accelerated with subsidies and infrastructure expansion. While these efforts are steps in the right direction, scaling them further could significantly impact air quality in urban hubs like Delhi.

The issue of Air pollution in India isn't fixed because it hasn't yet become an election-worthy topic. Unlike tangible benefits like free water, electricity, or transport, cleaner air is harder to quantify and politicize. Voter priorities often lean toward immediate, visible gains, and political incentives follow suit. Until public awareness grows and clean air becomes a collective demand, the issue is unlikely to command the urgency it deserves. The day it overtakes popular freebies in the electoral narrative, significant change might finally take root. Until then, we wait.

The Crux: The Foundations

It's not about whether the Indian way of living is better or the Western way is superior; they are simply two distinct approaches to life. Each system operates within its own cultural and historical context, and when we selectively borrow elements from one and insert them into another, unintended consequences can follow. As Modi's India ambitiously pursues its goals, it's important to remain mindful of these dynamics. The unseen checks and balances that underpin systems are often not immediately obvious, but omitting these safeguards when adopting elements from the West can lead to significant issues.

Traditions and families, for instance, come with their own set of challenges, but the absence of these structures creates even larger societal problems. For example, traditional support systems within families often serve as safety nets in times of crisis, which can be difficult to replicate in individualistic settings. Similarly, social media is a double-edged sword—it empowers individuals yet can become dangerously addictive, distorting our priorities. It's alarmingly easy to lose oneself in the pursuit of likes and views, fostering superficial connections at the cost of deeper relationships. In the long run, however, quality always triumphs over quantity, as exemplified by systems that reward sustained excellence over fleeting popularity.

The reliability and trustworthiness of a nation's institutions are deeply intertwined with the cultural and social norms that shape daily life. For instance, when honesty is a shared value among citizens, institutions naturally reflect that integrity through fair governance and efficient functioning. However, when foundational values erode, these institutions often mirror the societal gaps, leading to issues like corruption, inefficiency, and mistrust.

Addressing these challenges requires not just structural reforms but also a cultural shift towards re-emphasizing shared values and accountability.

In navigating the interplay of culture, governance, and modernization, the key is balance—adopting progressive elements without losing the strengths of traditional systems. It is this harmony that ensures institutions remain robust and societies flourish in the long term.

EPILOGUE

When my cousin informed me that the government had invalidated the 500 and 1000 rupee bills, at first, I dismissed it. "So what if the government invalidates certain currency bills?" I thought. Little did I know, this seemingly simple announcement would herald one of the most dramatic economic decisions in India's modern history, shaking not just wallets, but the very fabric of the nation. It was a seismic event that jolted the nation awake—not just physically, as people queued for hours outside banks, but emotionally and spiritually. For the first time in decades, it felt as though the very soul of the country had been stirred.

There was a small section of around 3-4% of Indians who were happy—those few who had been paying taxes all along. For a change, they had the last laugh. Their lives had often revolved around complaints about high taxes in a country where a large section of the population comfortably evaded taxes. This time, that large section was hit hard. Many voiced frustration, some simply hid their activities, while others, especially those involved in illegal activities like hawala trading or counterfeit currency,or any other, were devastated but unable to be vocal. Then came the most intriguing group: politicians, high-profile lawyers, and bureaucrats. They were outrightly furious. Why? Because, for the first time, they were caught off-guard, their usual avenues of exploitation sealed shut.

The groundwork had been laid well before demonetization. For example, the Prevention of Money Laundering Act (PMLA) underwent significant amendments in 2015 to address long standing loopholes. One of the key changes was the expansion of predicate offenses, allowing a wider range of financial crimes, including tax evasion, to fall under its ambit. This ensured that illegal activities generating proceeds of crime could be prosecuted effectively. The amendments also strengthened enforcement powers by enabling agencies to provisionally attach properties suspected to be linked to money laundering, even before a conviction was secured. Furthermore, financial institutions and banks were required to implement stricter reporting mechanisms for suspicious transactions, aiding in the early detection of illicit activities. These measures collectively enhanced the PMLA's effectiveness, making it a crucial tool in combating financial crimes, especially during and after demonetization.

Additionally, right after demonetization in 2016, the Benami Transactions Act was amended to address loopholes in its earlier version. Before the amendment, the 1988 Act had a vague and narrow scope, making it challenging to enforce. Terms like "benami transaction" lacked precision, and there was ambiguity around who the "real owner" or "beneficial owner" of a property might be. With the stricter definitions introduced in 2016, the Act was able to cast a wider net. By explicitly defining "benami transaction" to include properties held in fictitious names or where the source of funds is untraceable, it became far more difficult for individuals to disguise illegal assets.

Moreover, the broader definition of "benami property," covered both tangible and intangible assets, ensuring that transactions involving shares, bonds, and other financial instruments were also scrutinized. For example, tangible assets such as real estate and gold purchased under fictitious names were targeted, while intangible assets like financial instruments, including stocks, bonds, and mutual funds purchased with untraceable money, also fell under the scanner. This comprehensive approach made it significantly harder for offenders to conceal illicit wealth. The inclusion of exceptions, such as properties held by family members using legitimate sources of income, not only protected genuine transactions but also gave clarity to enforcement agencies. These well-defined terms eliminated ambiguities, making the law actionable and reducing the scope for misinterpretation or misuse. In essence, these changes transformed the Benami Transactions Act from a dormant statute into a potent weapon against corruption and black money, aligning it with the government's broader efforts to create transparency and accountability in the economy.

In short, the elite section—accustomed to exploiting loopholes for personal gain—found no escape from demonetization. This time, they were caught unprepared. They called it fascism and decried the execution of demonetization, but for the first time, many in this group were forced to resort to illegal methods, like bribery, to protect their own wealth.

If nothing else, the government demonstrated meticulous preparation and foresight before implementing its measures. The chaos witnessed during Modi's decade of leadership was largely due to missing or minimal loopholes and ambiguities in the policies and laws, making their exploitation significantly more difficult. Had all the policies and laws that were enacted during the last decade had sufficient loopholes and ambiguities, we wouldn't have seen such chaos.

There is a very thin line between exploiting loopholes or ambiguities in the laws and committing a felony. Loopholes and ambiguities in policies have often been deliberately introduced to allow flexibility for interpretation, typically favoring those in power. It's fascinating, for instance, that in a country as diverse as India—where minority rights are a daily topic of discussion and even have a dedicated minority commission—the Constitution itself lacks a clear definition of "minority." Who constitutes a minority? What is a minority? Is it a religion with more than two hundred million followers? Since the first amendment in 1951, the Indian Constitution has been amended more than a hundred times. The 42nd Amendment in 1976, often called the "Mini Constitution," added words like "socialist" and "secular" to the Preamble, and the 105th Amendment in 2021 restored states' ability to identify and notify Other Backward Classes (OBCs). Yet, no one has deemed it important to define "minority" in clear terms.

The Citizenship Amendment Act (CAA), for the very first time, clarified the definition of minorities(although minorities in the neighboring countries and not in India), addressing ambiguities in earlier frameworks. It is not the Modi Government who introduced religion in the act, it was already there, but the word "minority" wasn't defined. By explicitly identifying minority groups based on religion—such as Hindus, Sikhs, Buddhists, Jains, Parsis, and Christians from Pakistan, Afghanistan, and Bangladesh—the CAA provided a concrete basis for granting citizenship to those facing religious persecution. This clarity helped streamline the application process and reduced room for interpretation or delay, making the Act more effective in addressing its core objective of protecting vulnerable groups. While the CAA generated significant debate, its precise definitions represented a step toward addressing long-standing challenges in India's citizenship laws.

Even though the NRC was mandated in the Citizenship Act of 1955, it was never exercised on a national scale. Before amendments like the CAA, there were ambiguities in how "citizenship" was defined for certain communities, especially those affected by partition and religious persecution. Without clear legal guidelines, implementing the NRC would have been contentious and prone to misuse. Logistical and social challenges, combined with fears of social unrest, delayed its implementation, rendering it a dormant provision for decades.

The hard truth is that while India has laws and policies covering nearly every aspect of governance, loopholes and ambiguities remain rampant. We have strong child labor laws, yet "*chotus*" work in tea stalls. We have compulsory education policies, yet countless children remain out of school. Green tribunals exist, but stubble burning continues unabated. Prostitution is illegal, yet red-light districts operate in the open. Similarly, despite defined taxation laws, a significant portion of the population evaded taxes until demonetization forced compliance. The list goes on.

Demonetization was one of the rare moments when policies on paper came closer to aligning with the reality on the ground. However, the chaos it caused also revealed a harsh truth: while we demand honesty and corruption-free governance from others, we often fail to hold ourselves to the same standard.

Critics often argue that "development did not start after 2014; the Indian GDP was growing before as well." While this statement is technically correct, it overlooks a vital point: development should not be viewed in isolation but rather in conjunction with other factors. The speed and scale of transformation play a crucial role in its effectiveness. Simply ambling along and claiming effort doesn't suffice when the potential for rapid progress exists.

Even countries with unstable or absent civilian governments have achieved some level of growth. Take Pakistan, for instance, which endured significant political instability—characterized by the absence of democratic power transitions, frequent military coups, and prolonged periods of martial law that disrupted civilian governance. This volatile environment hindered the establishment of consistent policies or long-term developmental strategies. Yet, Pakistan managed to maintain a higher GDP growth rate than India until the 1990s, with average annual growth rates of around 6% compared to India's 3.5% during much of the post-independence period. This stark comparison begs the question: was the government in India acting as a brake on growth rather than a catalyst?

India, with its vast population of over a billion, has always had the capacity for significant economic and developmental strides. However, the pace of progress has often fallen short of what was achievable. A culture of poor political judgment and a lack of visionary leadership eroded the risk-taking appetite among decision-makers, stifling opportunities for bold and transformative actions. A sobering comparison lies in examining nations that gained independence after India but have since outpaced us in critical development indicators. This disparity isn't just about numbers on a graph; it underscores the immense untapped potential of a country that possesses abundant resources yet struggles to consistently maximize its opportunities?

India's progress hinges on leaders who possess vision, unwavering intent, and the courage to confront entrenched inefficiencies and implement transformative solutions. These are the qualities required to fix what's broken and pave the way for meaningful change. The abrogation of Article 370 stands as a powerful example of such intent. It was a decision that showcased unwavering resolve—one that previous governments had the opportunity to make but chose not to. Instead, they exploited Article 370 for electoral gains, avoiding the tough choice that this government ultimately made.

While critics often argue that these policies were flawed in their implementation and execution, it's worth asking: were they "not good" because they closed loopholes and left little room for exploitation? Not good for whom? Consider GST—criticized for its rollout—but wasn't the discomfort largely for those who thrived on the ambiguities in the earlier tax structure? Aadhaar linking faced similar resistance, but its goal was to foster accountability and reduce fraud. These controversial yet decisive actions reflect the intent to address systemic flaws rather than perpetuate the status quo.

This book is a testament to the fact that the policies and directives that stirred intense debates in India between 2014 and 2024 were not unique to India. The developed world has implemented similar policies at different points in time.

After a decade of transformative reforms and witnessing the remarkable pace at which change can unfold, India and Indians once again stand at a crossroads. Do we aspire for another decade of such transformative progress, or will we settle into the complacency of the "*chalta hai*" and "*aise hi hota hai*" mindset?

Either way, life will continue. We will still have elite institutions and organizations thriving, while importing electronics and defense equipment from other countries and exporting skilled Indians abroad all at the same time. The top 10% will continue to own 80% of the nation's wealth, while more than 50% of the population will still remain entrenched in agriculture, producing diminishing returns and engaging in protests. Politicians will still grow cauliflowers worth crores on their terraces, while small farmers will continue to bear the brunt of misguided policies and, tragically, resort to taking their own lives. Of course, we will continue fighting for them, but instead of addressing systemic issues, we will persist in fighting for farm loan waivers—a band-aid solution that does little to fix the systemic issues at the heart of the crisis.

This stark reality is not inevitable; it is a call to action. If we truly aspire to declare that India is a great country to live in, we must embrace another decade of bold and transformative reforms akin to those seen between 2014 and 2024. Agriculture needs structural changes—beyond subsidies—to ensure fair pricing, sustainable practices, and equitable access to markets. The judiciary must address its inefficiencies and backlog of cases to deliver timely justice. Our education system needs to pivot from rote learning to skill-based, future-oriented pedagogy.Cultural values need to be strengthened. Environmental policies need stricter enforcement to tackle pollution and promote sustainability. These sectors—and many others—urgently require reforms to create a foundation for an equitable and prosperous India.

Transformative policies are not just about correcting the present; they are about shaping the future. If India truly aspires to be a global leader and a great place to live, it must consistently challenge the status quo and embrace difficult but necessary reforms. These actions, while contentious, will define the nation's trajectory and set the foundation for a stronger, more equitable, and united India.

If we want to leave behind a legacy of pride, prosperity, and unity, we must move forward with intent, courage, and a commitment to reform. The road will not be easy, but the destination—a stronger, more equitable, and united India—will make it worthwhile.

"The negligence of a few could easily send a ship to the bottom, but if it has the wholehearted cooperation of all on board; she could be safely brought to port."

— Sardar Vallabhbhai Patel

About the Author

The author, an embedded systems design engineer specializing in FPGAs and Firmware Development, has worked across industries such as software, automotive, healthcare and aerospace. Beyond his technical expertise, he is deeply passionate about history, culture, politics, and technology, exploring how they shape societies.

Having lived in various European countries and the UK for over a decade, the author brings a unique vantage point to "The Seven 'I's of Modi's India: Through the Eyes of an NRI." This insightful book explores India's social, political, and cultural transformation from 2014 to 2024, drawing thought-provoking comparisons with global trends. It aims to spark dialogue and encourage critical thinking about the nation's progress on the world stage.

For the author, writing this book has been as much a journey of learning as it is a platform for sharing. He invites you to share your thoughts and perspectives on these ideas. Visit his blog at www.infiniteseaofopportunities.com to connect, explore more content, and engage in conversations that matter.

About the Author

www.ingramcontent.com/pod-product-compliance
Lightning Source LLC
LaVergne TN
LVHW091149150826
845672LV00005B/1079

* 9 7 9 8 8 9 7 2 4 6 8 8 5 *